Arnold Bax

Arnold Bax

by Colin Scott-Sutherland

With eight pages of plates and
music examples in the text

J. M. Dent & Sons Limited London

First published 1973
© Text, Colin Scott-Sutherland 1973

Made in Great Britain
at the Aldine Press · Letchworth · Herts
for J. M. DENT & SONS LTD
Aldine House · Bedford Street · London

This book is set in 11 on 13 point Baskerville 169

ISBN 0 460 03861 3

Contents

Illustrations

Acknowledgments

Throughout the making of this book I have had the willing and friendly co-operation of so many people that acknowledgments, for reasons of space alone, must be inadequate in relation to my indebtedness. It is to their tolerance, generosity and helpful advice that credit is due for whatever virtues this book may possess. The faults must remain my responsibility and to those who might well have expected something quite different from the pages which follow I offer my apologies as well as my gratitude. I should like to express particular thanks to the Bax family for their unfailing courtesy and encouragement—and to the late Miss Harriet Cohen whose unflagging enthusiasm illuminated many gargantuan meals at her mews flat. To all the following I owe a great deal for their contributions, stimulating conversation and letters:

Professor Gerald Abraham
the late Arthur Alexander
Sir Thomas Armstrong
the late Clifford Bax
Dermot Bax
Miss Evelyn Bax
Mr R. E. V. Bax
Mrs Vera Bax
the late Francis Colmer
the late Padraic Colum
Daniel Corkery

Alan Denson
the late Eleanor Farjeon
Eric Fenby
Hugh Fitch
Professor Aloys Fleischman
the late Mrs Tilly Fleischman
R. L. E. Foreman
the late Rolf Gardiner
Clifford W. Gillam
Eric Gillett
the late Cedric Glover

Mrs Ella Grainger
Frederick Grinke
Professor Patrick Hadley
John J. Horgan
Daniel Inman
Tamara Karsavina
Michael Kennedy
Maria Korchinska
the late Peter Latham
Malcolm McKellaig
the late Sir Compton Mackenzie
Frank Merrick
Donal O'Sullivan
Norman Peterkin
the late Montague Phillips

Patrick Piggott
Mervyn Roberts
Stanford Robinson
Mrs Anne Rust
the late Charles Kennedy Scott
Graham Royde Smith
Ronald Stevenson
Lionel Tertis
Helen Thomas
Kenneth Thompson
Harold Truscott
Ursula Vaughan Williams
Guy Warrack
Pamela Willetts
Mrs Undine Wilson (Bax)

I wish also to thank the staffs of the many libraries—at Edinburgh, Campbeltown and Strathaven—who have dealt with my innumerable queries with kindness and patience; Miss Margaret Murray, who coped with the typing of many pages of indecipherable script; and most of all my wife and family, who have never lost their invaluable sense of humour.

I am grateful to the following for granting permission to reproduce copyright material:

The Arnold Bax estate.

The Clifford Bax estate.

The estate of the late Æ ('Parting').

George Allen & Unwin Ltd (*Reminiscences and Reflections of a mid and late Victorian*).

Boosey & Hawkes Music Publishers Ltd (*The Life and Works of Tobias Matthay*).

Chappell & Co. Ltd (music examples on pp. 24, 53, 73, 81, 88, 96, 101, 106, 120, 126–9, 139–40, 153–4, 185).

J. & W. Chester Ltd (music example on p. 77).

The Daily Telegraph.

Faber & Faber Ltd (*A Bundle of Time*).

Roger Lancelyn Green (Gordon Bottomley letter).

Longman Group Limited (*Farewell, My Youth*).

Music and Letters.

The Musical Times.

A. D. Peters & Company (*Farewell My Muse, Inland Far, Many a green isle* and *The Traveller's Tale*).

The Society of Authors on behalf of the Bernard Shaw Estate.

The Times.

M. B. Yeats and Macmillan & Co. (*Four Plays for Dancers* and 'The Wanderings of Oisin').

COLIN SCOTT-SUTHERLAND 1973

And in a year
The loveliest singers of the time will come
With news of other kingdoms; and with tales
That shall make winter sweet and summer-time
Past all forgetting.

Clifford Bax,
Aucassin and Nicolette,
Orpheus No. 26, April 1914.

Introduction

Arnold Bax was almost exactly contemporary with Berg (b. 1885), Webern (b. 1883), Bartók (b. 1881), Kodály (b. 1882) and Stravinsky (b. 1882), a few years younger than John Ireland and the junior by eleven years of Vaughan Williams. At the date of his birth, Liszt, Franck, Gounod, Tchaikovsky and Brahms had still a few years to live; and Wagner had only just died.

Bax confessed himself a 'brazen Romantic'—acknowledging the presence in his nature of something which he saw as Celtic. His music is both Celtic and Romantic, but neither term will do as a pigeon-hole into which we may unceremoniously bundle his work without closer scrutiny. Within the man and the artist was a dichotomous personality, possessed of immensely fertile imaginative gifts which found expression through a prodigious and often intuitive technical ability. He was a 'tireless hunter of dreams',[1] a poet of vision and a mystic. He pursued his inspiration with singleminded purpose, regarding it as Celtic, and disagreed with Renan[2] who, he said, was mistaken in declaring that 'the Celt has ever worn himself out in mistaking dreams for reality'. On the contrary, the Celt, clearly recognizing the difference between the two, deliberately chooses to follow the dream.

The combination of the romantic and the Celtic made him a dreamer and a visionary. But the dichotomy within his personality, whose inner conflict unleashed an almost cosmic energy, prevented that lassitude of purpose with which both Romantic and Celt are so often charged.

[1] Arnold Bax, *Farewell, My Youth*, Longmans, 1943, p. 42.
[2] See quotation prefacing Chapter 8.

In a letter to Arthur Benjamin[1] Bax wrote: 'I am absolutely certain that the only music that can last is that which is the outcome of one's emotional reactions to the ultimate realities of Life, Love and Death. (All damned romantic, but I believe true.)' To equate imaginative with imaginary is a denial of life itself. The Romantic adventure has as its purpose a high ideal. It is not free from conflict and experiences the strange amidst the apparently commonplace. It touches upon the realms of the spirit and, therefore, upon unreality. Pursuit of such high adventure demands more than mere imagination. It demands purpose and tenacity. The 'tireless hunter of dreams' in Bax was endowed with prodigious energy, both physical and spiritual. And, in spite of the dark and forbidding forces in his work, there emerges from the conflict a kind of Nietzschean 'yea-saying', an ecstatic moment of truth, a penetrating insight into the ultimate realities before man's vision again clouds over.

Those who knew Bax have spoken and written of his generously warm nature—retiring though not shy; of his wit and charm, of his humour and powers of mimicry. For his human qualities he was held in high regard, not only by those whose lives and professions made them articulate, but by the people of Donegal, Sussex and Inverness-shire, amongst whom he lived and worked.

Most photographs in later life show him inclined to heaviness, his slightness of stature unrevealed by the camera. There is a hint of humour—sardonic humour—at the rather tight lips. Powys Evans's sketch shows him approaching middle life, the finely drawn sensitive features of the youthful portraits beginning to loosen and sag, the receding hair accentuating the high brow.

But in the eyes, Bax the composer is glimpsed. A friend[2] once remarked on the dissimilarity of his eyes—one visionary and Irish, the other practical and English. The eyes were indicative of the paradox in his nature: the Master of the Queen's Musick, the guardian of English musical respectability who, as Dermot O'Byrne, was the author of treasonable Irish verse; the English symphonist who sought inspiration on the craggy coasts of Scotland rather than on the Downs and Malverns. At the heart of all Bax's music is conflict—a deep inner conflict that reflects not only the duality of his musical nature but the basic predicaments of mankind. It is from the stress of this conflict that the motive power of his work is derived, although the

[1] Quoted in *Music and Letters*, Vol. 35, No. 1, Jan. 1954, p. 3.
[2] Anne Crowley.

Arnold Bax, sketched by Powys Evans

resolution of these stresses is not attained, except momentarily, in any single composition. The conflict is ultimately too cataclysmic for resolution on a personal level, and the final three symphonies show not an objective victory, nor objective surrender, but the expending of that conflict, effortlessly, in spacious terms that have reference to something elemental—something that is heard also in Sibelius.

This conflict in Bax is expressed in key (between vagueness of tonality and an aggressive assertion of a fundamental diatonicism) in rhythm (a loose and often nebulous web of sound which crystallizes into a trenchant Holstian beat); in register (where high and low registers in instrumental colour are juxtaposed); and in texture (where a deliberate cloudiness of sound is penetrated by the incisive thrusts of some powerful upsurge that illuminates the shrouded canvas like a shaft of light).

If 'a dancing star' was ever given birth out of chaos it is in music like that of the second Symphony, whose strange phantasmagoric beauty and catastrophic upheavals represent the other side of the composer of *Summer Music* and *Morning Song*. Bax's duality is clearly defined in the symphonic works whose tremendous surges of power, passionate incandescence and dark orchestral splendour are strongly contrasted with remote loveliness, austere beauty and wistful melancholy—culminating, its conflict reconciled, in the epilogic pages whose vigorous and joyous serenity is shot through with the all too human realization that such beauty is not, after all, attainable.

No great artist can be fully understood without proper appreciation of the environment from which he emerges. Either he is part of that environment and, in his greatness, towers above it, or a part of him is not of it at all but a spirit born out of time. Just how far the artist may transcend these chronological confines and become great not only among his contemporaries but in the eyes of posterity is something that cannot be measured and has no degrees.

But greatness is recognizable and, except for those isolated figures whose restless exploring genius has pushed further and further the frontiers of artistic experience, the greatness is firstly significant within the environment that gave it birth. For not all time is ripe for the appearance of the great explorer and innovator who comes opportunely at a new beginning and an end.

Bax's vision was one vouchsafed to few. Only a great heart and mind could follow such a dream in such a tempestuous century and achieve what he achieved. Bax was not only a great Romantic—he was a great artist and a great man.

Part One

1 Childhood

'All we had of joy endures, a joy within us
And all the rest of life is lovelier for those years'

Clifford Bax, 'Musician' in *Farewell My Muse*.

The history of the Bax family in England goes back at least as far as the earliest days of the Quakers, to which religious body Thomas Bax of Kitlands in Capel pledged his allegiance in 1655 and was imprisoned for his faith. A prosperous family of Surrey yeomen, the Baxes owned several properties in the Capel and Ockley district, half way between Dorking and Horsham. They were among the first adherents to the Quaker cause and were regarded in the district as a family of influence and prosperity.

Arnold Bax's great-grandfather, Daniel Bax (born 1777), the eldest son of Thomas Bax and Leah Leman, or Lemmon, of Ockley, left the rich Surrey pasturage of his forbears and settled in London, in the suburb of Hackney. His son by Elizabeth Haynes, also Daniel by name, was born in January 1812, married Eleanor the daughter of John Carter of Greenwich and substituted for the yeomanry of his fathers the mundane but profitable business of dealing, with his brother Edward, in the novelty of mackintosh waterproofs.

The establishing by the Bax brothers of a factory in London and a showroom in Orchard Street was instrumental in pioneering this new outdoor garment, and it is quite possible that some portion of the family's wealth derived from a share in the patenting of the process first discovered by the Scottish scientist Mackintosh. The possession of a number of properties also in that area of Oxford Street where the frontage of Selfridges now stands, and of which they were ground landlords, was a valuable asset.

Eleanor Carter was a forbidding woman, stern-lipped, puritanical, of firm, rather narrow, views. Of her large family the best known was Ernest Belfort Bax, a philosopher of some reputation, particularly in Germany where he went to study music at Leipzig in 1875. There, as Berlin correspondent of the *Standard*, he met Eduard von Hartmann and began to pursue the doctrines of Hegel and Marx. In his book, *Reminiscences and reflections of a mid and late Victorian*,[1] he describes rather

[1] Allen & Unwin, 1918.

bitterly the narrow evangelicalism and sabbatarianism of his early years. A master of French and German, he translated Kant's *Prolegomena* and wrote a number of important books—notably *Socialism, its growth and outcome* in collaboration with William Morris. A handsome giant of a man and a frequent visitor at his brother's home, the leonine E.B.B. impressed the young Arnold more by his prowess at the keyboard than by his doctrines.

Eleanor Carter survived her husband by eight years and, an impressive figure in the household of her son Alfred (with whom she went to live on the death of her husband), she presided at the birth of her grandson Arnold at Heath Villa, Angles Road, Streatham, on 8th November 1883.

Alfred Ridley Bax, barrister at law, born 25th April 1844, was a mild, serious and reserved man of considerable culture and learning, a dreamer rather than a thinker like his brother Ernest, and a Fellow of the Royal Society of Antiquaries[1] within whose dusty realms he escaped too vigorous a reality, content to leave the organizing of his household and the raising of his family to his energetic young wife.

Charlotte Ellen Lea was born at Amoy in China on 24th June 1860. Sixteen years her husband's junior, Arnold Bax's mother was a strong-minded inquiring woman, attractive, sympathetic and full of restless energy. As socially alert as her husband was retiring, she was a born organizer and contrived, in the rather dull social milieu in which she found herself, to gather around her people of distinction and taste. 'I have always said,' wrote Arnold Bax of her in 1943, 'that she would have made a very good Queen.'[2] On her mother-in-law's death in 1890 she assumed full charge of her household and the fortunes of her four children—Arnold Edward Trevor (b. 8.11.83),[3] Clifford Lea (b. 13.7.86), Aubrey Vernon (b. 1.12.84) and Evelyn (b. 12.4.87).

Over her young family this vital woman exercised a powerful influence, tempering the Victorian severity of the day with her warm sympathetic understanding and illuminating, for her perceptive sons in particular, areas of beauty in the matter-of-fact world around them.

---

[1] His researches into the Bax family history form the basis of a book *The early Quaker Baxes of Capel and Ockley in the district of Surrey* by Bernard Thistlethwaite, Headley, London 1936.

[2] *Farewell, My Youth*, p. 11.

[3] The picturesque fancy that Arnold Bax was born in the middle of a bog-lake in County Mayo was, perhaps almost reluctantly, dispelled by the composer himself in a short volume of autobiography, *Farewell, My Youth*.

In the creative work of Arnold and Clifford this maternal influence was deep and lasting, and was soon to provoke that violence of emotion that is so often the result, in those endowed with unusual intellectual power, of the conflict between a precious, markedly feminine intuition underlying a heightened perception of beauty, and the more aggressive emotions of the male. This violence is seen in Clifford's writings, notably in *The Traveller's Tale*:

> The magician ceased,
> And muttering under his breath, unsheathed a knife
> And took up a bowl of strong black earthenware.
> I thought I had shrieked, but no noise left my lips,
> For now I beheld him setting the bowl with care
> Up to my brother's throat. And muttering still
> He chose a point, like a sacrificial priest,
> And pushed the blade far in. With a gentle sigh
> The boy let one hand slip: and the streaming blood
> Gushed to the bowl and ran in glistening skeins
> Down to his belly.[1]

But Clifford's imagery is nowhere as savage as that found in almost all of the tales and verses which Arnold wrote under the psuedonym of Dermot O'Byrne:

> The pain-clouded eyes of the doomed harper regarded her with a kind of dull surprise. For a moment she stood looking through her tangled hair into those eyes. Then she shook herself like some wild animal, and with a scream swung the clairseach above her like a battleaxe. As it fell one of the drunken women lying upon the floor cried out in terror and began to whimper, but the blows still continued to rain down. With the heavy embossed frame of the harp the amazon battered Airbreach's head until the bones of the skull were crushed and the blood spurted out upon the rushes. She laughed, feeling the hot dark drops dripping from the harp upon her hands and bare arms.[2]

Such passages, with their overtly barbaric ferocity, are echoed in the violent upsurges of power that drive the symphonic works of Arnold Bax, and contrast so strongly with the moments of exquisite peace which he achieves in the symphonic Epilogues.

The boys were not discouraged from intellectual pursuits. There were many books in the library and Mrs Bax used often to read aloud

---

[1] Clifford Bax, *The Traveller's Tale*, Blackwell, 1921.
[2] Dermot O'Byrne, 'The Death of Macha Goldhair' from *Children of the Hills*, Maunsel & Co., Dublin, 1913, p. 142.

to the children (a practice which continued in later life, for Arnold liked his mother to read aloud while he was scoring many of his orchestral works), and both Arnold and Clifford were voracious readers. Their tastes were catholic, ranging from their favourite Dickens to the poetry of the Romantics, Keats, Shelley and Swinburne and to Ibsen, Björnson, Turgenev and Tolstoy, Celtic and Scandinavian mythology—in all of which Arnold was widely read before he was out of his teens.

Although the atmosphere of the Bax household was less rigid than most, Mrs Bax's encouragement of the artistic development of her sons did not preclude concern for their spiritual welfare. Each Sunday the family attended worship in the Congregational church. The afternoon was spent in painting texts, a little service was taken by Mrs Bax for the children in the schoolroom at which the staff of maids attended, and family prayers were conducted daily in the dining room, at which both family and domestic staff were present, presided over by Alfred Ridley Bax.

It was not, however, an oppressive atmosphere and while Evelyn and her mother gradually moved towards Roman Catholicism in later life, Arnold and Clifford, encouraged to think things out for themselves, drifted quickly from the conventional patterns of religious behaviour and began to explore more exotic paths.

Distinction of taste, increasing wealth and social position, and cultured and elegant pursuits channelled, but did not subdue, the vigorous creative energies that soon became apparent in Arnold and Clifford.

At the age of nine Arnold drew and painted, as a present for his mother, 'The Ladies own book of Volcanoes', a pamphlet stitched together by the nursemaid. He also had a passion for building with stone bricks (though he never improvised the architecture, but always copied the instructions from the accompanying book). His early addiction to puzzles—crosswords in particular—earned for him some superiority over his younger relatives, who nicknamed him 'Little Puffed Up' in consequence.

Although home circumstances played a part in the future artistic development of both brothers, much of their energy was active, not passive, and no restraint was placed on the healthy expression of youthful spirits for which the garden afforded an ideal playground. It was in these surroundings and spurred by a catholic taste in literature that the creative instincts of both began to stir. Amid the ploys of childhood, there began to develop an awareness of the beauty of external Nature that was to haunt Arnold Bax throughout his life and which he crystallizes in his autobiography into one moment of experience:

> I distinctly remember my first conscious apprehension of beauty. It may have been in 1889. Whilst staying with my parents in Worthing I was taken one September evening to the top of Arundel Park. It was the hour of sunset, and as we stood there an unimaginable glory of flame developed in the west so that all the wooded heights seemed on fire. Even the east was stained with pale coral. It might have been Ragnarök, the burning of the Gods in Norse mythology. I watched speechlessly. To my childish perception this visitation was sheer all-conquering splendour and majesty, untroubled by the sense of the transitoriness of all lovely things. The hour was immortal.[1]

In the early nineties the three brothers attended a small preparatory school known as Argyll House (in Balham Park and later in Nightingale Lane) not far from the rambling Marlborough House to which the family had moved from Streatham. After Aubrey's death from meningitis in 1895 the family moved again, this time to the more socially congenial district of Hampstead. There they took a house named Ivybank—a large red-brick building on Haverstock Hill which both Arnold and Clifford came to love. Here were spent the happiest hours of their youth, and the next decade was to prove valuable in the development of their artistic expression.

Arnold and Clifford have written of the garden at Ivybank whose formative impact upon both was fruitful. On its spacious lawns were played out the engrossing pastimes of childhood. There were several large houses and few flats at that time in Hampstead, and the district, before the days of bus and tube, was pleasantly remote from the city. Diagonally across the grounds of the house ran a row of giant sycamores and chestnuts, the only remaining indication of what had once been Belsize Park. And on the largest of these lawns their games of cricket were played.

The schooling that the brothers received at Argyll House and later at a small day school, Heath Mount, in Hampstead, was their only experience of communal school life. Concerned for the health of the younger Clifford, who had on two successive years been dangerously ill with pneumonia, Alfred Ridley Bax engaged a private tutor, Francis Colmer, an exhibitioner from Exeter College Oxford, and 'a

[1] *Farewell, My Youth*, p. 9.

man of most winning eccentricity'.[1] 'Col', a scholar of considerable erudition and a lovable personality, was soon on excellent terms with his young charges, and took a keen interest in their literary and musical activities.

He encouraged their writing, and before long Clifford's talent was expressed in a juvenile family production *The Ivybank Gazette*, the precursor of those sumptuous art periodicals he was later to edit.[2] Col joined also with enthusiasm in their leisure and cricket and the game became a kind of midsummer madness. Arnold, a stubborn bat and a deceptively accurate left-handed bowler, Claude Bax (a cousin), Francis Colmer, Clifford and the two Ivybank gardeners[3] made up the three-a-side matches which were eagerly resumed at each break in the routine of irregular verbs and Latin conjugations.

Other friends were added to the circle. Mrs Bax's generous hospitality and social instincts brought many people to the house—to play cricket and croquet (sometimes by moonlight) or wild games of hockey on Hampstead Heath (even in winter); to consume mountainous teas in Arnold's 'den'; to play chess, and paper and pencil games of all descriptions and to talk with all the impetuosity of youth. She allowed her sons full scope for their activities and the relaxation of domestic protocol extended so far as to allow them to sit down to supper in their cricket flannels. These 'social Saturdays' at Ivybank rapidly gained the distinction of a tradition (largely, as Clifford suggested, due to the excellent suppers which were provided) and many of the friend- ships formed at that time continued into later life—or until they were tragically cut short in 1914.

Alfred Ridley Bax was a musical man[4] and had for many years subscribed to the Saturday concerts at the Crystal Palace. The analy- tical programmes of these concerts that he had had bound dated back to 1860 and these, with their music illustrations, held the young Arnold spellbound. Poring over them he would improvise 'absurd symphonies and overtures from the musical excerpts'.[5] At about the

---

[1] Clifford Bax, *Inland Far*, Heinemann, 1925, p. 180.

[2] *Orpheus* with Edgar Davies, and *The Golden Hind* with Austin Spare.

[3] Appropriately named Eden, the elder of whom, as fielder, 'stoppeth one of three' and was promptly dubbed The Ancient Mariner by Clifford.

[4] The Bax family were later granted a coat of arms: 'Sable on a Chevron between three Martlets, argent, a lyre of the field: on a chief of the second, three beech leaves slipped vert: And for the crest, on a wreath of the colours two arms embowed, vested sable, cuffs argent, the hands proper, holding a lyre or.'

[5] *Farewell, My Youth*, p. 12.

age of nine he could already play most of the Beethoven sonatas and, while his father mildly discouraged the boys' passion for verse (Clifford had begun to emulate Shelley in manner both of life and thought), he saw no reason to discourage the signs of a growing musical awareness in Arnold. He sponsored a private choral society that met in a building adjacent to the house, to which Arnold, sitting upon three bound volumes of *Punch* in order to reach the keyboard, became unofficial accompanist at the age of thirteen. He was possessed of uncanny facility at the keyboard in improvisation and sight-reading, attributes he later likened to the natural acquisition of strong teeth or thick hair. Finding that no score held secrets from him, his reading in music became more and more adventurous and, though his talents were as yet unchannelled, he began to compose. One day, whilst recuperating from an overlong exposure to the sun at the wicket, he wrote a Sonata in two movements for piano,[1] and Alfred Bax could ignore the signs no longer. A consultation with Sir Frederick Bridge, then principal of the Royal College of Music, ended with the decision that the young Arnold should become a student at Hampstead Conservatoire to study piano, theory and composition under Dr Arthur Greenish, a one-time conductor of the Bax choral society and an enthusiastic teacher.

Alfred Bax was now strongly advised to consider his son's future musical education and, on the advice of John Attwater (Greenish's predecessor as conductor of the choral society), Arnold was allowed, when he was almost seventeen, to sit the entrance examination for the Royal Academy of Music in Tenterden Street, a choice that was to prove significant in the moulding of his future career.

---

[1] The MS of a Piano Sonata in two movements, marked 'Opus 1', now hangs in the Memorial Room at Cork University College. This, however, cannot have been his first composition (perhaps not even the Sonata referred to here—see *Farewell, My Youth*, p. 16) since it is clearly dated 27th February 1898, by which date he had already written a quantity of short pieces for piano.

2 Royal Academy and Dresden

'Music fierce as fire, or hazed with unrelinquished
Adolescent dreams of more than life can give'

Clifford Bax, 'Musician' in *Farewell My Muse.*

Arnold Bax entered the Royal Academy of Music together with
Benjamin Dale in September 1900. Amongst his fellow students were
Adam Carse, Paul Corder, Eric Coates, York Bowen and Montague
Phillips. The Academy at that time trembled under the principalship
of Sir Alexander Campbell Mackenzie, a fiery Scot whose outspoken
criticism of modernist tendencies in the work of his students was
belied by his liberal-minded policies for their musical education. It
was to his enlightened thinking that many young musicians owed
their first appreciation and understanding of the late works of Liszt.

At the R.A.M. Bax took piano with Tobias Matthay[1] and composition with Frederick Corder. Mackenzie's admiration for Liszt, Corder's
for Wagner, and their adventurous policies in education brought the
students into contact with new and exciting fields of musical thought
at a time when these might have their greatest impact. The marked
effects of the stimulus of Liszt and Wagner clearly differentiated the
students of the Royal Academy from those who, at the Royal College
under Stanford and Parry, were taught to look to Bach and Brahms
for models. This dividing line was to be quite clearly marked in the
course of English music over the first few years of the twentieth century
and one has only to look at the work of the first generation of these
composers—Vaughan Williams, Ireland and Bliss on the one hand,
Bax, Dale and Bantock on the other—to appreciate the difference in
outlook inculcated by the two environments.

Corder's influence on his pupils was considerable. John Ireland once
expressed surprise, on looking through some compositions of a pupil
of Benjamin Dale, that he could recognize the influence of Corder
extending to a second generation. But it was a permissive rather than
a restricting influence. It might perhaps have benefited Bax had his
professor been stricter. For the tendency to complexity in his writing
caused him considerable struggle throughout his life and perhaps

---

[1] 'A benevolent Svengali', *Farewell, My Youth*, p. 19.

barred the way for many to his work. At all events Corder's methods would not have been countenanced by Stanford, whose teaching made perpetual war on inessentials and was ruthless in its advocacy of stylistic purity. But the young Bax found much to admire in his teacher:

> A man of emotional and somewhat melancholy temperament, Frederick Corder seemed to me to be still living in the exciting period of his own youth, the late 70's and 80's. The Pre-Raphaelites were then at the height of their reputation and influence, and Wagner's empire was at last fully established throughout the world of music. These masters—together with William Morris of whose Kelmscott books he possessed a fine collection—were the aesthetic gods of Frederick Corder. I fancy that after Wagner his choice amongst composers would have fallen upon Dvořák.[1]

He became a frequent visitor at the Corder home in Albion Road, Hampstead, where he began a close friendship with Paul and Dolly Corder, and their companion Eleanor Farjeon. Many years later Miss Farjeon recalled him as he was then: 'He had no pretensions, was as sensitive as a candle flame that flickers with every breath, ardent in talk or at the piano, swift to respond and swift to withdraw and swift to appreciate his friends' talent and humour. He had one of the least ponderous natures imaginable.'[2] And at the Corders' home he became first aware of Harriet Cohen: 'I think the first time Arnold took any real notice of me was when I appeared at the Corders', at a tea party early one January, wearing a single daffodil as my only decoration. That meeting resulted in the piano piece.'[3]

Encouraged by the permissive atmosphere at the Academy, Bax was supremely happy and immersed himself in all that the musical world of the day had to offer. The excitement of creative work, new discoveries in music and literature, and the subtle adolescent currents of romance enveloped him: 'When I was young I was thankful for youth and could have shouted for joy in my consciousness of it—and indeed in my music, I frequently did so. In my 'teens I decided that twenty-two was the golden number in the count of a man's years. I longed to be twenty-two and to remain at that age for ever, and I am not sure even now that I was not right.'[4] Under the paternal eye of his professor he

[1] Obituary notice in *The Times*, 27.8.32.
[2] Letter to the author, October 1960.
[3] Harriet Cohen, *A Bundle of Time*, Faber, 1969, p. 30.
[4] *Farewell, My Youth*, pp. 23–4.

composed prolifically. With a set of Symphonic Variations[1] he won
the Charles Lucas medal for composition, and several of his compositions were played at college concerts under the direction of Mackenzie,
among them a work for viola and orchestra dedicated to Lionel Tertis.
An orchestral overture *A Connemara Revel* was premièred by Mackenzie
on 4th April 1905 and *A Celtic Song Cycle* with words by Fiona MacLeod
was first performed by Ethel Lister at Queen's Hall on 21st November
1904. These performances were well enough received, although Parry's
comment on one occasion was that 'young Bax's stuff sounds like a bevy
of little devils'.[2]

Several compositions were published, among them the *Celtic Song
Cycle*, which had drawn from one critic the admonition that 'this
composer had best be kept from further study of Debussy', a composer
of whom Bax had not at that time heard so much as a note! The early
Trio in one movement, marked Opus 4, has a youthful exuberance
(that same youthful exuberance which reappears in the last works of
his life) and makes use of a springy, ecstatic waltz-rhythm (which he
also used later in, for instance, the Violin Concerto) but the music is
not particularly interesting. The Song Cycle, although characteristic,
owes more to Wagner and Strauss than to the poet and the heavy
chromaticism is only momentarily lightened here and there by the
hints of a pentatonic melodic line which he was beginning to assimilate
from Irish music.

A few prentice compositions have come to light since Bax's death—
perhaps the most important being the tone poem *Cathleen Ni Houlihan*
written in 1903, a work which shows that he was by no means groping
for a personal style even at that early date. Other manuscripts are
incomplete.

But it was not only as a composer that Bax had attracted attention.
His piano professor Tobias Matthay held him in very high regard:

> They [Myra Hess and Irene Scharrer] had an especially interesting fellow
> student in Arnold Bax, much beloved and appreciated by Matthay for he was
> composer-pianist and greatly after his own heart. Bax was not a prodigy
> though his gifts were well-nigh uncanny. He cared not a straw for public
> performance, but the avidity with which he absorbed music both old and new
> not only made one marvel, but made him a centre around which lesser lights

---

[1] So far as is known this work, the occasion of Bax's one and only appearance on
the conductor's rostrum (see *Farewell, My Youth*, p. 26), has no relation to the later
work of the same name for piano and orchestra.
[2] *Farewell, My Youth*, p. 27.

revolved. He did not as yet bear evidence of the great work he was to achieve. One of his earliest productions was 'A Concert Waltz' which Matthay got Boosey to publish and which all his fellow students had to have a shot at. But very soon what Arnold was doing was one of the most important things on their musical horizon.[1]

His piano technique was prodigious, as many of his later published piano compositions show. But although he won the Gold Medal for piano playing in 1905 he did not pursue his piano studies and it was his uncanny sight-reading ability that above all else won him a fame that amounted almost to notoriety. It was this legendary ability that led him on one occasion to play from sight, and in the composer's presence, some early songs of Schoenberg, at a musical evening at Alfred Kalisch's music club. These powers impressed all who heard him play, and York Bowen, in an obituary tribute, later wrote: 'The other unmistakable sign of his growing creative gift was his power of extemporization, altogether beyond anything I have ever heard since at the piano keyboard.'[2] These were gifts about which he was characteristically modest, but they stood him in good stead as a composer. It is no mean tribute to his hawk-like proficiency that the Symphonies were in publisher's proof before he had heard a note played of these intricate scores. (Brahms himself made innumerable corrections to the score of his First Symphony after hearing it performed.)

Bax had already determined to write music, and within him began the stirring of that *wanderlust* which provoked his restless imagination. Relinquishing the Macfarren scholarship when it had still a year to run, he left the R.A.M. and his college days behind him and set off in search of adventure. After he had left, Bax's father, like York Bowen's, returned the entire scholarship money in the form of a hundred-guinea endowment for the free training of a promising but impoverished student.

In 1905, his love of Wagner undimmed, he set out for fashionable Dresden to savour the delights of the concert halls and the splendour, in the heyday of the Dresden opera, of Schuch's direction of *Siegfried*, *Tristan*, *Elektra* and *Salome*.[3] With his companions, Paul Corder, Roland

[1] Jessie Henderson Matthay, *The Life and Works of Tobias Matthay*, Boosey & Hawkes, 1945.
[2] *Music and Letters*, Vol. 35, No. 1, Jan. 1954.
[3] 'She stands within the giant gates
  Of night, and in the flame she sings'
        Dermot O'Byrne, 'To Frau Wittich as Isolde' (MS).

Bocquet and Archie Rowan Hamilton, Bax gloried in his freedom with all the exuberance of youth, steeped in Wagner and exhausting, in a wild exciting bohemian existence, the reservoirs of adolescence. This expeditious sowing of wild oats unburdened him, in an orgy of creative activity, of the remaining vestiges of the direct influences of his German idols and prepared the way for the swift development of his creative personality.

The most vital experiences however were not musical and, one snowy March day, he fled from Dresden with 'a tall, calm-eyed Scandinavian girl':[1]

We huddled together for warmth, stealing rather awed sidelong glances at the white-drifted rides of that vast and gloomily romantic Bohemian forest. It was getting towards dusk, and it seemed not impossible that trolls from her country and native kobolds lurked behind every tree, or that—seeing that we were on the verge of Slavonic earth—the Baba-Yaga herself might come blundering through the branches with her monstrous pestle and mortar. However, after bumping through ever deepening snow for some miles, we at last drew up at the warm and hospitable Rainwiese inn, where we reckoned on staying for two or three days.

Unforgettable days they proved to be, poignant—sweet in recollection to my dying hour. By day we wandered in the endless glistening forest, gazed up at the mighty Prebischthur, or were ferried by a silent one, who may have been Charon himself, upon an ice-green water mirror, its breathless surface reflecting the tall frozen cliffs of the canyon through which the scarcely flowing stream sluggishly crept. Later, with the intense silence of the snow-curtained pines beyond the dark blue of the window, we lay wakeful in one another's arms half the night.[2]

Like that earlier experience of the Arundel sunset, it is this kind of encounter—largely sensual, imbued with the mystical spirituality that is essentially pantheism—that is the true key to all Bax's later music and especially to the seven symphonies. The strongest influences in his life were those physically encountered and sensually perceived, and he confided the magic of such experiences first to his notebooks and then, by a process more subtle, to the pages of the music:

On my strange virgin bridal night
While shadows crept on silent fell
And delicate snow-blossoms beat
Upon my lips, upon mine eyes
The multiple-woven veil that lies
O'er unseen things was drawn apart

[1] *Farewell, My Youth*, p. 38.   [2] ibid., p. 39.

And in the mirror of the snow
I saw when the last light sank low
And chill lay on the forest heart
The wedded flames of Love and Death
One star—and when the latest breath
Of Day was spent, peace came and she
The pale bride took me by the hand
And her eyes bade me understand
And lifted the dead fear from me
For Love and Death and the wood's heart
And my own soul no more apart
Shone in their dusk . . . and day was done
And in the dark house we were one.[1]

Bax had decided that twenty-two was the golden age in life and 1905 was a significant year. It was a year of prolific composition, and although much of this music is lost, there remain a number of pages, in manuscript and in short score, where Bax has recorded the growth of his own very personal idiom. In the score of a heavily Straussian (see Ex. 1(a)) symphony the influences are apparent, and an unmistakably Celtic lilt (Ex. 1(b)) has begun to make its appearance:[2]

Ex.1 *Sehr Langsam und Sëhnsuchtsvoll*

(a)

(b)

pp

[1] 'In a Bohemian forest' (from a manuscript notebook by Dermot O'Byrne in the author's possession).
[2] Fragmentary MSS of two symphonies at least exist—one in F (marked Opus 8) now in the Memorial Room at Cork University, and one in F minor in the author's possession. Both date from between 1905 and 1908.

Example 1(b), already sufficiently well defined to be recognizably second subject material—a kind of evocation of the spirit of Fintan[1] singing 'memories through the fainting light'—is lyrical and with a hint of that haunting Celtic nostalgia that has all too often led to the supposition that Bax was for ever lost in that limbo of movements whose impetus petered out in the noise of subsequent eruptive happenings.

The moment was of more significance than simply an echo of Celtic twilight. For Fintan sang not only in the long twilight, but along the warring plains and smote victorious chords from the harp of the winds. And in the mature works this Celtic element has a twofold expression, by turns eloquent and breathtakingly beautiful, and then suddenly harsh and warlike. From the same source, in the full flood of symphonic composition, came both secondary and primary material, added to and enriched by other experiences, but recognizably derived from this period in his life when he came into contact with the first major influence in his life—Ireland.

[1] 'Fintan—the spirit of Irish song', Dermot O'Byrne, in *Seafoam and Firelight*, *Orpheus* series, No. 2, 1909, p. 32.

3 Ireland

'At the grey round of the hill
Music of a lost kingdom
Runs, . . .'
W. B. Yeats, *Four Plays for Dancers.*

Bax was nineteen when he first encountered Yeats's *The Wanderings of Oisin*. Both brothers had shown an early sensitivity to poetry and both reacted sharply to this new discovery. Clifford, a young art student at Heatherly's, was introduced to Yeats by Ernest Rhys. In the poems of Yeats he found yet another clue to that spiritual accomplishment of which his questing intellect was constantly in search:

> Whence are all the starry legions traversing the sky?
> Whence the olden planets and the sun and moon and earth?
> Out of what came all of these and out of what came I?[1]

and which led him to Eliphas Levi, *The Golden Bough* and the esoteric doctrines of Theosophy.

Arnold, on the other hand, found in Yeats a release and direction for the emotional forces pent up within him. 'The Celt within me stood revealed', he wrote in *Farewell, My Youth*.[2] Celticism seemed an antidote to age, an elixir preserving forever the vigour of youth—and with youth, joy.

> . . . his was the key that opened the gate of the Celtic Wonderland to my wide-eyed youth, and his the finger that pointed to the magic mountain whence I was to dig all that may be of value in my own art. . . . his poetry has always meant more to me than all the music of the centuries. . . . All the days of my life I bless his name.[3]

It was to Ireland, where he went that same year, that the discovery of Yeats first led him. Together with Clifford he set out for Ireland 'in a state of considerable spiritual excitement' that was primarily mystical. And while Clifford found what he sought in the intellectual society of Dublin in the company of Æ,[4] O'Sullivan, Stephens, Colum and others,

[1] 'The Meaning of Man', Clifford Bax, in *Poems Dramatic and Lyrical, Orpheus* series, No. 9, 1911, p. 81.
[2] pp. 41–42.
[3] ibid., p. 48.
[4] George Russell, the Irish poet, painter and economist.

Arnold went on, beyond the enmeshing circles of the city, to the remote corners of Old Eire, to ancient Donegal and to the windswept Atlantic seaboard.

There he found the tiny village of Glencolumcille:

> I like to fancy that on my deathbed my last vision in life will be the scene from my window on the upper floor at Glencolumcille, of the still, brooding, dove-grey mystery of the Atlantic at twilight; the last glow of sunset behind Glen Head in the north, with its ruined watch tower built in 1812 at the time of the scare of a Napoleonic invasion; and east of it the calm slope of Scraig Beefan, its glittering many-coloured surface of rock, bracken, and heather, now one uniform purple glow. In winter I would often linger at that window, too fascinated in watching the implacable fury of that same Atlantic in a southwesterly storm to sit down to work. At one end of the little Glen Bay was a wilderness of tumbled black rocks, for some reason named Romatia (a particularly 'gentle'—or fairy-haunted place, I was told in Dooey opposite), and upon this grim escarpment the breakers thundered and crashed, flinging up, as from a volcano, towering clouds of dazzling foam which would be hurled inland by the gale to put out the fires in the cottage hearths of Beefan and Garbhros. The savagery of the sea was at times nearly incredible. I have seen a continuous volume of foam sucked, as in a funnel, up the whole six-hundred-foot face of Glen Head, whilst with the wind north-west a like marvel would be visible on the opposite cliff.[1]

To this remote and magical place came Bax in a mood bordering upon ecstasy. But if the poetry of Yeats had revealed to him the shadowy realm of Ireland's legends and history, the land itself turned that poetic image into reality. 'He derived a pure happiness, I think, from the wild loveliness of the islands and lakes and windy heights, and from the charm and vivacity of the peasants.'[2]

The impact of this land he was to love 'better than any land beneath the visiting moon'[3] was recorded first of all in his notebooks. The mood and the ways of Ireland captured his imagination. As he travelled —to the corners of Donegal, to Clare and Sligo, to the islands of Lettermullen and Gorumna, and to that 'other Aranmore where nobody ever goes'[4]—he took pains to learn the language and the ancient script[5] and to note down, not snatches of tune, but the idio-

---

[1] *Farewell, My Youth*, pp. 50-1.
[2] Clifford Bax, *Inland Far*, Heinemann, 1925, p. 126.
[3] See Preface to *Music in Ireland* by Aloys Fleischman.
[4] *Farewell, My Youth*, p. 45.
[5] Mastering both, he translated the first part of *In the Shadow of the Glen* into Erse.

syncratic extravagances of language he encountered amongst the
people: 'An Irishman enjoys the use of language as an athlete the use
of his limbs'.[1] Stimulated by their strange ways and poetic speech,
Bax began to write. The name 'Dermod McDermott' began in June
1905 to be recorded under passages of Yeatsian verse in closely written
note-books.[2] And gradually, under the triple aegis of Yeats, Synge
and Æ, a second self—a literary *Doppelgänger*—began to emerge in
Bax's personality. Dermot O'Byrne—the name he finally used—was
the measure of his affection for things Irish and was partly a cloak to
conceal his other self, Bax the musician. O'Byrne was the true projec-
tion of his Irish/Celtic self as far as he found it possible to give it form
and shape, and beneath the wild extravagance of language there hid a
sensitive and visionary soul. Most of O'Byrne's literary work has been
collected into the three titles that can still be found in Dublin book-
shops. Of his verse note-books a selection entitled *Seafoam and Firelight*
was published in 1909, the second of the *Orpheus* series, 'devoted to
work by artists who desire to give their productions an atmosphere more
spiritual than that which is characteristic of the present age and of most
contemporary art' and the product of the combined talents of Clifford
Bax and Edgar Davies. These booklets, which included the work of Æ,
Eleanor Farjeon and Gwendolen Bishop, as well as both Bax brothers,
were issued in connection with the art magazine *Orpheus* that Clifford
had inaugurated in 1907.

The poetry is marked by a delicate, sometimes bitter, but always
haunting beauty. There are evocations of legend, where names like
Deirdre ring with potent magic. But the lines are shot through with a
sense of wonder at the endless phenomena of natural beauty which for
the Celt had an especial meaning. The sea, omnipresent, flows through
the lines like some elder deity, and though the poems bear decided
traces of the influence of Yeats and others, they are often of high
quality and show how deeply Bax had absorbed the Irish characteristics:

The Aran Isles in ocean's arms lie low
In stony sleep, their crumbling agelong piles
Feed death with dreams, no summer spirits know
The Aran Isles.

[1] *Inland Far*, p. 131.
[2] In June 1908 (although not a member of this society, to which Clifford belonged)
he contributed two poems to the third volume of Transactions of the Theosophical
Art-Circle over the pen-name of 'Diarmid'.

No careless mood of the gay old sun beguiles
The shades that wander there like midnight snow,
The endless grey sea-sorrow and the murmuring miles,[1]

The windy riders trampling the waves that flow
From the sombre west; yet sometimes still the smiles
Of elder gods must lighten as long ago
The Aran Isles.[2]

Clifford spoke of O'Byrne to his friends in Dublin, and when in 1911 Arnold rented a furnished villa in Bushy Park Road, Rathgar, he found himself closely involved in the literary society of the city to whom he was introduced by Clifford.

It was the practice in Dublin society to hold open house on certain evenings of the week—the James Stephenses on Mondays, the Colums on Tuesdays and the George Russells on Sundays. It was at the Russells' house that the principal gatherings were held and there Bax was to meet frequently the most prominent figures in Irish life: James Stephens ('an intellectual leprechaun of a fellow'[3]), Maud Gonne, Con Curran, Seamus O'Sullivan, the Pearce brothers, Thomas McDonagh and many others.[4] In Dublin Bax diffidently presented a copy of *The Sisters & Green Magic* to Æ to whom he had inscribed the volume and was delighted to find that the poet was enthusiastic about his work. Æ spoke of O'Byrne to Colum, then editor of the *Irish Review* (a paper devoted more to literary matters than to politics), to Darrell Figgis, Lord Dunsany and to the red-bearded Ernest Boyd, then reader to the Talbot Press. Some of the tales which began to appear in the pages of the *Irish Review* at the instigation of Colum were later collected (by Maunsel & Co.) into a volume entitled *Children of the Hills*, and the Talbot Press put out another collection under the title *Wrack*. Both were well received. 'I was particularly attracted [says Colum] to a tale which began: "A man woefully out of breath, with eyes dilated by fear burning in his hollow grey face, hammered with a ragged thorn stick on the gate of the Glengariff School of Poetry".'[5]

[1] A line which impressed Clifford. See 'Buried Treasure' in *Evenings in Albany* by Clifford Bax, Eyre & Spottiswoode, 1942, p. 38.
[2] *Seafoam and Firelight, Orpheus* series No. 2, 1909, p. 30.
[3] *Farewell, My Youth*, p. 96.
[4] Although Bax met Yeats on a number of occasions, the poet was not at this time a frequenter of those circles in which Bax moved.
[5] Letter to the author, 1963. O'Byrne's fame was not confined to Ireland. The poet Gordon Bottomley later wrote to Bax (in 1923) of those stories to which he had been

Figgis, too, was impressed with the tales and asked Bax to visit him. Bax found him 'woefully unstable and vain' but fell deeply in love with Keel in Achill where Figgis had his home. Writing from there to Molly Colum, at the height of the winter storms, he described the scenery and the wildness of the weather:

> The weather still remains rather lurid, but the flying glimpses of golden or purple islands—Inishclare, Inishturk and others—throw a kind of enchantment over me, which they might not possess to the same degree under summer skies. At the present moment Inishturk is flooded in a bewitched haze of sunlight and flying foam. There is a curious tone about the light surrounding these Western islands into which one is tempted to dip one's dream with almost a sense of physical languor. It seems to paralyse one's thought and will and encourage even the most energetic and passionate temperaments to become quietists . . .

But the idyll was shortlived and, in language that echoed the fire and devastation, O'Byrne sang an elegy for those who died in the bloody Easter of 1916.

No fiery breath

Of holy rage can stir you more, no land
Under the moon break up your soul with love;
Shocked to stark peace one hour you stand above
All memory that could hurt you or assail;
Down smashed familiar streets and haunted shore
Long may the suffering winds of Ireland wail,
Here in our world you shall be seen no more.[1]

In *A Dublin Ballad and other poems*, published in a limited edition of 425 copies by the Candle Press, Dublin, in 1918, Bax sang the heroes of the revolt—and found himself in conflict with the English censor by whom the book was banned as subversive (a strange position for the future guardian of English musical respectability to find himself in).

---

introduced by Edward Thomas: 'They have that charm of firstness, the elusive magic that is always the final marvel and desiderium of art for me— . . . they are of the world of Christabel and St Agnes' Eve, Hand and Soul, The Blessed Damozel, The Blue Closet, and At Arthur's Tomb, and The Hollow Land, Denys L'Auxerrois and The Countess Cathleen: plain gifts from the gods of the kind that no one knows how they arrive . . .'

[1] Dermot O'Byrne, 'In Memoriam Patrick H. Pearse' in *A Dublin Ballad and other poems*, p. 8.

The book was warmly praised by Yeats[1] but it was the end of a chapter.

If O'Byrne was highly thought of in Irish literary circles, Bax the musician was scarcely known at all—except to Dr John Larchet, the musical director of the Abbey Theatre. Neither Æ nor Yeats thought of him as anything other than a writer. The magic of Eire was not, however, lost upon Bax the musician. Had he not encountered the liberating force of the music of Ireland, the oppressive influences of Wagner and Strauss might well have stifled his originality for many years to come. But almost at once the curves and inflections of Irish folk music began to be felt in his work. His reaction to this discovery did not lead him, as the English folk music revival did so many of his colleagues, to collect or arrange those folk songs with which he came into contact—or even to relate words and melody. With a single exception (see pp. 80-1) Bax made no specific use of folk song as such and had little use for arrangements, drily commenting 'there's more enterprise in walking naked'. His most Irish moments bear little relationship to the music of Petrie or of Herbert Hughes. His attitude to Irish folk song was that of the romantic and poet, rather than that of collector or scholar, and although he was quick to absorb into his own musical language the elements of a recognizably Irish idiom—the poignant cadences, the modally ornamented melodic line, the repeated notes,[2] he was able more quickly and more naturally to absorb the essence of Irish music into his own personal style than was his *alter ego* with the encrustations of the extravagant imagery of the Irish literary movement. One is even tempted to regard the figures that move so abundantly against O'Byrne's backcloth of the Irish scene as grotesques, even caricatures, were it not that Bax evokes characters every bit as strange in the remembered world of his autobiography, and that many of his Irish friends confirm that such odd creatures were indeed to be seen on the Irish roads in those days.

But while this extravagant imagery is a predominant characteristic of O'Byrne's writing, such is far from the case when one examines the

[1] In a letter to John Horgan, now in the Memorial Room at Cork, Bax expressed his great pleasure at the poet's commendation 'in public, in a Dublin drawing room', of *A Dublin Ballad*.

[2] These repeated notes occur most often at the beginning and at the end of a phrase. And in such instances, as at the final cadence of his setting of Clifford Bax's 'Youth', they could be said to relate to the thrice repeated tonic of the plagal cadence—which was, according to Glinka, the characteristic cadence of Russian folk song.

music. For here the Irish Bax is inseparable from the Bax of the symphonies, and in many moments where he does not indeed sound particularly Irish he may yet well be employing a musical terminology that could be so considered if taken out of context. Bax absorbed from Ireland something more fundamental and in the end more important than simple folk modality or an archaic pleasure in tales and legends. For it was in Ireland that he first began to probe, perhaps unconsciously, into those forces that motivated him as a creative artist.

In September 1912 he stayed for a week with Æ in a country cottage at Breaghy, rented annually to the poet and painter so that he might paint. Bax had often gone to lonely places in company with Russell and had watched, in the dusk, 'the flame-like people', those dancing lights along the ridges of the hills which Russell attributed to the Sidhe, and whose iris-hued forms he professed to be able to see and to paint. Though a little sceptical about Æ's famous clairvoyance, Bax never lost that deeply mystical sense in which he shared these experiences. On this particular occasion, as he later relates in *Farewell, My Youth*, he was aware of hearing in a moment of quiet a strange sound, a 'mingling of rippling water and tiny bells tinkled, and yet I could have written them out in ordinary musical notation'.[1]

> ... During that week he made me try to concentrate on certain elemental ideas and to discover their associating images. 'Think of the sea and do your best to exclude any other preoccupation. You won't be able to keep it up for more than a few seconds at first, for true concentration is the most arduous exercise the mind of man can attempt. But try, and you may find a visionary symbol suddenly form in the depths of your consciousness' ... Obediently I left him to walk awhile by the seashore, and on my return I said, 'I saw a white sword in a quivering circle of deep red.' 'Quite correct,' said Æ, 'that was the Druid sword of Mananaan Maclir, the sea-god of the ancient Irish!' 'Perhaps,' I ventured, 'the test was not so very severe, for I believe that water is my natural element.' His 'long grey pantheistic eyes' peered at me seriously from behind his spectacles. 'Beware of believing any such thing,' he cried earnestly, 'unless you are certain of it, for water of all the elements is the most dangerous for evil!'[2]

Bax's self confessed 'Celticism' had been aroused by the discovery of Yeats and of Ireland. But, while he related this directly to Ireland in the tales and verses of Dermot O'Byrne, the music reveals it to be a kind of nature mysticism, whose origins are pantheistic and not

[1] *Farewell, My Youth*, p. 103.
[2] ibid., p. 103.

nationalistic. It is the spiritual aspect that is the true key to the music
—and in his early love of Shelley, his predilection for wild land- and
seascapes, and for those aspects of Nature with which civilized man
comes least into contact, we recognize, through his music, a nature
mystic of the most profound kind.

And with the westward progress of the nomad the sound of the sea
grew ever nearer and nearer. If Bax's pantheism has a focus, then it is
in that element of which he was warned by Æ. In *The Garden of Fand*
it is the enchanted ocean upon which the legend unfolds that dominates
the score, and it is by the waters that all is finally engulfed. Bax turned
again to the sea in *Tintagel* and in the fourth Symphony, which he
admitted to be an evocation of a rough sea at floodtide on a sunny
and breezy day. And throughout his music the sea is heard as a deep
pulse—the swell of the limitless waters over which he looked from
Glencolumcille and from Morar. (See Sonata for Two Pianos, Ex. 2.)

At the end of it all Bax stood, in spite of *A Dublin Ballad*, apart from
the harsh realities that turned the Celtic stage into the scene of a long
and bloody conflict. He looked out not on the strife-torn streets of
Dublin but over the sea—riding with Niam and Usheen towards a
distant dream. And while this vision affected his whole life and his
work, the reality of the music he was later to write was to vindicate
completely the final subjugation of O'Byrne by Bax. But the symphonies
were still some ten years ahead. And from Ireland in 1910 Bax returned
to England to meet the second great emotional encounter of his life
which was to swing the needle from magnetic to true north.

4 Russia

'And then, tearing his soul up by the roots,
she declared, without equivocation, that for
several months in the previous year she had
been the mistress of an officer in the Guards.'

Clifford Bax, *Many a green isle.*

At the home of a mutual friend in Swiss Cottage, one autumn day in
1909, Bax was introduced to a young Russian girl 'with the cold pure
face and spun-gold hair of a water nymph'[1] and before long he had
fallen in love with her. A Ukrainian by birth 'Loubya Korolenko'[2]
had settled in London after travelling extensively on the Continent
with her mother.

> Oh! Loubya was like a naiad for beauty—a golden Roussalka with ice-blue
> eyes! Lured by the fascination of her nationality and history how easily did
> I slip into absorbing love of her!—a disastrous and humiliating adventure, but
> one that I have never regretted, since it brought many an enlightening
> experience which I might otherwise have missed.[3]

On learning, early in 1910, that she had suddenly decided to return to
her homeland he returned from Connemara 'through a wild spring
storm'[4] determined to accompany her to that strange and exciting
land. With 'Fiametta'[2] as travelling companion and chaperone they
left England in April.

They arrived in St Petersburg on the eve of Easter to find the city
in a blaze of festive colour. 'Bells thundered and jangled from every
church with its crosses and cupolas awry . . . .'[5] There they joined the
throng of people, and finding the great church of St Izak's full to
capacity they made for the Kazan Cathedral.

> Very confused and blurred is my memory of that utterly bewildering scene.
> The blaze of a thousand sacred candles, the gorgeous vestments of metro-

---

[1] *Farewell, My Youth*, p. 64.
[2] The names Bax uses for the two girls in *Farewell, My Youth* are pseudonyms. Fiametta
is Olga Antonietti, to whom jointly with Natasha (presumably Loubya's real name)
May Night in the Ukraine for piano is dedicated.
[3] *Farewell, My Youth*, p. 64.
[4] ibid., p. 66.
[5] ibid., p. 67.

politan and priests, the awed ecstasy on the faces of that superstitious Slavonic
mob as those mysterious, complex and colourful rites were enacted. A dim
phantasmagoria of sound and light—that is all that remains.[1]

With a kind of romantic exaltation, intensified by the fantastic
backcloth of the Russia of the Czars, Bax was involved in a love affair
of great passion. But it was entirely one-sided. Loubya, with a theatrical
sense of the drama, was beginning to enjoy herself and led the romantic
young composer a merry whirl.

Bax was sorely tempted to return home. But partly for the sake of
Fiametta, and partly for the novelty of the experience, he determined
to see the adventure through. The social pleasures of St Petersburg
were attractive enough and Bax contrived to make the most of the
opportunity—but gypsy cabarets, theatrical outings and other social
occasions did little to soothe his wounded spirit. One of the most
important occasions, however, was the last performance of the opera
season where for the first time Bax saw *Prince Igor* and the Russian
Imperial Ballet Company. 'By the latter I was so headily excited that
I came near to casting myself from the dress circle into the stalls.'[2]

In the end it became quite apparent that in permitting his attentions
the faithless beauty was merely indulging her vanity. The edge of his
passion whetted by this realization, Bax alternated between moods of
excited exaltation and gloomy despair, and accepted her ultimate
decision to return to her native Ukraine with resignation.

The journey to the Ukrainian town of Lubny seemed interminable.
But in spite of the strained and unsatisfactory relations with his companion and the agonies of frustrated love, Bax found his imagination
fired by the countryside in which he found himself. In the velvety
nights, the shimmering forests of silver birch, the night stars hanging
'almost to hand like ripe fruit',[3] in the haunting song of the nightingale
and the languors of the not very remote Orient, Bax found ample
inspiration.

At Lubny he and Fiametta were allocated rooms in the second
house of the estate which belonged to Loubya's sister, '. . . a gaunt and
neglected palace of wood with a shabby verandah along its entire
front.'[4]

[1] *Farewell, My Youth*, p. 68.
[2] ibid., p. 70.
[3] ibid., p. 72.
[4] ibid., p. 72.

Before leaving St Petersburg Bax had summoned Dermot O'Byrne in a mood of savage rebellion to write the grisly tale of 'The Sisters' '... wherein the vanity of women met with a nemesis of peculiar savagery ....'[1] Bax the musician now turned for solace to composition. A piano was found for him and the troubled opening of the first Piano Sonata expresses quite adequately his mood.

> ... I endured in a vast but, in the end, quite tranquil loneliness, accumulating impressions for future service to my art, and holding a firm control over my ever present pain. I felt very detached from this alien life, detached now even from the imaginary Loubya of my early dream. Herself I seldom saw except at mealtimes, and if we did meet by chance at another hour her only greeting was usually a wooden resentful stare.

But Loubya's flirtations had re-awakened her affection for a young man with whom she had been a student at Kiev and within a short time the two were engaged.

> ... I stayed over her betrothal party, a protracted and—for a time—very ceremonious affair. Guests arrived from all over the countryside—amiable military gentlemen, and various young Natashas and Olgushkas, alert and twittering with curiosity and excitement. The feasting began some three hours late. ... According to plan most of the company, including the bride-to-be and myself—though not Fiametta—became very drunk.[2]

The flighty Loubya's sudden betrothal had put an abrupt end to his stay in Russia, and with a kind of relief he returned to England.

Back in London the Russian escapade seemed like an exotic dream. The affair had left him, however, in an emotional agony. He had had the mortification of being present at the betrothal of the girl he had so idolized. He returned to England much disturbed, still suffering the unhappiness of unfulfilled longings which he courageously but vainly endeavoured to throw off. He was bruised in spirit (his own description in his autobiography, written over thirty years later) but he comforted himself with the feeling that this experience would be of profit to him as an artist. It was perhaps an appropriate frame of mind for work. In a kind of ecstasy of agonized emotion he became absorbed in a number of important works, the first Piano Sonata particularly, and the earlier version of the first Violin Sonata.

The influence of Ireland and of Russia in Bax's music is strong, although musically both appeared first as peripheral rather than as

---

[1] *Farewell, My Youth*, p. 69.   [2] ibid., p. 77.

fundamental forces. Of the two, the influence of Ireland is more liberally indicated—in the curves and twists of melody which very quickly became an integral part of his style. But the effect of the Russian adventure was deeper and more complex. The specifically Russian moments (particularly in the earlier music such as *May Night in the Ukraine* and *Gopak*) have something of a picture postcard atmosphere, rather like the Spanish element in French music. Russia had aroused depths of emotion and touched strange primitive aspects of his personality. The quasi-liturgical note that had sometimes been heard in his music grew stronger and was to be heard in the later symphonic works as something of considerable spiritual importance. Russia too awakened some deep affinity within him—not only the nature mysticism aroused by the impact of the Russian countryside, but a spirit that was reflected in the Russian character.

> The Russian creative mind in seeking inspiration from oriental art (or perhaps through its natural affinity with Eastern mentality) has absorbed two curiously antithetic ideas of beauty—a love of monotony, of endless repetition and of meditations on the more sombre aspects of Nature, and a love of most vivid, even violent contrasts of bright colour.[1]

The rich and sensuous harmony of Wagner and Strauss in Bax's work now seemed to be blown through by a cold northerly wind that had howled over the frozen wastelands of the North.

The experience of St Petersburg and the Imperial Ballet had left an indelible impression. And in London, amidst the approaching festivities of the Coronation, the Russian ballet of Diaghilev burst like a bombshell. The voluptuous and barbaric spectacle[2]—*Igor*, *Schéhérazade* (in Bakst's gorgeous settings), *Thamar*, *Firebird*, *Coq d'Or* and Roerich's *Le Sacre*—the oriental tang of the music and the flagrantly pagan exoticism of the ballet in its richest and most opulent period, went to Bax's head like wine.

> I am indulging deeply in the Russian ballet—which is absolutely a new art. Before them there was no such thing as dance and dramatic gesture and the figuring of the Spirit of romance on the stage. I wish you could all see them. I am sure you would find a new zest and vitality in life as I do. Of course, it is all frankly pagan but none the worse for that.[3]

[1] Gerald Abraham, *Borodin*, Reeves, 1927.
[2] 'Today's performances by comparison might grace the parish hall . . .', Eugène Goossens, *Overture and Beginners*, Methuen, 1951.
[3] Letter from Bax to Padraic Colum.

But even these splendours could scarcely cauterize the wound that the
Russian adventure had opened in his sensitive soul.

Shortly before going to Russia Bax had met a young girl who was
dark, attractive, warm-hearted and of a generous nature. Her parents
—Carlos Sobrino, the eminent Spanish concert pianist, and his German
wife, a fine singer and teacher at Hampstead Conservatoire who had
given some lessons to an aunt of Bax's at Ivybank—were on friendly
terms with the Bax family. And with Elsa, or Elsita as she liked to be
called, Bax had begun a warm friendship. They had met on several
social occasions, and Elsa had sung some of his songs.

During his absence in Russia several things had happened that were
greatly to disturb him on his return. His greatest friend Godwin
Baynes[1] had married Rosalind, the daughter of Sir Hamo Thorneycroft,
the sculptor. The Bax family had decided to leave Ivybank (the house
was pulled down the following year) and to take a house in the West
End of London. The house was already in an upheaval in preparation
for the move. But most disturbing of all was the news of Clifford's
sudden marriage. Returning from Russia he found himself deprived
of the company of the brother with whom he had shared all his confi-
dences. Unable to unburden himself to his mother (in spite of her
gifts of sympathy) he turned to Elsa in whom he found both sympathy
and understanding. With the ripening of their friendship and confidence came the ease that Bax's wounded soul craved, and their engage-
ment followed quickly in the winter of the same year.

Since Ivybank was to be given up in the early part of 1911 it was
imperative that the arrangements for the marriage should be under-
taken quickly and, on 28th January 1911, the ceremony took place
quietly at Marylebone Registry Office. Alfred Ridley Bax provided
the young couple with a large house in Chester Terrace overlooking
Regents Park and within easy reach of Cavendish Square to where the
remainder of the family had moved from Hampstead.

But the irksome ties of domesticity and the surroundings of the city
of London began to disturb Bax. He wrote to Colum:

> London seems to me possessed with an absolute whirlwind of excitement,
> entirely without direction of any kind. I find it impossible even to read for
> ten minutes together. The whole of life for me here is like an endless concert—
> or rather rehearsal for a concert—quite exhilarating, but rather bewildering. I
> cannot imagine any literary person producing anything at all whilst living in

[1] See footnote 1, p. 45.

this place. I know I never could. Yet I think it is good for one occasionally to imbibe sensations in flood—like the saturnalia of the Greeks. Kilmasheogue seems very desirable though at times . . .

This *wanderlust* led them first to Dublin where they set up home in Rathgar in a rented villa in Bushy Park Road, conveniently near Æ. Here two children, Dermot and Maeve, were born, but his restlessness, in spite of visits from Clifford, and the society of his new-found Dublin friends, had not abated.

In 1913 they returned to England to a house in Station Road, Marlowe. In November 1915 they moved to Riversleigh, a handsome residence close to the bridge, on the south side of the river. It had a pleasant garden running down to the water's edge where a boat could be moored.

We often played chess there in the garden. He took that house to cover a period extending well into 1916. I occasionally visited him there and stayed a week or so, with Tim Braithwaite (studying for a professorship at the RAM, but who later developed a talent for etching for which he became well known) and also (Arthur) Alexander, a student at the RAM from New Zealand. We made some very pleasant trips up the river—one, a two-day jaunt up to Sonning. On this occasion Alexander (who of course must be termed Sasha by Arnold), Arnold and I, were the 'Three Men in a Boat', with Elsa taking the place of the dog 'Montmorency'. And when it came to hauling the boat from the tow-path, Arnold and Elsa would be harnessed together and did not spare themselves in pulling us upstream.[1]

From Marlowe they moved again, to Beaconsfield, not far from Spean in the Chilterns where Clifford's wife and daughter, Undine, were living.

Arnold would come to see us (always unexpectedly), about three times a year. He always came when the cherry blossom was out because there was an avenue of fine cherry trees by us and he loved them: and we would walk in our lovely Chiltern beech woods which inspired his 'November Woods'.

Sometimes I would stay with my cousins at Beaconsfield and we loved to sit under the grand piano when he was playing and composing. The bass strings were particularly resonant, which inspired us to growl and play bears round the piano legs—but Arnold carried on quite oblivious to us. Like all people who achieve anything worth while he had fantastic powers of concentration.[2]

But the shadow of coming events had already darkened the sky and the tensions of war and a growing spiritual unease within him combined

[1] Letter from Francis Colmer to the author, 1963.
[2] Letter from Mrs Undine Wilson (Bax) to the author, 1963.

with disastrous results upon Arnold's domestic life. Neither he nor
Clifford settled happily into domesticity. The qualities that were to
distinguish the creative artist in both brothers were also those qualities
that were to disrupt their lives. Their restless and passionate sexual
natures were not something which could be disseminated in the usual
flights of adolescence, but a fundamental and vital part of their make-up.
Arnold perhaps more successfully than Clifford was able to channel
this force in a more remedial way into his work.[1] He remained within
the domestic hearth for several years—not unhappily, for Elsita had a
kind and generous nature. In the end, however, they agreed to separate.
Leaving her with the two children, with whom she moved to Golders
Green, Arnold took rooms in Fellowes Road, Hampstead, and threw
himself into his work.

[1] In Clifford's *The Traveller's Tale* the strength of this force within him is apparent.
It shows in all his work, this strong sexual drive, and especially in his only novel,
Time with a gift of tears (Eyre & Spottiswoode, 1943), whose title is taken from one of
the choruses in Swinburne's *Atalanta in Calydon*, 'Before the beginning of years . . .'

5 Early Music

In November 1928 Arnold came to Fontmell Hill. Balfour (Gardiner) persuaded him to help him plant a few trees on a poor piece of run-down arable downland. Balfour pretended that none of Arnold's plants would live; whether they did so or not it is impossible to tell. But today there is a magnificent forest of beech, oak, ash, sycamore and larch—(some 18 acres)—which we call Arnold's plantation. When, in 1951, at Balfour's memorial concert, I told Arnold that I had, with great labour, high-pruned most of the 40,000 trees in his plantation he snorted, 'Yes, I can well imagine all the priapic rites that you conducted in that wood!' Anyway, there is a memorial to Arnold Bax on the Dorset Hills, and if the ruddy grey squirrels (enemy of all good trees) will only leave it alone it will become one of the finest woods in England, the haunt of wild deer, foxes, badgers, and birds.

Letter from Rolf Gardiner to the author, 17th November, 1962.

Different writers have taken different dates as the precise moment when the English musical renaissance became fact. The exact date, if there is one, is of little consequence if the burgeoning of this reborn creativity is recognized and its character made apparent. It will serve the present purpose if we take a date somewhere in 1898, when the *Standard* in a long and appreciative article hailed the emergence of English genius in music:

> Coming down to breakfast at Ivybank one autumn morning in 1898, I found my father seated at table, his favourite *Standard* open between his small and beautiful hands and looking quite excited. 'You should read this, my boy,' he exclaimed before I could take my seat. 'A new English composer has turned up and the paper says that he is something like a genius!' He handed me the sheet, and I read a long and highly laudatory account of the first performance of 'Caractacus'.[1]

From this date the English musical renaissance gathered momentum. This particular period is perhaps less understood than any other development in music. It has been the subject of many a final chapter and of at least one full-length study which clearly illustrates the diverse expressions with which this creative energy manifested itself. It is this very diversity which has so far bedevilled the historians who, in a catalogue of events and personalities, have not yet properly traced the

[1] *Farewell, My Youth*, pp. 28–9.

evolution of a specifically English musical character in the early years of the twentieth century.

It is all too often thought that the renaissance was something quite new, springing *sui generis* from a barren soil. In fact the term itself implies the truth—that the quickened musical creativity of those years was a rebirth, a resuscitation of something long dormant, dormant but never dead. If new developments in technique and a growing awareness of the Continent gave the movement a more modern sound, the creative impetus came from the source that had always prompted artistic creativity. It was in fact a nationalist movement, though lacking the catalytic influences of war and oppression, whose roots go back to 'The Reading Rota' and 'The Agincourt Song' and the first substitution (c. 1500) of the English language for the Latin in the august surroundings of the Mass.

The Janus-headed genius of Elgar, charting the course of English music and putting this country back on the musical map of Europe, was both prophetic and retrospective, and involved inextricably in the final processes of dissolution that attend the end of an era. Elgar was perhaps the most important figure in English music. But it was not from Elgar that the music of the renaissance took its character. His aloofness probably helped to prevent the establishing of a national 'school', while at the same time his work attracted the acclaim and admiration of all Europe.

The nationalist in Elgar—recognizable though not always easily defined—looked westward to the Malverns, drawing from them the earthy spirituality that is an abiding characteristic of the English musical voice and of which *Caractacus* was a direct expression. Parry had shown that once again English music and poetry might come together, and it is scarcely surprising that, in their search for textual material, the younger composers should have turned to the literature of the late nineties and of the early twentieth century, which was distinctive in character. It is this fact, more than any other, that gives the English musical renaissance its special character, to which the influences of the rediscovery of folk-song, the unearthing of the glories of Tudor music, the impact of Debussy and of the new Russian ballet added new facets of exotic colour.

Each composer involved in the renaissance, however, made his own discoveries, casting about for a personal means of expression and bringing his own solution to the problems of a new century. Movements, or schools, within this revival (with the possible exception of the folk-song movement) were virtually unknown and the definitions around which the composers of the time tend now to be loosely grouped are seldom specifically musical but drawn from the other arts.

In 1905 the Society of British Composers was formed under the presidency of Corder. Under its auspices the work of many young native composers found its way into print. Although Bax himself fared indifferently in this (the single movement Trio sponsored by the Society was later disowned by its composer as 'a derivative and form-less farrago'[1]), the Society was symptomatic of the new vigour in English music, championed in a very practical way not only by the Society but by such men as Henry Wood, Dan Godfrey and the individualistic Joseph Holbrooke. The latter's concerts at Steinway Hall (and in the provinces) provided a platform for the music of many young men, amongst them Bantock, Cyril Scott, Ireland and Bax, as well as many whose names are now forgotten. And within a few years the equally individualistic Beecham kindled new fires with the music of the then unknown Delius.

When in 1908 W. H. Bell (later Principal of the South African College of Music) and Beecham prepared a manifesto on behalf of English music, spreading it around London, literally, in the form of leaflets, it was to Ivybank, where Mrs Ridley Bax had organized a musical recep-tion for the intelligentsia of Hampstead, that they came to speak.

The Musical League, with the backing of Elgar and Delius, came to life in March 1908 with a letter to *The Times* bearing the signatures of Mackenzie, Bantock, Wood and others. In one of its earliest concerts (on 25th September 1909) Bax's *Fatherland*, a setting for tenor, chorus and orchestra of words from Clifford's translation of 'Vaart Land' (from 'Fanrick Staal's Sanger' by Runeberg), was sung by John Coates at the Philharmonic Hall, Liverpool.

In the following year, however, Bax made what was to be his most important contact to date with the public, an impact that was to further his success as one of the rising hopes of British music but at the same time to present to both listener and critic an aspect of his work that was to have far-reaching consequences in its future evaluation, and was in a way responsible for the neglect into which his music fell after 1939. In 1901, whilst on holiday with a college friend in Malvern, Bax met Elgar. It was a happy encounter[2] since the older composer,

[1] See *Farewell, My Youth*, p. 89.
[2] In a letter written in March 1921 offering Elgar the dedication of his first String Quartet, Bax spoke of the memory of an 'unforgettable day'.

while offering Bax little encouragement in his choice of a career, spoke
later of him to Henry Wood. And in response to Elgar's introduction
Wood commissioned Bax to write an orchestral work for the 1910 series
of Promenade Concerts. Bax had already written two tone-poems
directly influenced by Yeats, *Cathleen Ni Houlihan* and *Into the Twilight*
(the latter had been premièred by Beecham at Queen's Hall in April
the year before). *In the Faery Hills*, written in answer to Wood's
request, was the second of a trilogy of tone-poems on Irish subjects of
which, in a list supplied by the composer to the 1912 Society of
Musicians annual, *Into the Twilight* was given as the first.[1] *In the Faery
Hills* is based on an episode from *The Wanderings of Oisin* which tells of
Niam's luring of Oisin to the isles of revelry. There he is greeted by
the immortals; but his song proves too sad for them and seizing his
harp they cast it into a deep pool, drawing the singer into the unending
revels. Its thematic material bears the strong imprint of Irish song,
with the reiterated notes, jig-like dances (with the suggestion of a
double tonic), and decorative ornamentation. Undoubtedly this work,
with its successor *The Garden of Fand*, linked Bax's name inextricably
with the so-called Celtic twilight.

The Celtic movement in English music was not, however, confined to
the music of Bax. Other Corder pupils, Bantock and Paul Corder[2]
among them, had written music with Celtic connotations. But Bax's
strong attachment for Ireland set his Celtic music apart and attracted
most interest. The undue emphasis placed upon this aspect of his work
has persisted overlong and to some extent (at least until the recent
recording of several of the symphonies) has obscured its true nature.
For the chief protagonist in both *Faery Hills* and *Fand* is the sea—an
environment upon which the figures of ancients and heroes appear
shadowy and insubstantial, just as the 'druidical' element in the
music of John Ireland, such as *Mai-Dun* and *The Forgotten Rite*, is the
backcloth against which dark forces move and enact their mysterious
ceremonies. This pantheistic nature mysticism is the principal constituent of Bax's Celticism, and its focus is the sea:

[1] The third is an even more interesting work, the MS of which is now in the British
Museum, called *Rosc-Catha* (Battle Hymn), a piece which, it was later discovered by
Graham Parlett (see Bax Society Bulletin Vol. 2, No. 2, November 1970), grew out
of the music projected for the opera, *Deirdre*.
[2] The son of Frederick Corder and a fellow student of Bax. He wrote a symphonic
poem *Morar* which Bax must then have known, and his Nine Preludes for piano
show strong similarities with the early piano music of Bax and York Bowen. Many
of the predominating influences of the day can be heard in these pieces.

Sky and sea are still calm and radiant here, and the tranquillity is quite extraordinary. I think if I were to live in Scotland or Ireland I should write entirely different music, no more fierce symphonies with the alleged perpetual conflict. I should give myself entirely to nature's moods . . . nature does give one something definite, and there is probably more stability in The Garden of Fand than in any of my symphonies . . .[1]

To this not only Bax but Bantock, Scott, Grainger and Delius were susceptible.

Bax had become involved in the awakening of English music. The Musical League, however, came to little in spite of the enthusiasm it had engendered, and in the absence of an efficient administrator its practical effect was slight. But the impetus was not to peter out. Other champions were soon to come forward, amongst them Bevis Ellis and Balfour Gardiner.

If, apart from the folk-song revival, there is any kind of distinctive movement in British music prior to the 1914–18 war, it was given expression in two series of concerts sponsored by Balfour Gardiner in 1912 and 1913. In these concerts Gardiner took over the role of the Musical League in sponsoring native music.[2] Balfour Gardiner was a close friend of both Bax brothers and of Delius. He had trained with Ivan Knorr at Frankfurt where he had met Percy Grainger, Norman O'Neill, Roger Quilter and Cyril Scott. The 'Frankfurt Gang', as they were known, were perhaps the most interesting and least predictable of all the groups within the renaissance. Balfour Gardiner, whose unconventional attitude to music[3] did not prevent him from writing some fine and now unjustly neglected music, was generous, wealthy and fully qualified for the role of Maecenas. He gave unreservedly of his time and of his wealth to the cause of English music, and the series of eight concerts sponsored by him in 1912 and 1913 were probably the most important single events in English music before the war. Elgar and Parry were both represented, the former by the second Symphony

---

[1] Letter from Bax to Harriet Cohen, 1930.

[2] The only strangers in these concert programmes were Tchaikovsky's first Piano Concerto (played by Grainger on 27th March 1912), Borodin's *Polovtsian Dances* and Grieg's two Psalms.

[3] Balfour Gardiner professed to have no reverence for the past. He once alluded to 'Old Bach and that congregation' and referred to Beethoven as 'that desolating old monkey'—the Frankfurt Gang were apparently united in their detestation of Beethoven. The composer he seemed to enjoy most, if not exclusively, was Tchaikovsky. He wrote many fine works, such as the justly popular *Shepherd Fennel's Dance*, *News from Whydah*, *Overture to a Comedy* and *Philomela*.

(conducted by Elgar himself), and the latter by the Symphony in B minor. Works by Grainger, Quilter and O'Neill, as well as by Cyril Scott, Vaughan Williams and Holst, appeared in the programmes. The series opened with Bax's *Enchanted Summer* and the second concert (on 27th March 1912) began with a work that might appropriately have heralded the series, Bax's *Festival Overture*. Taking part in these concerts were the newly formed Oriana Choir, whose conductor, Charles Kennedy Scott, wrote me this account of those days:

I settled in London about the turn of the century, when I founded the Oriana Madrigal Society (Beecham had a hand in it then) and it was through this organisation that I came to know Balfour and Arnold, when the former, in 1912, decided to give a series of choral and orchestral concerts at Queens Hall and (as far as unaccompanied singing was concerned), the Oriana Society was the only group he could turn to in order to do what was wanted. By that time the Oriana had made something of a reputation and it was not only that no alternative to its services was available but that the standard of its choral work almost inevitably drew the Society into this particular movement. For it *was* a special movement: not merely the giving of Concerts in an ordinary way but with the express purpose of providing a foothold to a dozen or so of our young active composers who were more or less unknown to the public at this date. Balfour Gardiner was their natural leader: not perhaps the most outstanding musician amongst them, though he was a considerable composer, but by reason of his taste and judgement, his enthusiasm, his financial re- sources, and utterly unselfish personal character. Everyone loved Balfour as a dear friend, who not only helped us all with unsurpassed largesse, but steered music into channels that literally inaugurated a new era of artistic freedom. If anyone deserved the title of a Maecenas it was Balfour. He generally lived in the country at that time, at Ashhampstead in Berkshire, but had a small house in London, just off Edwardes Square, Kensington, opposite to that of his friends Norman and Adine O'Neill. Here we would meet: Gustav Holst, Delius, Percy Grainger, Frederic Austin, Roger Quilter, Benjamin Dale, Cyril Scott, Norman O'Neill, Arnold Bax, and occasionally others—though it was strange that Vaughan Williams was never of the number. I doubt whether before or since there has been such musical fervour in our midst, or such a banding together, in comradeship, of alert musical intelligence. The time had come to establish the work of these new men, and Balfour Gardiner's two series of concerts—in 1912 and 1913—eight concerts in all—were the ap- pointed means. Many were the delightful evenings spent at Balfour's house when, with Balfour as a perfect host, the general project was aired, and works were submitted for approval. It was at these meetings that Arnold Bax was so invaluable. None of us had his powers of sight-reading. He could play any- thing that was put before him at the piano, from a big orchestral score to a two-stave arrangement so that it was possible not only to select what was required with greater assurance but to have a pretty good idea of what was wanted in performance. It was all very stimulating and helpful and it could hardly have come about in any other circumstances.

. . . The extent of Balfour's generosity will never be known, but it was the discerning quality that went with it that made it so unique. Bax's orchestral work naturally figured a good deal at the Balfour Gardiner concerts. 'Enchanted Summer', the 'Festival Overture', 'In the Faery Hills', and 'Christmas Eve in the mountains' all had place in the programmes. His unaccompanied motet for double choir, 'Mater Ora Filium', came later, when I had the satisfaction of performing it with the Oriana at Messrs Murdoch's concert of the recent works of Arnold at Queens Hall in November 1922. I have no doubt that this and Arnold's other motets can be associated with what Arnold heard the Oriana do at Balfour's concerts ten years earlier . . .[1]

No one was freer from pedantry than Arnold. Even his most intricate polyphony seemed somehow to work out to the expressive simplicity of a song. Counterpoint dissolves into lovely harmony. We forget the ingredients that make it.

My impression of Arnold is of an artist of outstanding personality; no one is quite like him, nor can he be associated with a school. But these were also the marks of his contemporaries. It was the almost sudden differentiation of musical character and achievement that appeared about this time (linked of course with the development of technical resource) that is remarkable; but it was a differentiation that had not yet passed beyond the bounds of common sense and common communication.

1912 was the year of *Pierrot Lunaire, Duke Bluebeard's Castle* and *Prometheus*. And in 1913 *Le Sacre* was to achieve a *succès-de-scandale* in Paris. On 24th May 1911, after the first performance of Elgar's second Symphony at the third concert of the London Music Festival, Bernard Shaw was heard to remark to the composer: 'The harmonies, for an Englishman, are surprisingly modern', to which Elgar is reported to have replied: 'Perhaps so, but you mustn't forget that it was Cyril Scott who started all that.' The mood of the Balfour Gardiner concerts, undeniably English and expressive of the late-romantic ethos of the nineteenth century, had something of this adventurous spirit. Grainger's and Scott's music, with experiments in free rhythms and strange harmonics, must have sounded very modern at that time.

Unlike those whose sanction rested upon folk music and the folk-song movement as the only permissible deviation from rectitude, the Balfour Gardiner group gathered not around Elgar but around the expatriate Delius whose music, then only beginning to become known in England,

---

[1] Bax may well have remembered these performances vividly, but the immediate source of his inspiration was hearing the Tudor singers sing Byrd's Five-part Mass —an experience that made a tremendous impression on him. It is significant that he thought this music far greater than Bach. (*Author's Note.*)

proved heady wine. Natural reaction to now outmoded religious beliefs and the cocoon of Victorian sentimentalism, together with the new philosophies of the twentieth century, and the liberating influences of Grieg, Strauss, Wagner and the Russians, had set almost every composer to seek a new kind of spirituality in the only alternative field— Nature. The music of Delius, gloriously pagan and pantheistic, was intoxicating. Even Elgar made the pilgrimage to Grez.

Bax visited Delius on a number of occasions, where he met Eric Fenby:

> Few ventured on Delius at his home in rural France, but Bax was always welcome. Routine for visitors was usually the same: descent at Bourron or Fontainebleau stations: a drive through the forest in the old Ford to Grez: lunch: a stroll by the river whilst Delius had a nap: tea: departure. My first impression of Bax remains: Bax in his prime with Delius at Grez: quick, ruddy, shy, untidy, reticent about music, expansive about books, and constantly searching for matches for his pipe. The aged owl-like figure who greeted me years later at Balfour Gardiner's memorial concert in London seemed strangely out of context. I never saw him again. (Did truth or eccentricity conspire with Balfour to plant his Dorset trees and name them after his friends—Arnold's plantation, Gustav's plantation—should their music not live? I have often wondered since.)[1]

Delius has almost always been considered as a singular figure within the English musical scene—a 'sport' without ancestry and without followers. That this is far from the truth time has shown, and the music of Delius provides a link with Europe and with the progress of the English musical renaissance that the music of Elgar does not.

Bax admired Delius, liking especially *Song of the High Hills* which he thought was his most convincing and virile music. Delius (whose antipathy for music not his own was well known) professed a liking for *Tintagel* and *The Garden of Fand* but had no patience at all with the symphonies. After one of Bax's visits to Grez, Delius remarked to Eric Fenby: 'I like Bax. I'm glad he came. If only that boy would concentrate he'd do something fine. His forms are too loose. He should concentrate.' (May Harrison's comment on hearing this was: 'Strange! What strikes one most when rehearsing with Bax is his absolute passion for form!')[2]

[1] Letter from Eric Fenby to the author, 1962.
[2] ibid. Bax had been rehearsing with May Harrison for a recording of the Delius First Violin Sonata. He had proposed to Delius a cut in the score, to which Delius returned a flat refusal.

Each new experience gave Bax a fresh stimulus, and music poured from him. Several works followed *In the Faery Hills* which showed other aspects of the composer and made apparent the true source of his Celticism. The principal influences in this music were those of Shelley and of Swinburne. *Spring Fire*, an attempt to describe 'the first uprush and impulse of Spring in the woods',[1] was written in 1913 for performance at the Norwich Festival in the following year. Because of its extreme difficulty it was withdrawn and the first performance, postponed because of the war until 1916, did not take place until it was finally given under Leslie Head on 8th December 1970. Complex, and scored for a very large orchestra, *Spring Fire* is a symphony in five sections[2] drawing its inspiration from the first chorus of Swinburne's *Atalanta in Calydon*. It is very characteristic Bax, with its opening harp *ostinato* and cello solo (later used in the slow movement of the Cello Sonata), and the clarinet's dance-like tune (which later found its way, rather incongruously, into the music for the Royal Wedding in 1947). The 'Dawn and Sunrise' of the Introduction quickens into a joyous Bacchanal, whose coarsely blown flute fanfares usher in the *Allegro vivace*, 'Full Day', which bears a prefacing quotation from the poem:

Come with bows bent and emptying of quivers
Maiden most perfect, lady of light,
With a noise of wind and May rivers,
With a clamour of waters, and with might

And later, in this same section of the work, four solo violins, *teneramente*, sing a melody which Bax later echoed in the opening bars of 'Apple Blossom Time' for piano. The 'Romance' which follows, a nostalgic acquarelle, is followed by another riotous movement entitled 'Maenads', again prefaced by Swinburne's words, and full of boisterous gaiety:

The dryads, maenads and bassarids fly dancing and screaming through the woods, pursued relentlessly by Bacchus and Pan and their hordes of goat-footed and ivy-crowned revellers. Gradually elements from earlier parts of

[1] Bax's programme note.
[2] Bax himself regarded the work as in four linked sections or movements; but it is almost possible to see a complex three-movement pattern (the opening to the end of the 'Full Day' section, the Romance and the final *Allegro vivace*) like that of the later symphonies. Its predecessor might perhaps be the Third Symphony of Raff, 1869, which has an equally colourful programme.

the composition become mingled into the thematic weft of this musical daphne-
phoria. It is as though the whole of nature participated in the careless and
restless riot of youth and sunlight.[1]

This is music perhaps less polished than *The Garden of Fand*, but it is a
mood echoed even in the last works of his life.

The score of *Nympholept*[2] 'a nature poem for orchestra' was begun in
1912 and completed in 1915 (though it waited until 1961 for a performance). Bax dedicated the score to Constant Lambert, and prefaced
it with a quotation from Meredith's 'The Woods of Westermain':

Enter these enchanted woods you who dare.

Here again, in the hushed sunlight of the midsummer wood, Bax
enters a pagan, pantheistic world, which for him had a deep spiritual
importance. In the score there appears an important figure (see Ex.
4(b)) which reappears in *November Woods* and significantly (though
slightly decorated) in the Alleluias of *Mater Ora Filium*. Like the quasi-
liturgical motives of the symphonies it has affinities with plainchant
and is imbued with a kind of earthiness in keeping with the pagan
mysticism of these atmospheric works. After Bax's death Vaughan
Williams wrote of him: 'Arnold Bax, like Shelley, seemed to have
something of the faun in his nature. One almost expected to see the
pointed ears when he took his hat off. This reflected itself in his music.
Though no ascetic, he seemed not to belong to this world but always
to be gazing through the magic casements, or wandering in the shy
woods and Wychwood bowers waiting for the spark from heaven to
fall.'[3]

Vaughan Williams, however, goes on to say (probably touching upon
one reason why these exceptionally beautiful works have suffered
neglect): 'But for Bax, unlike the Scholar Gypsy, the spark fell continually and abundantly, perhaps even too abundantly; the very
fertility of his harmonic and melodic invention sometimes prevented
us from seeing the wood for the trees.'[4] His tribute, 'Bax had probably
more poetry in him than any one else alive', he qualified, and there is

---

[1] Bax's programme note.

[2] Nympholepsy—a condition of frenzy or ecstasy caused by desire for the unobtain-
able. The poem occurs in Swinburne's *Astrophel and other Poems*, Chatto & Windus,
1894.

[3] In an obituary tribute, *Music and Letters*, Vol. 35, No. 1, Jan. 1954.

[4] ibid.

no doubt that Bax was unwilling to prune his material or to control the rush of inspiration that fills these scores with the riot of colour and texture of a Brangwyn canvas.

With yet another important work, *Enchanted Summer*, Balfour Gardiner's series of concerts opened. Bax's setting, for two sopranos, chorus and orchestra, of words from Act 2, scene 2 of Shelley's *Prometheus Unbound* was written in 1909. It is a sensuous pastoral in which

> ... the voluptuous nightingales
> Are awake through all the broad noon day.

The *Allegro vivace* is Tristanesque, with many important and characteristic figures of Bax's later music, and reiterates the mood of the earlier works:

> There those enchanted eddies play
> Of Echoes, music-tongued, which draw
> By Demogorgon's mighty land,
> With melting rapture or sweet awe
> All spirits on that secret way.

6 Interlude

'I can well remember having occasion to call on relations on the afternoon of
that eventful Saturday, the first of August itself—I found them preparing to
go to a cricket match!'

Ernest Belfort Bax, *Reminiscences and Reflections of a mid and late Victorian.*

'Those who decry cricket,' wrote Clifford Bax, 'decry it for its principal
virtue—not understanding that it is the best of all games for building
up permanent friendships. Who ever made a lifelong friend by constantly rushing about?'[1] By friendship, Clifford, who had the same
magnetic personality as his mother, set great store, as his books show.
And although in 1911 he had immersed himself in rural Wiltshire, he
was not prepared to forgo the intellectual companionship which he
had gathered around him in London. In 1908 and 1909 he had conceived the idea of perpetuating the companionship of those summer
days at cricket in the garden at Ivybank by a series of 'cricket weeks'
using North Walsham, where he was then living, as a centre. And in
1911, from his lovely Wiltshire manor at Broughton Gifford, not far
from the seventeenth-century village of Lacock, he issued the invitations
that brought together the 'Old Broughtonians'—a stimulating company
of literary and musical friends whose convivial interchanges brought
Arnold Bax into contact with a number of men who were to exert
considerable influence on him.

The manor house, with its stone-tiled roofs, triple gables and
mullioned windows, was an ideal setting for such a company. It had
been built in the days of Charles I by Sir John Horton and had
atmosphere.

If Europe was poised then, in the summer of 1911, on the brink of
disaster, there fell no shadow on the square lawns of Broughton Gifford
nor upon the cricket fields of Box, Lacock or Corsham where the team
tested their strength. The nucleus of this not too strictly literary eleven
was formed from the participants of those garden matches at Ivybank:
the Bax brothers, Francis Colmer, the two gardeners and Lynn Hartley.
But others were soon added to the circle such as Arthur Waugh and
Edward Thomas. To their coming Clifford looked forward with
eagerness:

[1] Clifford Bax, *Ideas and People*, Lovat Dickson, 1936, p. 103.

On the morning of the day that was to bring us all together, I awoke early. An elfin breeze turned back the summer curtains of my window, and I saw that the sun had been up for two or three hours, and that the day would be clear and hot. Across the fields came the voice of a labourer calling to some one: and a cock still crowed in the nearest farm. 'Coming from London,' I thought, 'they will like these noises: and thank heaven, it looks as though we shall have a week of perfect weather.' And then, getting up briskly because of my gay mood, I considered the various men who, at that moment perhaps, were anticipating a holiday in the west country as gladly as I was anticipating their companionship. I had been friends with J. C. Snaith for three or four years, and had honoured him as the author of *Broke of Covenden* and that unique fantasia *William Jordan, Junior*. He was somewhat senior to the rest of us: a dark, lean, ruminative figure: known by none, liked by all: a man whose grave personality was respected by others even in their most high-spirited moments. Within a few hours the house would be filled with the overwhelming Baynes;[1] and we should all be laughing, a fraction late, at the witticisms of Maitland Radford. I remembered that some one had said, in a letter, that Stacy Aumonier, having abandoned his landscapes, was now entertaining the public with humorous monologues: and I knew, from experience, that he would maintain his position as chief jester to the company.[2] If any player was doubtful of being able to come, I had only to write in a nonchalant postscript 'Stacy will be here' in order to make quite certain that I should not be short of a man. And Herbert Farjeon, too, and my brother,—they would both send up the barometer of our gaiety: and 'the Major',[3]—he would provide a good-humoured objective for ingenious ribaldry. And what of Reginald Hine, —he who had always loved the nooks and crannies of history, who looked like

---

[1] Dr Godwin Baynes, friend and translator of Jung. He was hero and habitué of many of London's cultural circles. In *The Golden Echo* (Chatto & Windus, 1953, p. 261) David Garnett says of him: 'Godwin and Rosalind (Thorneycroft) were married and set up house in Bethnal Green. I had also brought in friends of my own to Godwin's circle, perhaps the most important being Edward Thomas who, through Godwin, got to know Clifford and Arnold Bax and a new world of leisured people. I believe indeed that the friendships he formed at this time did more to liberate him as a poet than anything he had experienced before.' Baynes and Arnold Bax became close friends and on his death in September 1943 Bax wrote of him: 'A great mountaineer and mighty swimmer, he was also declared by Holst to be the best amateur singer whom that famous composer had ever met.' The adventurous Baynes had volunteered for medical service in the Balkan war of 1912 and soon found himself in Constantinople reorganizing the Army hospitals. 'Later,' continued Bax, 'he performed hectic feats of surgery among Turkish refugees from the savagery of the Kurds. It is characteristic of him that he once found himself engaged in lonely combat with a golden eagle in the Persian mountains . . .'

[2] A famous tale in the Old Broughtonian annals tells of a telegram from Aumonier being delivered to the team, with whom he was not on this occasion present, at the cricket field. Opening the telegram it was found to read 'Have just had tea—Stacy'.

[3] R. H. Lowe.

a poet from the age of chivalry, who could improvise a story more skilfully than men could write it? Hine would add scholarship and a tinge of romance to our assembly. I foresaw him associating in particular with Francis Colmer, who had tutored me when I left school; a man of most winning eccentricity and of seemingly boundless knowledge in the fields of history, literature, and art. Finally we should have Lynn Hartley among us.[1]

The manor house weeks ended on 9th August 1913 with a draw at Melksham. Twenty-two matches had been played, 10 won, 7 lost and 5 drawn. Arnold Bax figured high in the bowling tables (6 for 30 and 5 for 21 against Box in 1912 and 1913) and the champion scorer was Arthur Waugh. Clifford had the score records privately printed—'the little green book that is now so rare'—and with the copies to his friends of those days he sent an 'Envoi':

> For Christmas Eve to you, my friend,
> This tale of summer days I send,
> That in its leaves may yet live on
> The hours long looked for, but soon gone.
>
> Nor only may this book recall
> Our ups and downs with bat and ball,
> But sense of days without a care,
> And cool blown clouds and August air,
> And fields of corn and fields of hay,
> And rambling farms of Shakespeare's day.
>
> Life can be grim, but when at last
> Our annual interlude is past,
> And in the dusk alone I sit
> At that long table, candle-lit,
> Made from a Kentish cherry-tree.
> I know how goodly life can be
> With ancient pipes and cider new
> And eight or nine such men as you.
>
> So take my gift and in it find
> That subtle influence best designed
> To keep a friendship sound and fair,—
> The happy memories that men share.

The projected tour of 1914 at Clifford's new home in Spean was not to materialize. But this was not the end. When the shadows of war had lifted, the ranks of the Old Broughtonians had thinned.

[1] Clifford Bax, *Inland Far*, Heinemann, 1925, pp. 178–80.

Arthur Waugh had died in 1915; John Eden had been killed in 1916; and the last days of the war had claimed Edward Thomas and Lynn Hartley. Seven years had passed since the company had parted on the field of Melksham before Clifford once again put the old spirit to the test.

Newbury and Bath were to be the settings—and any doubt about 'getting past it' on the part of those older 'Broughtonians' was quickly dispelled by the zeal of the new enthusiastic recruits like Alex Waugh and Cecil Palmer, A. D. Peters and Eric Gillett, R. O. Morris, Ralph Straus and Harold Monro. And Armstrong Gibbs came along to compose the 'Old Broughtonian Battle Song'; 'the words of the song represent the composite efforts of certain members of the team who for obvious reasons prefer to remain anonymous: the music is by all the composers who ever lived'.

Filled with a new spirit of adventure, the Old Broughtonians set out against Marlston ('August 4 1922—the wicket was like a suet pudding'); Aldermaston ('August 7th—the outstanding feature of this match was the splendid bowling of Arnold Bax—14.4 overs, 2 maidens, 27 runs and 6 wickets'); Kingsclere ('August 8th—the most pleasant event of the match was the taking of his 100th wicket for the OB's by Arnold Bax')—against Fifield, Newbury and Hampstead Norris.

The succeeding weeks at Bath took those who had known the Periclean pre-war encounters back to familiar places—to Trowbridge, Lacock and Corsham, and the prosaic score records[1] began to include anecdotes and verses compiled by Clifford and printed in yearly volumes (by Charles and Ursula Birnstingl at the Favil Press in Church Street, Kensington).

The stout bowling of the Major (R. H. Lowe) at Box (12th August 1926) is celebrated by Clifford in heroic couplets:

Again and yet again the wickets fall,
And one man's genius triumphs over all.
Nine times the Box men, as the records show,
Had fallen to, as they had fallen, Lowe [2]

And Arnold recalled a memorable marathon against Corsham on 14th August with a victorious saga, 'The Korshejm Saga', in which the OB's (in spite of Julius Harrison, Stacy Aumonier and Knox-Shaw

[1] To the initiated, the score record reads like a sonnet, Edward Thomas once said.
[2] *Old Broughtonian Cricket Weeks*, Vol. 5, 1933, privately printed, Favil Press, London.

having fallen three successive ducks to the Corsham bowling) had gone on to snatch a narrow victory of 143 to 138, with Lowe's glorious last-wicket stand of 21.

1933 was Clifford's last year—and at Corsham on 19th August he looked back over the years:

> Our game with Corsham had in it an inevitable tinge of sentiment. I had announced that it would be my last cricket match . . . I was therefore saying farewell to my team after 22 years. . . . The sky was now a patchwork of large white clouds and rich blue estuaries, and my thoughts turned to some of the earlier matches which I had played within earshot of those Elizabethan alms-houses—the great game which is immortalised in the Korshejm Saga, another in which the Baron [Keith Henderson] and I had the joy of making a record stand for the 9th wicket and a 3rd game long ago on the other side of the war. I remembered how the Major, then in his prime, scored 98 and with me at the other end made a stand of 112 runs: how we bicycled homeward to the Manor House on a golden evening: and how a clergyman (now possibly a bishop) playing for Corsham and being shot out by a demon ball from Willy Eden had observed as he departed, 'You sim to hey pleed befah . . .'[1]

[1] *Old Broughtonian Cricket Weeks*, Vol. 5, 1933.

7 Symphonic Variations

This for the maiden with the daffodil
Whose fingers' intricate enchantments fill
Our ears with far-strayed echoes of Romance.
Let us forget all churlish circumstance
And gather aught we may have said or sung
Of life's most honourably remembered days,
And while dreams burn and she is fair and young
Bring her each one his meed of love and praise.

Written by Bax in Harriet Cohen's autograph album, 10th May 1918.

Whatever Bax's concern for the fate of humanity, he expressed it in no documentary fashion in his music, leaving Dermot O'Byrne to write of the horror and grief he felt for the tragic events of Easter 1916:

You can leave your slane to rust, old man
And stretch all day in bed;
No more I'll rinse out crock and pan,
Or soak the flour for bread;
But think my fill of Mount Jerome
And a heap of nettles far from home
Where Dan lies stiff and dead.

But first I'll burn the creepy-stool
His little naked feet
Would dangle round and him from school;
(O! nice they were and neat!)
Yon creepy's pain that's fit to kill
Since Dan went whistling down the hill
To die in Sackville Street.[1]

The death of Padraic Pearce prompted Bax to write *In Memoriam*, a funeral elegy (originally entitled *An Irish Elegy*), for cor anglais and string quartet. But he mourned his friend more than the cause. The horrors of the Great War, too, are veiled in the shrouded harmonies that envelop the grotesque genuflections of the Spectre of Death which appears as 'the grey dancer in the twilight' in the second Violin Sonata. And the only indication of outward events in the music with which Bax was chiefly occupied during the years of the

[1] Dermot O'Byrne, 'In Glencullen' from *A Dublin Ballad and other poems*, Candle Press, Dublin, 1918, p. 14.

war is a pencilled note in the score, 'maroon announces signing of the Armistice, 11.11.18.'

This work was the Symphonic Variations for piano and orchestra. During the early years of the war Bax had heard a young pianist play some of his own compositions with a deep and uncanny sympathy. The girl, of Lithuanian ancestry and a pupil of Matthay, later described as 'the piano witch' by Einstein, was the nineteen-year-old Harriet Cohen. Captivated by her playing and by her elfin beauty, Bax entrusted to her the fortunes of this new and important work with which she made her Prom debut on 23rd November 1920. It was an auspicious occasion. 'There was a mighty success at the concert: I think we had about twelve recalls. All the composers, young and old, were there.'[1]

Yet in spite of this success, repeated in ensuing years, a note of perplexity could be heard in the reviews of the first performance:

> The season has brought forth no work of such stature as this . . . the Variations are great music in the sense that they are built of great material,—but the theme itself is too small for the work. (*Morning Post*, 24.11.20.)

> This extended scale is their main attraction . . . there is a grateful pause in the middle,—which means more to the composer than to the audience, who have no clue. (*The Times*, 24.11.20.)

> In the earlier portion of the work the music seems to be writhing in an effort to express something, becoming at times exceedingly impetuous and emphatic without gaining in coherence . . . (*Daily Telegraph*, 24.11.20.)

The critics' perplexity was not, however, shared by everyone. In *Around Music* the perspicacious and outspoken critic, Sorabji, wrote of the work: 'It occasionally reaches a pitch of fantastic and imaginative beauty that Bax touches nowhere else, except in "The Garden of Fand". It is incontestably one of the finest concerted works of the present day . . .'[2]

The Symphonic Variations is not a concerto. Although there are brilliance and virtuosity in the piano part, there is a total absence of the interplay of soloist and orchestra that marks the concerto form. It is conceived, like the later *Winter Legends*, in concertante style for piano with orchestra, dominated throughout by the keyboard which is silent only for about 250 bars of the entire composition—and these

---

[1] Letter from Harriet Cohen to the author, 1962.
[2] *Around Music*, Unicorn Press, 1932, p. 70.

are spaced, a few bars here and there, throughout. Nor is it a classic example of variation technique. The use and manipulation of the thematic material are directed by what seems an almost capricious waywardness. The individual beauty of the music, the magic of the piano writing, particularly in the Nocturne, and the vistas of Bax's poetic imagery, are striking enough. His dual nature, riven by the opposition of two conflicting forces, produced music of almost frightening grandeur in the symphonies. But in the Symphonic Variations, written in the full flood of his romantic ardour, it is Eusebius who is uppermost and its strength lies in its beauty.

The Symphonic Variations is unquestionably a major work, flawed though it may perhaps be. In the critics' uncertainty the composer's own doubts about the work are reflected, for, on the advice of Sir Henry Wood, and against the pianist's, Bax allowed the first variation to be omitted and the *Scherzo* to be severely curtailed at the second performance in the following year. But this did not provide the solution. The problem of the Symphonic Variations, if problem there is, remains one of form and of balance. It was not a new problem for Bax even then, but one with which he had already grappled with varying degrees of success in the earlier sonatas and in *Spring Fire*. In the Symphonic Variations Bax chose to hang the immense fabric of the music upon skeletal framework, balanced upon a central pivotal pause which occurs after the third variation. (See p. 52.)

Bax's arch-like form is one of considerable strength. The first section opens in E major and closes, before the central pause, in G major. After the pause, and an appropriately modal variation, 'The Temple', the tonality of F major established in the *Scherzo* drops, through a long and characteristically hypnotic pedal point, through E to D (the flat 7th) and is firmly resolved in the opening E major.

The opening bars of the work point the problem. With their curious parallel with the Sarabande from Grieg's *Holberg Suite* they are full of cadence, drooping from the tonic through the flat 7th and back, a nexus of harmonic chains that prevents the flight of the melody from achieving anything more positive than a tranquil and fragrant loveliness.

The enigmatic subtitles with which Bax saw fit to cloud the issue still further, far from having a direct bearing on the formal structure, other than the obvious one of contrasted movement, have a deeper and more important psychological significance. The sensuous beauty of the Symphonic Variations is that of a love poem, an idyll whose 'Strife' is

INTRODUCTION	VAR. I	VAR. II	VAR. III		VAR. IV	VAR. V	VAR. VI	CODA
10 bars	*Allegro*	Slow	*Allegro*	CENTRAL PAUSE	Slow	*Allegretto*	*Moderato*	
E major	YOUTH	NOCTURNE	STRIFE		THE TEMPLE	PLAY	TRIUMPH E major	
						INTERMEZZO		

23 minutes

23 minutes

'I believe, furthermore, that there should be one interval, not two, in this or in any other type of drama . . .' (See Clifford Bax, *Ideas and People*, p. 221.)

finally resolved, not in the peroration of the ultimate development of the 'theme', nor even in the passionate concluding bars, but in the quiet serenity of the section which Bax entitled 'Triumph'.

The key to the whole work lies not in the seemingly inadequate 'theme' but in a song, written earlier the same year to words of Æ:

As from our dream we died away
Far off I felt the outer things;
Your windblown tresses round me play,
Your bosom's gentle murmurings.

And far away our faces met
As on the verge of the vast spheres;
And in the night our cheeks were wet,
I could not say with dew or tears.

As one within the Mother's heart
In that hushed dream upon the height
We lived and then we rose to part,
Because her ways are infinite.

Ex.3

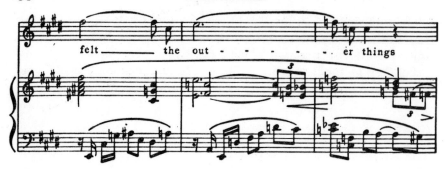

felt —————— the out - - - - - .. er things

'Parting', composed 1916, published by Murdoch, 1921. Words by Æ, in *A Golden Treasury of Irish Verse*, ed. Lennox Robinson, Macmillan, 1927.

This, both music and text, is the true theme of the Symphonic Variations, adumbrated in a misty haze at the entry of the strings in bar 16, and is not fully revealed until the conclusion of the first variation, when it is stated, quite simply, by the piano alone.

The 'Triumph' variation, whose first eight bars exactly duplicate the eight bars of the piano accompaniment given in Ex. 3, thus becomes the kernel and also the *dénouement* of the work, the spiritual counterpart of the more earthy (or less ethereal) ten-bar opening passage which is seen in retrospect as a kind of *epilogue* as well as prologue, recurring again just before the climax of the final thirty-two bars.[1]

The recurrence of the 'theme' at the end of the 'Triumph' variation marks in fact the beginning of the Coda, with its passionate assertion of the essentially transient nature of all beauty. By contrast, the foregoing 'Triumph' is a victory of spirit—of the eternal power of love and beauty over the frailty of created things. The Coda is a cry of agonized passion. There is nothing in British music to compare with these bars for sheer intensity of inexpressible emotion—except perhaps the closing music of *A Village Romeo and Juliet*, where, in almost identical terms, Delius consummates the hopeless passion of Sali and Vreli in the embrace of oblivion. The Symphonic Variations ends with the same kind of finality: 'Heigh ho, Travellers We, a-passing by'. It was a mood both knew well.

After the war the artistic climate changed. Overnight it seemed that men and their ideas had grown old and new young men had appeared. As the 'silly season' of the twenties began, the world turned its back on the past: new words became current, new ideas were propounded

---

[1] Rosa Newmarch's programme note for the first performance is, I think, misleading on this point.

and new freedom of thought extended the horizon. And, although Bax's music (like that of Sibelius) appeared unaffected by the experiences of 1914–18, no artist could remain unscathed.

Bax had not lost sight of his goal, but in *Farewell, My Youth*, written some twenty-three years later, he chose this moment for a valedictory glance at the world he had known.[1] He was then thirty-seven. And at this same point Dermot O'Byrne wrote his poetic epitaph:

> Out of that beautiful and treacherous West
> I will call home my fragile fleet of dreams,
> Nor seek again those vain Isles of the Blest
> Nor heed again the phantom sun's behest
> Nor sea-allurements in his last red gleams.
> With swords and spears agleam about their sides
> I will launch out new ships upon new tides.[2]

Pearce and McDonagh were dead, the Colums and Boyds were in America. Even the food in Dublin seemed to Bax to have lost its savour. However, post-war artistic society in London, though scarcely burning with the fevered fire that had lit pre-war Dublin, had yet a good deal to offer.

Harriet Cohen, now Bax's interpreter and constant companion, had, like Mrs Bax and Clifford, a magnetic personality. And her infectious enthusiasm for causes and people, which drew around her the most diverse and interesting personalities, began to involve Bax in a new and exciting society. Her autograph book, produced at those musical gatherings which she called 'serenades', and at which many of Bax's works were first performed, records many celebrated names—Shaw, Bennett, Lytton Strachey, Dulac, Edward Clark and Elizabeth Lutyens, Constant Lambert, Adeline Genée, Karsavina, Colum, Enesco, Heifetz, Rubinstein, Kodály, John Ireland, Ramsay MacDonald, Laura Knight and many more. Known to her intimates as 'Tania'— the name was Bax's—she was widely respected as a champion of British music (and of Elizabethan music, a policy for which she was rebuked by Vaughan Williams because of its effect on her career). Not only in England was she so regarded, for she was held in high esteem by Kodály, Janáček, Sibelius and Bartók, (the last of whom dedicated his *Six Dances in Bulgarian rhythms* to her).

Bax was one of the most receptive of all creative artists. It would

[1] See *Farewell, My Youth*, pp. 109–11.
[2] 'The Ships', in *Seafoam and Firelight, Orpheus* series No. 2, 1919, p. 34.

have been strange had this society, rich in its diversity of creative genius, not been reflected in his music. Between the early years of the war and 1921, when the opening bars of the first Symphony were conceived, his music became even more kaleidoscopic. The revision of the first Piano Sonata was followed by the second and a number of piano pieces were written for Harriet Cohen—*The Maiden with the Daffodil*, *Nereid* (originally entitled *Ideala*), *The Princess's Rose-Garden*, *Sleepyhead* (all dreamy evocative pages of romantic enchantment, almost Eastern in their subtlety of colour and sound, rather like Clifford's exquisite verse)—and, in contrast, the gay *Whirligig*, *In a Vodka Shop* and the dark, menacing *Winter Waters*.

But the 'new ships upon new tides' set out from rocky shores and were to voyage less hospitable waters. And from that moment the seven symphonies were perhaps the inevitable outcome. Sibelius had already dealt austerely with his own vision in the fourth and fifth Symphonies, and although Bax's first attempts at austerity produced the engaging and approachable first String Quartet (and the *Lyrical Interlude*—all that remained of an earlier quartet), he began to find, in the more exacting field of chamber music, the discipline that had become necessary. It was both technical and psychological discipline. He had added the sonorous coda to the first Piano Sonata, but had allowed the peroration of the second to appear as a simple melody, as uncomplicated as the tunes of the first Quartet. And in *In Memoriam* the emotional impact of Easter 1916 is expressed all the more intensely as a result of this new-found and self-imposed discipline.

One single event, however, had the furthest reaching consequences for his future work. For it brought uppermost and satisfied that need for discipline and emotional austerity that besets the artist in the moraine of war. One evening at Wyndham Place Harriet Cohen's 'serenade' consisted of a recital by the Tudor Singers in which Bax heard for the first time Byrd's Five-part Mass. He was immediately attracted by this spiritual, ornate, yet emotionally austere music and found it infinitely satisfying. In spite of the rich and sensuous colour of his orchestral works Bax possessed a fluent contrapuntal technique that (often obscured in textural treatment in the orchestral works) was melodic and horizontal rather than vertical in impulse. In the complex web of sound of many of Bax's scores can be discerned the simultaneous weaving of several melodic threads. And now Bax began work on a number of choral compositions of which the most important is the motet for unaccompanied double chorus *Mater Ora Filium*. In this magnificent work we are conscious of some transcending element, a spark of fire that moves it out of the realm of the concert hall and ranks it among the greatest choral and spiritual masterpieces of all time:

> I remember Arnold coming to Addison Road where I lived then and playing me Mater Ora from the MSS. I was probably the first to hear it. This splendid composition is I feel the finest purely choral work that has appeared since Elizabethan times. Of course it is nothing like Elizabethan work in style[1] but in texture, expressive range and spaciousness it can be compared without detriment to anything in our English vocal repertory. I doubt whether it has ever received a wholly adequate performance in which the vocal lines have been uniformly clear or its poetic quality fully realised. Its first performance[2] was the best I ever gave. But in spite of imperfections of treatment in singing, the grandeur of the work invariably seems to make itself felt with an audience.[3]

For the text Bax had the sensitivity of the poet. But both sound and image in his score belong to the present day. There is no trace of pastiche. It is deeply felt music, and the great cumulative Alleluias of the motet make use of that same pattern that occurs in *Nympholept*, and in 'Your eyen two', and which has a spiritual significance in Bax's work.

At the end of 1911, fired by the experience of the Ballets Russes which had taken London's theatre world by storm, Bax wrote the score of a ballet, *Tamara*, based on an old Russian folk tale and dedicated 'to the divine dancer Madame Tamara Karsavina whose wonderful art inspired this work'.[4]

For Karsavina, whom he did not meet until 1920, he also orchestrated a Ballade of Chopin, scored a Liadov prelude and wrote the piano pieces

[1] Bax was almost alone in English music completely to assimilate the Elizabethan influence into his own very personal style. The nearest to him in this respect is Herbert Howells, in whose organ music this amalgam of old and new is fused into one recognizable and authentic voice.

[2] 13th November 1922.

[3] Letter from Charles Kennedy Scott to the author.

[4] Karsavina had no knowledge of this work although she became a close friend of Bax in the 1920s. The piano score of the ballet is in U.C.C., Cork, the title altered to *King Kojata*. The reason for this is suggested credibly by Professor Fleischman (*Recorded Sound*, Jan.–Apr. 1968, Vol. 29–30) as partly owing to the reticence of the composer and partly because of the success in the following year of Balakirev's *Thamar* in which Karsavina had the leading role. (The title is the same but the two stories are quite different.) That Bax should be capable of 'silently burying a major work of such attractiveness' is quite characteristic of him. Harriet Cohen once told me that Bax had travelled some distance on board ship with the conductor Toscanini but had not liked to make himself known.

The Slave Girl[1] and *Lullaby*. Already he had made some tentative excursions into the theatre with the ballets *Between Dusk and Dawn* and *The Frogskin* (the former had already been given at the Palace Theatre). Now Karsavina commissioned him to write the music for a new play by J. M. Barrie called *The Truth about the Russian Dancers*. Although described as 'a whimsy', this light-hearted piece gave the dramatist considerable pains—some dozen different versions of the play in typescript were found in a suitcase after Barrie's death. It was produced on 15th March 1920 by Gerald du Maurier at the Coliseum with décor by Paul Nash. Bax's music for this rather frivolous conception (in which Karissima, the Russian prima ballerina who marries into the English nobility, expresses herself by dancing her part throughout), was 'exceedingly clever' (*Dancing Times*) and worthy of listening to for its own sake. It was, said A. B. Walkley (in *The Times*), 'woven into the action with a curious felicity'. Karsavina was enchanted with the music: 'I own I was awed at the task of first choreographing my part within the weird framework of Barrie's play. Music of the quality that Arnold Bax composed shaped into form my first gropings—I knew that if I listened to the music the shape and curve, the rounds and angles of the movement just sprang as it were from the sound.'[2]

But the production was not an unqualified success for Bax. His ideas for the theatre that had been aroused by the Russian ballet were no more capable of fruition in the 1920s than were Clifford's, whose *The Poetasters of Ispahan* had brought him some acclaim on its production at the Criterion in 1912. In the early twenties Clifford began to write a number of plays without forsaking his role as poet and philosopher. *The Rose without a Thorn*, produced by Nancy Price in 1931, was perhaps deservedly the most popular. But the esoteric philosophy and the poetically sculpted lines of Clifford's rather delicate-seeming art were soon unfashionable, surviving, like many other works of poetic worth, in treasured editions, read rather than performed.

Arnold had translated the first pages of Synge's *In the Shadow of the Glen* into Erse and in 1919 the Talbot Press published a three-act play, *Red Owen*. This had been originally conceived as a plot for an opera and was enthusiastically received in Ireland, to whose people the character of Red Owen Hanrahan was not unfamiliar. But neither

---

[1] To which Karsavina danced a 'fierce and strange' dance.
[2] *Dance Perspectives*, U.S.A., 1962. Several numbers from the score were later arranged for piano and published separately under the titles *Water Music*, *Serpent Dance* and *Ceremonial Dance*.

Yeats nor Douglas Hyde had portrayed a character of such enormous stature as O'Byrne's 'gigantic and tragic figure who reels out of some night of the Gods onto a terrestrial stage pitifully mean and narrow for a being who has all the consciousness of vast powers but who appears to his fellows as a drunken tramp with an evil reputation gained by the spell his extraordinary songs lay on women'.[1] It was a subject well suited to O'Byrne. No bald outline of this rather ferocious tale can convey any real impression of the power of O'Byrne's drama or the ornate language which is used to convey that power. The solution presented by opera Bax found unsatisfactory. There are many so-called 'stage works'—Delius's *Village Romeo and Juliet* and Barrie's *Mary Rose* among them—that however well produced and performed cannot be satisfactorily realized in actual performance and whose beauty and magic are only perfectly conveyed to the mind that is oblivious of all else save its own imaginings and visions. Perhaps the medium of film, with its boundless possibilities and artifice, might be the ideal medium for such work.

Bax chanced at this time upon the work of Gordon Bottomley who was a friend of Clifford's but who lived in the north, at Carnforth. He read several of Bottomley's plays and wrote enthusiastically (though probably diffidently) to the poet. Earlier, in his first flush of love for Ireland, he had thought of an opera on the subject of Deirdre. Some sketches are all that remain of this project. 'The gathering of the Chiefs' and an Adagio exist in piano score, and some of the material was later used in the tone poem *Rosc Catha*. Acutely conscious of the dual role of poet and musician, and sensitive to the incompatibility of poetic image, speech rhythms and the melodic line of song or instrument, he spoke of this to Bottomley. Bottomley's long and interesting reply takes up these points and expresses the same ideas:

> . . . the conviction grows on me that no one can do the poet's job for him except himself, and that great music-drama does not need full poetry. Music is not a way of supplementing and completing poetry: music and poetry are different ways of doing the same thing, often incompatible though sometimes magically at one for a brief space. I believe the point you so justly make about the musical phrase being longer than the poetic and the rhythms different is a symptom of this: and as with the phrase the imagery of music is rarely identical with the imagery of poetry and makes the latter unnoticeable and the music of notes obscures the music of speech. That matter of the imagery is most salient, for when a poetic image is sung it is very hard to take in.

[1] S.L.P. in the *Irish Times*.

For these reasons I believe that opera texts should be written on purpose very simple and immediate in statement, avoiding complexities of metaphor inference and suggestion and not relying much on the atmosphere and quality of words. Such a drama as *Pelléas* fulfils these conditions: but oftenest I believe they will have to be written on purpose—on Wagner's principles if not by Wagner's methods. The austere result may well be a work of great poetry and worthy of the greatest poet's attention: but it will have to be poetry in a narrow range and content to forgo, for the musician's sake, three-quarters of the sources of its power in order to let the musician reach their common aim in his way. If it does more the musician will sometimes have to ignore it.[1]

Although Bax had established himself with the performance of *In the Faery Hills*, the perplexity with which the critics had received the Symphonic Variations seemed to indicate that the direction in which the composer was going was not altogether clear. The only available music in print was a handful of works for piano and some songs (in the catalogues of Ascherberg, Augener and J. & W. Chester), and with characteristic reticence Bax did not actively seek performance. But by the beginning of 1922 *The Garden of Fand, November Woods*, the new Piano Quintet, the first String Quartet and *Mater Ora Filium* had all appeared in print in the catalogue of Murdoch Murdoch & Co. (later Chappells). Two performances of *November Woods*—the first of the tone poems to appear in print—had taken place in Manchester and London under Hamilton Harty. *The Garden of Fand* had been performed here, and in the U.S.A. where it was given its first performance on 29th October 1920. Dan Godfrey, who had conducted *The Garden of Fand* in Bournemouth later in 1920, also did *Tintagel* in the following year. The Quintet, the String Quartet and the Violin Sonata (No. 1) had all received public performances. But recognition of his music was still hindered by its seeming complexity and by the composer's astonishing versatility (Edwin Evans's list at the end of the *Musical Times* article in 1919 listed more than a hundred works of which over thirty were full-scale or large orchestral works). It seemed to have become even more difficult to decide just where Bax's incredibly fertile genius was leading him.

With this perhaps in mind, Bax's principal publishers, Murdochs, sponsored a programme devoted to his music at Queen's Hall on 13th November 1922, a programme designed to show the diversity of his creative achievement. The concert, which included his best and most important work, was given by Eugène Goossens, who conducted *The*

[1] Letter from Gordon Bottomley to Arnold Bax, 6th February 1923.

Garden of Fand; Lionel Tertis, who played the Phantasy for Viola and Orchestra; Harriet Cohen, who played several piano works including the new second Sonata; and John Coates who sang several songs, including the justly popular 'I heard a piper piping' (Joseph Campbell). The concert also included the first performance by the Oriana choir, under their conductor Charles Kennedy Scott, of the motet *Mater Ora Filium*.

No one questioned Bax's achievement or doubted his stature. But, as with the Symphonic Variations, the critics sounded a note of bewilderment at this *embarras de richesses*:

> We came away thinking what an extraordinarily versatile composer Mr Bax is and remembering that there are several other phases, some of them containing his best things such as the instrumental chamber music, which this programme could not attempt to include in its three hours. It would be difficult, however, to say at the end of it all what it is that Bax stands for in music.[1]

It was not altogether surprising that this extraordinary display of versatility should puzzle the English musical establishment who had begun to fall under the spell of the tone poems and had allocated Bax his place, not undeservedly, within the rather misty confines of the Celtic Twilight.[2]

To those who were, in the circles of his acquaintance, privileged to know more of Bax than most, the problem was less acute. Edwin Evans in an important article published in two parts in *The Musical Times* for March and April 1919 had surveyed Bax's work to that date with splendid insight, had put the Celtic twilight image into true perspective and had suggested where the composer's greatest strength lay:

> The Celtic influence is plainly visible in all his musical work which has frequently been described as the equivalent in music to the poetry of W. B. Yeats. Its special quality is a paradoxical blend of musical thought which, however evanescent its expression, is as definite as it is concise, with a sense of mystic beauty that demands a continuous softening of outlines. The word 'atmosphere' has fallen into disrepute through being so constantly associated with nebulous writing but here it will serve. As with many artists who have come under the fascination of the Celtic fringe Arnold Bax's musical thought is, in its essence, so lucid that it loses nothing by being placed in an atmosphere which would reduce ill-defined ideas to a state of solution. He can afford the luxury of surrounding it with mystic vapours because they do not obscure it, and because

[1] *The Daily Telegraph*, 14th November 1922.
[2] J. & W. Chester's 'Miniature Essay' on Bax, however, makes no mention of this.

his sense of beauty is so keen that he can express it by hyperbole when it suits him, though his method is generally more direct. In the end his inventiveness can always be relied upon to bring to the point of his pen whatever may be necessary to counterbalance the Celtic mirage. The sense of atmospheric beauty and the inventiveness are in fact compensating qualities in his work. Where one tends to fuse and decentralise, the other is always at hand to supply new elements of cohesion. It is a curious beauty, eminently sane, and yet tinged with a certain wistfulness wherein resides at once its charm and its paradoxical nature, for to be wistful and at the same time robust is a combination of qualities that falls to few. In his larger works it enables him to allow his ideas to become fluid with the full confidence that they will not lose their plastic shape, and in the smaller compositions, such as his pianoforte pieces, it gives him an unusual degree of liberty in dealing with the background before which the musical idea is presented in motion.

And in 1931, in *The Sackbut* for March, L. Henderson Williams wrote, in one of the most important and most penetrating articles ever written on Bax and his work: 'Younger than Holst and Vaughan Williams, he is today at meridional creativity, the noblest English musician of the young century.' Between the writing of these two estimates of Bax the composer came the first of the seven symphonies.

But in 1921 the Symphony was only beginning to form within Bax's mind. If this was to be a new direction then it was not altogether apparent even to the composer himself. No composer in England was so driven by his inspiration, and if the direction in which this force was taking him was not clear at the time, it is less difficult to understand in restrospect. Bax demonstrated through all the diversity of his utterance an undeniable unity of musical personality. Neither the seductions of the theatre nor the demands of his literary *alter ego,* Dermot O'Byrne, could more than momentarily divert him from the path on which he had set out. His chameleon-like virtuosity, though expressed in seemingly disparate attitudes, was harnessed to one purpose. Beauty was his goal—and the pursuit of beauty and its perfection in terms of human perception was his purpose. If this purpose was, outwardly at least, unacknowledged, even to himself, his creative instincts were borne by an urge powerful enough to achieve that perfection, if only momentarily, and human enough to express the hazards of the pursuit in terms of human endeavour. For a time the virtuosity—the intellect—seemed to cloud his purpose. But the new forces that were now heard in his music, which at length dominated the symphonies, and which by their very nature lent strength to that purpose, had only begun to work.

In the course of a vocal recital by Adeline Delines at the Aeolian Hall on 17th November 1922 a new composition for viola and piano was given its première by Lionel Tertis and the composer. In three movements, *Molto moderato*, *Allegro energico* and *Molto lento*, the Viola Sonata upset customary procedure and placed the slow movement last, making the central movement a demonic *scherzo*. In the Sonata, Tertis had gained a new and important work for his instrument and one of considerable distinction. From the opening bars, in which the dark tones of the viola's lower register are contrasted with the delicate high register of the piano, the Sonata drives towards the climax of the last movement with the same inexorable logic that John Ireland shows in his fine Cello Sonata. And the huge emotional climax of the eloquent and elegiac final movement which derives from the opening motif on the viola seems to mark quite clearly the end of a phase in Bax's music. It was chosen for performance at the 1924 Salzburg Festival of the I.S.C.M., strangely neighboured by the music of Krenek, Pizzetti, Vycpalek and Weill.

Some time after the first performance of the sonata Bax played over to Harriet Cohen and Arthur Alexander at Wyndham Place a new composition for piano. Without hesitation both listeners impressed upon the composer that this was something new, bigger than the piano, and symphonic in scope. A new direction had begun.

Part Two

8 Musical personality

Its history is itself one long lament: it still recalls its exiles, its flights across the seas. If at times it seems to be cheerful, a tear is not slow to glisten behind its smile: it does not know that strange forgetfulness of human conditions and destinies which is called gaiety. Its songs of joy end as elegies; there is nothing to equal the delicious sadness of its national melodies . . . the essential element of the Celt's poetic life is the adventure—that is to say, the pursuit of the unknown, an endless quest after an object ever flying from desire. It was of this that St Brandam dreamed, that Peredur sought with his mystic chivalry, that Knight Owen asked of his subterranean journeyings. This race desires the infinite, and pursues it at all costs, beyond the tomb, beyond hell itself . . .

J. E. Renan, *Poetry of the Celtic Races and other studies*, trans. W. G. Hutchinson, 1896.

By his own confession Bax was 'a brazen romantic', a definition which he went on to explain: 'My music is the expression of emotional states —I have no interest whatever in sound for its own sake'.[1] Taking this at its face value, the 'emotional state' most often expressed in Bax's work is that of gentle melancholy. This accords well with the popular and undiscriminating classification of his music as 'celtic'. But the terms 'romantic' and 'celtic' will not of themselves do as a description. Both terms are appropriate, but neither is free from misconstruction and neither is fully understood in the musical climate of today. The 'tireless hunter of dreams' in Bax's make-up pursued, by choice, the vision of Renan's other world and in the search found the adventure that is both celtic and romantic.

The true romantic is an adventurer whose extravagant realism carries with it the spice of danger. There is energy and conflict, both physical and spiritual. Within Bax is the genesis of conflict, productive of that music 'fierce as fire', unleashing a cosmic energy that propels the music with the power of some dark leviathan. It is this power that drives Bax, the Romantic, in those moments when Bax, the Celt, is forced to cease contemplation of the melancholy beauty of his visionary inspiration and seek action. Thus his music is the expression of both unity and opposites.

Bax's philosophy strongly asserts his romanticism. His truth or beauty was intuitive, and at the same time primitive, ecstatic, unhampered by the artificialities of civilized accretions, and reduced to the basic elements. In a letter to Harriet Cohen he wrote, in 1930:

[1] *Musical America*, 7th July 1928, p. 9.

I can't help being (fundamentally) a very primitive being. I believe in conditions of extasy—physical or spiritual—and I get nothing from anything else.
I think all the composers who appeal to me—Beethoven, Wagner, Delius,
Sibelius—were primitive in that they believed that the secret of the universe
was to be solved by extatic intuition rather than by thought . . . all our unrest
and melancholy is caused by conscience and remorse inhibiting nature . . . I
do believe that all original ideas derive from some condition of untrammelled
passion and extasy . . . something that only man can feel (not an animal) . . .

The most urgent need of Bax's inner nature was beauty—of line
(melody), of colour (harmony) and of shape or form. His pursuit of
this vision was perhaps more single-minded than that of any other
composer since Wagner, but this romantic temperament and his
mystical affinities with the natural forces of his environment were
characterized by a wayward and wild spirit that bred conflict. And
the conflict between the intellect and emotion is as much a part of the
music as the duality of Arnold Bax and Dermot O'Byrne.

Bax was both sensualist and philosopher. Darwinism and the
alienation of many from conventional religion had brought those
endowed with spiritual qualities that could not be satisfied with
sensuality alone into an intolerable predicament. It was the byways of
a romanticism which led him to other worlds within this one and
where Bax found assuagement for the never dormant sensuality within
him. But in choosing to 'follow the dream' he was seeking not only
satisfaction for that sensuality but peace for the questing intellect that
impelled his creative urge.

The pursuit of such revelations is fraught with danger, but through
all the conflicts and hazardous encounters, the romance and enchantments, Bax ventures, certain only of one thing—the reality of his
ultimate vision. The vision itself does not go unchallenged. The strongly
masculine diatonic basis which underlines those passages in his work
by which escape from the besetting dangers of the quest is made possible
—and which leads in the epilogic passages not, as might be expected,
to the moment of ultimate consummation, but more often to a tranquil
recollection of that moment, seen as if from a tremendous distance—also
drags the spirit back to the nearer reality, to its human doubts and
fears, to face again the interrogation of the intellect.

The flight of the music and the falling cadence are controlled and,
at the eye of the hurricane, there is a pool of deep and unutterable
peace, the source of all the whirling cosmic energy generated by the
stress of the conflicting powers. In his work Bax seems to subjugate self

in a kind of mystical unity with those elemental forces. If this is anything, it is pantheism—a more accurate description might be pagan.
And 'suckled in a creed outworn' Bax is more concerned with man as
a solitary individual than as a representative creature of a social genus;
going beyond the conception of the Romantics, he sees man in relation
to his natural environment as a rational and sensual being with an
inner spiritual existence.

This kind of reality, which found expression in the work of the pre-
Raphaelites, is itself Celtic (cf. the inverting of the otherworldly vision
in legends such as the voyage of Bran) but without any of the limitations
of time and place such as those that might seek to place the Celt in
Bax only in Ireland. Celtic art, that of a warrior aristocracy, is the
evocation of that same earthy spirituality that emanates from nature
worship and nature mysticism. Its altars were found in the midst of
thick woods, open only to the sky—altars and sacrificial emblems alike
decorated with intricate, even virtuosic, designs in stone and metal
whose curious curved and ingrowing patterns are re-echoed in the
rich curvilinear ornament of the Art Nouveau period of the early
twentieth century.

Bax's spirit soars into strange and beautiful realms. But although
Bax himself recognized this he is not shorn of his links with the earth:
'I am an appreciative inhabitant of this world . . . yet a part of me is
not of it.'[1] The music of Mahler, gloriously rich in sunset hues, exulting
in a frenzied and despairing song of protracted farewell, ends with the
music silent, as in a cavernous void. It is not destruction but total
annihilation. Bax on the other hand exults in the same agony at the
transience of beauty. But the pantheism of his inner being clings
tenaciously to earth, in which there is promise of new birth and new
growth. The final epilogic quiet of Bax's symphonic works tells us
nothing of the outer darkness into which Mahler so irretrievably casts
himself, but is a brilliantly illumined peace. This pantheistic and
spiritual element is found in the quasi-liturgical passages that recur
with frequency and have some affinity with plainsong and with
organum. In this element, liturgical in feeling and expression, we are
conscious of a deeper, darker side to his personality.[2]

But in the symphonies this force has the power of some primeval
incantation: a power that seems fearsome enough to call up elemental

[1] *Farewell, My Youth*, p. 42.
[2] If one compares this liturgical element in Bax with that, for instance, in Respighi's
Feste Romane one realizes how potent and dark is this force in Bax.

spirits. This huge surge of power, in the first symphony, stalking up
majestically from the bass, holds Bax in a tremendous grip—a power
which Neville Cardus, in the review of the first performance of the
Symphony in Manchester, felt instinctively (see p. 119). This force
can also be quiescent, as if awaiting the command of the sorcerer-priest,
and is sometimes seen in barbaric, but less terrible, guise in another
frequent pattern—that of a kind of primitive 'war dance'.

The rapid temperamental changes in his nature, giving us the
pages of tranquillity, were closely bound up with his experiences in
literature—in Norse and Celtic legend, his readings in Tchekhov,
Tolstoy and Turgenev, in the writings of William Morris and the
literature of the Pre-Raphaelites, and in *The Ring*—but were even more
closely connected with his perception and experience of the forces of
Nature, to whose nuances of mood he had both a poet's and a mystic's
sensitivity. The conflict of those elements that bred the jagged torment
of the wilder pages of his scores is a part of that pantheism which also
infuses the pages of tranquil loveliness into which the wilder passages
ultimately dissolve. It is a beauty, remote and beyond human grasp,
like that of the sun glittering on the ice-clad barrenness of the endless
Polar wastes.

The strongest mystical affinity in this pantheism in Bax is with
the sea. For him the sea held a strange fascination. Just before his
death he stood, rapt in contemplation, on the old Head of Kinsale,
in County Cork, looking out over the Atlantic burnished to beaten
gold by the last rays of the sun, a scene which was for him the very
stuff of his imagination. There are pages in his notebooks, covered with
oceanographic data, meticulously noted. The sea is Fand's magic
garden, in whose depths the intrepid mortals are engulfed. It thrashes
at the cliffs beneath Tintagel castle, and its breezy freshness in the
fourth Symphony's opening bars, its shimmering splendour in the slow
movement of the third, and its dark menacing inscrutability in the
piano passacaglia *Winter Waters*, are all aspects of the legendary domain
feared and unexplored by man, ruled over by Mananaan MacLir, or
Manawydan fab Llŷr.

Images of the sea occur and recur in the poetry and prose of
O'Byrne:

> For all my heart's warm blood is mixed
> With surf and green sea-flame,
> And wavelight burns within mine eyes.
> When the Saints your soul shall claim,

Kneeling at Maurya's feet thoul't hear
The cold seas scream my name.[1]

And so also do images of the sea seem to ebb and flow in the music—
in the deep bass surges that rise and fall in the opening passages of *The
Garden of Fand* and *Tintagel*, the slow movement of the two-piano
Sonata (Ex. 2) and elsewhere. The 'sick Tristan' motif which, as Bax
points out, occurs in *Tintagel*[2] is also heard in Debussy's *La Mer*. This
sea-surge is also in the huge swelling waves of the slow movement of
the fourth Symphony where it has a direct relationship with that
arch-like pattern that is the structural skeleton of the seven symphonies.

In *Inland Far* Clifford Bax seems to suggest a key to one, or perhaps to
both, aspects of his brother's personality:

> Believing that men's emotions adhere to the physical things amidst which they
> have been experienced, I believe too that there is an emotional emptiness in
> wide spaces, in portions of the world like that through which we were now
> pounding our passage, where nothing has existed except the blind waters of
> the sea and the elementary sensations of the sea's inhabitants; and that this
> is why a traveller may feel in those places a brilliant clarity all about him, as if
> he were entering an unhandselled world.[3]

And into this macrocosm Bax ventures, the microcosm of a tiny human
spirit. Uniquely gifted for the expression of such phenomena, Bax
stands apart from the emotional forces he has unleashed, quiet amongst
the tossing branches and autumnal storms of *November Woods* and the
menacing swell of *Winter Waters*, a not quite human beholder. It is
this element of emotional detachment that frees Bax's symphonies from
the defects of the nineteenth-century programme symphony. There is
nothing of the artist-as-hero in Bax. He is driven by forces that take all
the composer's powers to control.

One reviewer of *Children of the Hills* by Dermot O'Byrne found the
writer 'lacking in heart', in common with other Celtic writers of high
endowment. But within Bax the musician there is at the same time a
deep knowledge and understanding of a man's humanity:

> He [Vaughan Williams] is on the opposite side of Bax from Holst, heart and
> soul everywhere taking the lead of head. A devotional predisposition removes
> from him that urge to seek and probe that is ever tormenting Bax. He hopes
> more than he fears and with all his mysticism he is more easily comprehended.

[1] Dermot O'Byrne, 'Love and the Sea', 14th June 1907 (manuscript in the author's
possession).
[2] Two bars before letter H and at *Allegro con brio* after letter M.   [3] p. 66.

He is larger but not deeper hearted. He takes you with him to the borderland of mortality or on the illimitable seas 'further, further out', and then, as on a Mount of Transfiguration, you feel for a moment 'it is good for us to be here'. But it is a white glow, a special moment and attitude in life. Bax is the common life of all shot through with something that is the very essence of humanity at its highest but is capable of descending with it to its despair. Bax's music speaks for the inarticulate: it asks more explicitly than the tormented soldiers in 'The Silver Tassie', 'Why are we here?' Vaughan Williams accepts mysticism as an escape from the responsibility of thought—Bax does not. He must escape also, for the pressure of that thought is more than mortal can bear for long. But he escapes by gates of sensuous beauty, as a student lifts his head to a window, refreshing himself with the serenity of sun on sward. Again and again in his music we meet this sudden turning away from tragedy, this lift from unremitting discord to major harmonies of extraordinary sweetness and simplicity. But we know it for an escape, not a resolution; and in that again it is the stuff of our common experience.[1]

And at the same time, the strange spiritual urge, felt in the symphonic liturgical motifs (see Ex. 13), appears throughout his music:

One instance in which conscious labour becomes suddenly lifted above itself occurs, I think, in the unaccompanied motet 'This Worldes Joie'. Up to 'all goth bot Godes will', at the close of the second verse, it moves on a broad and even road of no arresting quality. Suddenly, with the bass enunciation of this line we are aware that something new has entered the music, at first seemingly out of character. But it becomes of increasing significance: it dominates. An elemental weight of evil, more mighty than any skill of craftsmanship could devise, issues from the music and beats almost unbearably upon our hearts, inescapable as death itself. Slowly the tide recedes . . . the creative fire dies down, and the prayer for salvation comes in weakly. The spirit that sometimes possesses Bax, breaching his human boundaries and speaking through him some illimitable universal thing, has just carried us, too, beyond our little pre-determined limitations. But it has passed on and the world closes in. We see again a man, graving with man's tools his small designs . . . alone . . .[2]

It is not easy to analyse the character of a composer whose expression ranges from the simplicity of the first String Quartet to the complexity of *Winter Legends*. The duality of Bax/O'Byrne is the outward indication of a deeper dichotomy within Bax's creative personality. Dermot O'Byrne was a cloak for Celtic aspects of his being that required direct expression. Deeply involved in the resurgence of Irish art, this literary *alter ego* was a channel for Bax's affection for both country and people. It was a localization of the Celtic impulse in the immediacy of words.

[1] L. Henderson Williams, 'Bax—The Philosopher's Musician', in *The Sackbut*, March 1930.   [2] ibid.

And though it bred its own conflicts (between himself and the English censor in the matter of *A Dublin Ballad*), the music shows with greater clarity that the dichotomy is a much deeper division in his nature.

Gradually, within the earliest of his compositions, the general characteristics of his music begin to resolve themselves into two strongly contrasted elements, indicative of this duality—a delicate wistfulness, nostalgic contemplation of unassailable beauty; and a harsh severity, bleak and hostile, culminating in outbursts of shattering power.

The nostalgic, wistful element finds expression in the recurring use of several melodic patterns that occur in the earliest music.

Ex.4 'Morning Song Maytime in Sussex'

3rd Symphony

This drooping, quasi-Delian figure with its roots in *Tristan* is found in Bax, Grieg, MacDowell and Cyril Scott amongst others. This sighing figure, with its very English 'droop' so characteristic of Elgar, Ireland and of other composers of the renaissance has its corollary (loosely an inversion of the first pattern) in another Baxian figure:

(b) *Nympholept*

Mater Ora Filium

And here it is further noticeable that, as this theme is developed, the implied resignation of the 'droop' is almost always followed in Bax's music by a vigorous rising climb expressive of faith and joyous aspiration.

In moments of anguish the melodic curves are further elaborated by the use of decorative ornament, embellishing the simple, even pentatonic lines with quaver-group patterns (or some such figure, it may be triplets, in the context), that seems to indicate emotional stress. (This decorative element is strongly akin to that ornament found in Celtic/Irish music such as 'The Fair Dark Rose' and elsewhere.) The second of these two patterns, perhaps because of its mirror-like relation to the first or its Florestan-like reflection of Eusebius, has a feeling of affirmation as in the gloriously positive 'Alleluias' of *Mater Ora Filium*.

The other, darker, side of his character, though present to some degree in earlier works, does not find full expression until the first of the symphonies. And from that time its power to affect, even to transform, the more feminine side is indicative of its almost primitive origins. It is at once recognizable, for it rises most often out of the darkness of the bass, or from the enormous pedal points that gather the music into moments of unbearable tension. Its climax is achieved with chilling ferocity and is cumulative—its resolution obtained only by fusion with the more lyrical material. Bax's bass lines, from which this powerful element generally arises, repay close study.

His work does not fall naturally into stylistic periods. The course of his musical development was set by those influences which he encountered early in life and, while he quickly assimilated every later influence with which he came into contact and which affected him, it was into a style already very much his own. Although he tended to concentrate in roughly defined periods on one particular medium, writing the greater part of his piano music between 1915 and 1921, the songs from 1905 to 1911 (then a second group after 1916), the tone poems between 1912 and 1917, it is evident that two main dividing lines can be traced in his work. These mark off the period of the seven symphonies (1920–1939) from those periods which precede and follow these works in which Bax's 'credo' is enshrined. The 'symphonic period' (using the term only in relation to the seven) extends over almost twenty years, preceded by a twenty-year period of development and growth, and succeeded by an epliogue of some twelve years.

In the years before 1920 those elements that emerge in the seven symphonies as individual and characteristic are seen to grow and take form. To this first period an epilogue is sung in the lovely elegiac but disturbingly disquiet final movement of the Viola Sonata. In 1921 the fierce outburst of the first Symphony shattered the illusions of those of his listeners who, without recognizing the full strength of his creative powers, thought him becalmed in a celtic, romantic backwater.

Similarly a break is apparent after the final symphonic epilogue of the seventh. Although this last period produced at least two major works—the Concertante for three solo instruments, and the Concertante for Piano (left hand), the music belongs to a world intimate and withdrawn, a world less remote than that of the symphonies, less fierce also and more personal. It was as if he had turned his back upon those Isles of the West (see p. 55), had done with visions and contented himself with a closer reality and more present things. Unable, like his colleague Vaughan Williams, to re-orient himself within the swiftly changing artistic climate, he withdrew into a kind of retirement 'like a grocer', as he put it. Conscious of failing powers, and no longer under the compelling drive of the inspiration that had wrung the seven symphonies from him, he turned inwards but without resentment to the peace within. The beauty which Bax contemplated in 1939 was shared by few. And in spite of the apparent cheerfulness of much of the late music, the scores of these last works are essentially ruminative and contemplative—with only the occasional spark of the old fire. In these scores he returns to the vision of youth with the added wisdom of experience. It is not too fanciful to see in this perhaps arbitrary division of Bax's creative life a parallel in the symbolism of Youth, Maturity and Age—Age as in the legends where youth is refreshed and renewed —and a symbolic presentation of the formula A–B–A, where recapitulation embodies cyclically the renewal of the primary conception—and also reasserts the triple movement form in which the seven symphonies are framed. This is an illusion further strengthened by the pivotal nature of Bax's slow movements, where the impulse of each work seems to crystallize in a purely melodic affirmation, as if development and recapitulation were an approach to and descent from some mountain peak from whose pinnacle and in whose rarefied air the ultimate goal is glimpsed momentarily but clearly. It is not, of course, a conscious process. Few composers have been so led by the power of their inspiration. 'All that can be said with certainty is that the truly inspired artist does not possess a gift, but is possessed by it as by a demon . . .'[1] But

---

[1] Arnold Bax, from an essay (untitled) contributed to a booklet on 'Inspiration', published by J. & W. Chester.

it is an intellectual and philosophical design peculiarly in accord with Bax's artistic purpose.

One looks for the first indications of developing personality to the songs—to which a composer, his spirit in thrall to the poetic image, comes early. A Celtic Song Cycle (Opus 4) was dedicated to Gladys Lees and is a setting of five poems of William Sharp (Fiona MacLeod), a poet whose mood seems now perhaps half way between the heavy Teutonic romanticism which impelled the early MS symphonies and the more evanescent Irish/Celtic spirit that, strongly in the air in Hampstead in the early 1900s, had already begun to show in these early songs.

The oppressive Germanic atmosphere is gradually lightened as Bax turns from Bohemian pine forest and mountain, to the Hebridean seas and to the musical imagery inspired by this new vista to which his discovery of Ireland had led. The sombre element is first replaced by something that seems drawn rather from the Pre-Raphaelites and from Morris—with Nordic rather than mid-European origins. In 'The Fairies' (William Allingham) the two predominating forces of his youth are clearly defined. He drinks with Delius at the fount of Wagner and Strauss. (See Ex. 5.)

And in the central section of the song, clearly owing much to the folk impulse, is seen the new direction taken by his melodic invention, which in earlier songs shows little promise of originality and sometimes a curiously stilted sense of melodic balance. This Celtic tune is as beautiful as anything of its time.

Some time ago I came across a letter written to Bax by Shaw—from Ayot St Lawrence and dated 2nd July 1928: 'I couldn't come to the concert. I wish you would make the gramophone people record the quintet and the symphony; it is the only way in which they can be heard often enough to be really added to one's permanent, singing-in-the-bath musical stock.'

This suspect ability to write a tune has often been glossed over in reviews of Bax's work, or even strenuously denied him. Sibelius thought otherwise, recognizing in his use of the word 'ashamed' the predicament of the melodist in contemporary music: 'Bax is one of the great men of our time. He has a fine musical mind, an original personal style, a splendid independence, and, thank God, he can write a melody and is not ashamed to do so.'[1] This ability cannot be denied Bax, who was

[1] Quoted by Harold E. Johnson in his *Sibelius*, Faber, 1960, p. 159, n.1.

Ex.5 'The Fairies' (Allingham)

extremely modest about it, once asking Eric Coates what it felt like to have written 'world famous melodies'. Bax's own tunes have it in them to be equally famous, not their least attribute being that element of compulsion that forced him, in his consciousness of youth, to shout for joy.[1]

Our understanding of melody even today is still deeply rooted in song, a vocal rather than an instrumental faculty. The contemporary composer must take into account the accumulated impressions and associations of these same intervals that have served previous generations. That Bax did so unconsciously is, I think, demonstrable in the feeling (from which few British composers writing in the 1900s are free) that he is hinting at, or even quoting from, this or that composer or work. Like the music of his teacher, Corder, Bax's work shows an eclecticism

[1] *Farewell, My Youth*, p. 23.

that is astonishingly varied in its allusions. It owes much to Wagner,[1]
to Strauss, and to Liszt; something to Debussy, Dvořák, Grieg and the
Russian nationals such as Borodin and Glazounov. It has close affinities
with Elgar, Sibelius and Delius, and strong points of contact with
Fauré, Dukas and even with César Franck. Perhaps none of these
'influences' is unexpected in a young and inquiring composer emerging
from the R.A.M. in 1905.[2]

The catholicity of Bax's musical education gives rise to an amount
of cross-reference that is very revealing. As there are in every composer
configurations of melody and harmony that can be readily identified
with the music of other composers, there are inevitably such indications
in Bax. His 'borrowings', however, are the more important since, with
a few exceptions, they appear to be unconscious—indications of
predilection of taste rather than of influence as such. As indications
they are revealing enough, and show quite clearly the directions of his
creative musical intelligence. But they are primarily a musician's
dippings into the common pot of Western musical experience out of
which Bax, like all truly great composers, was to forge a language that,
as one becomes familiar with it, emerges as completely his own—giving
voice to a personal 'demon' whose thrustings have given us pages as
strangely beautiful and phantasmagoric as anything in Schoenberg.
One must not make too much of these 'borrowings'. Yet they are
significant in their indication of Bax's own artistic standpoint. For it
has all too often been ignored or even not been realized (since Bax's
music has scarcely yet been accorded its proper due in performance)
that he belonged as an artist fairly and squarely to the nineteenth
century rather than to the twentieth, and this in spite of the abundance
of apparent discord—discord arising from the clashes of a large-scale
polytonal interflow of melodic and harmonic strands derived from the
procedures of history and not from any desire for novelty or sensa-

[1] Francis Colmer once asked Bax after he had moved to Storrington, where he lived
in an hotel without a piano, what music he had taken with him from Hampstead.
'None,' came the answer, 'except *Tristan* and *Meistersinger*.'

[2] John Ireland on the other hand reacted sharply and specifically to the influences
of Debussy and Ravel and later to Stravinsky. In Bax these early influences were
more numerous and more far-reaching. The strong parallels between Bax and Dukas,
in a work like *La Péri*, and between Bax and Delius in 'Eventyr' are, in spite of
musically common ground, more immediately recognized in the quasi-programmatic
similarities—of idea, treatment and style. Bax had an infinitely receptive mind and
it was just this wide-openness of susceptibility that, encouraged by Corder, ensured
that his work did not become hidebound or rigid.

tionalism. The impress of mid-European thought had begun by 1905 to exert an oppressive influence upon his music. Two compositions which succeed the disinherited Piano Trio are symphonic sketches existing only fragmentarily in short score (*circa* 1905-7—one in Cork, a Symphony in F, Opus 8, and the other in F minor, in the author's possession), neither of which has much significance as a symphony. Both are almost tortuously involved in the kind of Straussian convolutions that, however exciting the momentary harmonic orgasm, might have relegated Bax to the graveyard of many of his now forsaken contemporaries. (To the slow movement of the first of these Bax appends a programme note which shows that this influence, derived in this instance from *Der Tor und der Tod* by Hoffmansthal, is not only or indeed simply a musical one.) But in both works there emerges at some point a strong melodic line of the kind now over conveniently pigeon-holed as Celtic (see Exs. 1(b) and 14). It is of course Celtic, and it was fortunate that Bax chanced upon this liberating source of melodic energy. He might have fallen under the spell of the English folk-song revival whose source material proved altogether more earthy and less spiritual than its Irish counterpart. At the same time, however, or within a few years of this discovery, he came equally under the spell of Russian music (and which composer of his generation did not?). It was an influence that accorded well with both elements of his nature. The music of the 'Mighty Handful', with its characteristics of melodic ingenuousness and barbaric ferocity, its kaleidoscopic colour patterns, semi-oriental associations, bright, sharp orchestration, sudden startling modulations, the tendency to repetition with variation rather than true development, the long pedal points and *ostinato* figures, and a penchant for the romantic/heroic, was calculated to appeal to Bax. In a work like *Prince Igor* we are, even more convincingly than in Wagner, transported to a plane where life is reduced to its simplest, barest passions.

Bax's first love was also the orchestra, scarcely the ideal medium for folk-song, and yet, as the music of the Kouchka showed, an excellent and colourful vehicle for the complex designs of the imagery associated with folklore and legend. This aura surrounds even the simplest of Irish folk melodies. And it was natural that Bax should ultimately see his own Hy Brasil at a point somewhere north of west.

These apparent 'borrowings' are indicated throughout Bax's work. Many of them can be readily identified with Russia—the Borodinesque themes of the Concertante for Piano (left hand); the *Schéhérazade*-like songs that occur in the symphonies and the concertos; and the echoes of Rachmaninoff and Glazounov.

Bax quoted from Wagner—acknowledging it—in *Tintagel*, using a motif known as 'sick Tristan', a motif which pervades his music and whose inflections strongly influenced his sense of cadence. He quotes from Elgar (in the first String Quartet) and from Benjamin Dale. (In the Violin Concerto, at the opening of the slow movement, there is a passage which occurs in Dale's Sonata, but which is itself a curious shadow of the slow movement theme of Elgar's own Violin Concerto.)

One of the strangest 'quotes' of all is concealed in the opening bars of the Symphonic Variations, where the music closely parallels the Sarabande from Grieg's *Holberg* suite (further underlined by the reference in bar 6 to the Grieg Concerto) with its characteristic chromatic step descent in the bass. There are also echoes of Grieg in the sixth Symphony, in *Serpent Dance*, in *Hardanger* and elsewhere—scarcely surprising since Grieg's influence (he was one of the most widely played and most popular composers of the day, and his piquant harmonies strongly influenced European and Russian music) is also quite apparent in Delius, MacDowell and others. At other times there are shadows—of Dvořák (in the fourth Symphony's principal theme, first movement), of Sibelius (*Tapiola* is plain enough in the sixth Symphony, and the wraith of *Finlandia* is heard at the opening of the fourth Piano Sonata).

All those influences, and more, Bax encountered and assimilated with a mind receptive beyond the average. Folk-song, Irish or English, was only one of those influences to which he was susceptible and his attitude to folk music was quite unlike that of Vaughan Williams or of Holst. Only once did he consciously use a folk tune[1] and he was not sufficiently a purist to leave it alone even then. The instance is the Phantasy for Viola and orchestra:[2]

---

[1] Recognition of folk-song influence was inevitable. At the first performance in Cork of the first String Quartet, the audience was convinced he had used the tune 'Ban Cnuic Eireann Og' and Mrs Tilly Fleischman drew my attention to the close resemblance between the slow movement of the Piano Sonata No. 4 and the tune 'Has sorrow thy young days shaded'. Such resemblances are natural enough. But the 'folk' melodies in his work are of his own devising.

[2] The tune in question is No. 933 in the Petrie MSS. Its title is 'A chailin donn deas na gciacha bana' which means 'O pretty brown-haired girl of the white breasts'. The title is incorrectly spelt in the published score.

Ex.6 (An Cailín donn deas na cíocha bána)

(A Chailín donn deas na gcíacha bána)

As at other times when this melodic urge is expressed in quasi-Irish dress—with the thrice repeated notes, the modal inflections, the pentatonic cell—the line is spun out, borne upon half cadences and attenuated climax, ever more decorated and ornamental. The decoration of the melody shows how deeply Bax had absorbed into his style the characteristics of Irish/Gaelic melody. This ornamental decoration of the line—usually in quaver patterns or other compound groups, dependent on the context—is expressive almost always of heightened emotion and excess of passion, and is born of a reluctance to complete the cadence or progression without dwelling on its beauties.

Also very characteristic of Bax's melodic idiom is its tendency to cling to or revolve around a central note—which may be the 3rd or 5th or, less usually, the tonic—whose repetitions he varies with shifting chromatic harmonies. It is a characteristic derived from the necessity for tonal polarity within the web of chromatic colour, and of Bax's reluctance to complete the cadential progression. It has also a dark corollary in the chant-like repetitions of the liturgical themes which are related to plainsong.[1]

Other characteristics of the melodic line—i.e. the chromatic 'sway' or Tristanesque 'droop' (in the fifth Symphony and the second Violin Sonata), the enharmonic twists (in *In a Vodka Shop* and in all the symphonies), the trills and oscillating figures (noticeably in the third Symphony's first movement), the 'galumphing' movement (in the sixth Symphony and elsewhere), the use of arabesque (in almost all the piano works) and the characteristic 'water' theme (in *Nereid* and the Sonata for Two Pianos (Ex. 2)) and numerous modally inflected passages—are closely related to the harmonic movement of the music. But Bax's Celticism is never truly localized—in Ireland or anywhere else. The impact of Irish/Celtic music was, however, deeply involved in the development of his own personal language. The expressive 'cantilena' of Irish song ('In singing Gaelic it is most important that the phrases should never be broken'[2]) infuses much of Bax's melodic writing. The decoration is exotic rather than florid ('We are really Orientals in our singing and the gravity of the Gaelic singers is that of the East'[3]). The avoidance of expressive directions in Gaelic music can also be traced in the purity of feeling which Bax achieves in the long melodic passages of the symphonic epilogues. But his feeling for the

---

[1] In a programme note for the tone poem *Christmas Eve in the Mountains*, when it was given a performance in Balfour Gardiner's series, Bax wrote: '[it] is based principally on two leading themes. The first is a slow passage of six notes (woven polyphonically through the whole composition) which will be recognized, by those familiar with ecclesiastical music, as an old Magnificat tone of the Roman Catholic Church.'

[2] Hannagan, *Songs of the Irish Gaels*, O.U.P., 1927.

[3] ibid.

cadential 'dying fall'—so characteristic of Grieg and the Russians— the long-breathed span of the melodic flight, its emotional power thrust in the third phrase of the melody (a concomitant of his intuitive use of a kind of ternary principle that operated on a broad scale in his symphonic thinking, whose powerful inner logic refutes the often-repeated charge of formlessness) and its open-ended suggestion of worlds beyond, together with a sure-footedness in appropriate harmonic texture, enabled him to write melodies somehow both spontaneously beautiful and yet logically bound up with the ebb and flow of his large-scale musical purpose.

Instances of this melodic ability are not hard to find. I have already mentioned the verse 'They stole little Bridget' ('The Fairies'). The 'Rann of Wandering' (Colum) contains such another. The delectable song of the enchantress Fand is echoed in the slow movement of the *Legend Sonata* for cello and piano. The *Tintagel* melody—a kind of variation process built upon a cell-like phrase of the first two bars— and the austerely beautiful central movement of the second Symphony (Ex. 14) or the final consummation of the seventh Symphony's Theme and Variations, are other instances. In all Bax's melodies there is the 'droop'—the downward curve of resignation—but it is followed with a gesture of defiance in the final phrase and with an upward surge, as if it were seeking a way beyond, buoyed up with an uncrushable hope that, in the denouement of all his sonata-form works, achieves something that is lacking in all but the greatest art: serenity.

The broad lines of Bax's melodies, many of which, like the principal melody of *Tintagel*, exist embryonically in phrases or cell-like groups from which the span of the tune is evolved by a subtle process of incessant variation, are basically related to the procedures of folk music. At moments of anguish or emotional stress the basic cell, in its proliferation, is forced into seemingly complex permutations of the chromatic scale often on two separate planes (as in the opening of the third Symphony) and the music is usually at those moments charged with strong emotion, between which and the development of the melodic line there exists a direct relationship. These inflections have their origin not only in the folk modality from which the thematic nucleus itself is often enough derived but in a variety of sources all of which Bax had assimilated and which have significant harmonic implications. For the jewelled clusters of colour strung upon the central thread of the melody are not mere harmonic decoration but are an integral part of the whole framework and design.

While those elements (Exs. 4 and 13) which I have suggested illustrate the dual nature of Bax's musical make-up are related basically to folk modality (as is the conspicuous use throughout his music of the sharpened fourth of the Lydian[1] and the flattened 7th of the Mixolydian[2] scales), the use to which he puts this language shows an approach to the problem of the use of folk material quite different from that of so many of his contemporaries. The chromatic decoration and quasi-oriental arabesques with which he embellishes his melodies have not only colouristic properties but a compulsion and inner logic of their own.

In a letter in February 1912 to Rosalind Thorneycroft he spoke of this harmony:

> I was very pleased with my Sonata.[3] It did not sound at all like anything else and I realised, for the first time, that my harmonic scheme is unlike that of other composers—an interesting thought. Also I realised an illuminating paradox, i.e., that one cannot know one's own work until one gets entirely outside it, which I did then as I listened to it from the next room.

Bax's personal use of the modal inflections found in folk-song and the polyphonic interplay of chordal blocks of sound derived from his experience of the Tudors, with their stimulating harmonic clashes and major/minor ambivalence, is part of his nature of opposites and temperamentally justifiable. He preferred the primitive clashes found in indigenous folk music types and declared that much folk-song had been tamed and civilized. Edmund Rubbra, in an article in the *Daily Telegraph* (14th October 1933), spoke of this 'virile cacophony'. The opening bars of the fourth Symphony suggest the double tonic of Irish/Scottish folk melody, a cacophony which even in allusion is virile enough. There is also conspicuous use in his work of fanfare-like chordal progressions, sharpened by the incisive tones of the brass or darkly outlined in lower wind or trombones each of which instances can be related to modal procedures, to folk music—and also to organum or plainchant, whose movement, following its own logic, results in strange-sounding and complex-seeming harmonic progressions. In this kinship with the polyphonic composers, Bax shows considerable

[1] In, for instance, the final movement theme of the sixth Symphony (Ex. 13(g^2)) whose Lydian colour is reminiscent of Grieg; and indeed the theme itself has a curious mirror-like relationship to that of 'Shepherd Boy' from the *Lyric Pieces*.
[2] In the central section of *Overture to Adventure* and elsewhere.
[3] Violin Sonata No. 1.

mastery of the interpenetration of strands of thought on several levels, through whose interaction the rich harmonic colour is produced. There are innumerable instances of the major/minor ambivalence, for example in the second Violin Sonata, whose principal theme is the 'germ' type which dominates his symphonic writing. There is nothing washy about the fluid pattern of 7ths in the Toccata for Piano or similarly in the setting of Hardy's 'Carrey Clavel', and static sequential effects are avoided by the skilful tapestry of line which goes to make up the pattern.

Bax has all too often been considered as a harmonist in the impressionistic sense. And while there is no doubt that the extreme subtlety of his methods often conceals the workmanship, closer scrutiny of the more intricate passages in the scores uncovers a wealth of significant detail which, when realized in sound, gives another dimension to the music.

The key to this is in Bax's notation—the orthography of the musician. For it is not unusual to find in Bax whole chords containing simultaneously flats, sharps and naturals as accidentals, and very often underpinned by a quite extraneous pedal note. It is quite possible that the practice of writing for the harp—or two harps as he does so often in the orchestral works—and the particular technical problems involved in the use of the harp pedals influenced him in this respect. But this notation gives an indication that Bax's harmonic thinking was closely bound up not only with the interaction of those notes grouped in the chord but with their development in the linear sense.

Bax's harmony must be read horizontally as well as vertically and this is particularly noticeable when one compares the piano and choral writing with that of so many English composers whose antecedents are found in that very English institution, the hymnal, rather than in the motet. No finer examples of Bax's powers of linear manipulation could be found than *Mater Ora Filium*, or in the intricate chromatic strands in the harmonic web which he weaves around the line of a folk melody in his Traditional Songs of France.

The younger English composers were not slow to react to the emotional stimulus provided by the expansions of the language of harmony in the early twentieth century. As in the pictorial arts colour or harmony became a dominant factor in composition with the simplest melodic line clothed in the richest harmonic dress[1] that, it must be

[1] In many of the folk-song settings by Scott, Quilter and Grainger.

confessed, was sometimes more cloying than the sentiment of the Victorian era. 'The Chord' became invested with an almost mystical significance.[1] But although Bax's harmonies are rich and expressive of excess emotion, they are rarely over-refined, but are sharpened with an acute sense of dissonance that has its origin in the horizontal movement of the music rather than in the chords themselves.

Bax took part in this expansion of the harmonic language of the nineteenth century, but by the time the *Harmonielehre* (1911) appeared he had already formulated his own personal style and remained not only uninfluenced by Schoenberg but quite without the ability to understand, from the point of view of musical aesthetics, the standpoint of the atonalists. For the origins of Bax's harmonic procedures one must look to the past. And there, in such works as Liszt's Piano Sonata, which were formative in the harmonic development, not only of Bax's music, but in twentieth-century music generally, the seeds of Bax's harmonic language were sown.

Bax's technical ability gave another dimension to his harmonic thinking, in the matching of harmonic colour with timbre in a unique and personal way. Although he made use of the keyboard as an intermediate stage in the process of composition, the 'colour' of his inspiration was a part of its conception. The idea germinated and was conceived wholly in the tone colours of its instrumentation. Bax's orchestration is not only vivid—it is purposeful. His virtuosity narrowed the gap that exists between inspiration and realization. He himself claimed that the 'idea' sprang, fully clad in instrumental colour, from his mind.

In the orchestral works Bax demands large forces which he uses in the same virtuosic fashion as Richard Strauss but with quite different,

---

[1] In his contribution 'Delius today' to the brochure of the Bradford Delius Festival in 1962, Sir Thomas Armstrong quotes a long and interesting letter from Grainger on this very subject, which refers specifically to 'pre-raphaelite influence'. He goes on to indicate specific instances of 'the chord' to which Grainger draws attention: 'It will be found . . . in the last bars of Grainger's setting of the *Australian Up-Country Song*—four bars from the end to be precise. It will also be found in Cyril Scott's *An Old Song Ended* and these examples are characteristic ones to which the composers themselves call attention. The music of Delius is full of this harmony. The chord appears to be a version of a chromatic chord on the major sixth of the scale with its ninth and appoggiaturas. It can oscillate by moving its bass up or down a semitone and thus incorporating the neighbouring 7ths and 9ths. . . . The significance of this harmony for many English composers of this generation was very great.' The chord can be found also in Bax.

more subtle results. Drawing on all the resources of the modern orchestra he evokes the varied moods of the sea in the tone poems *The Garden of Fand* and *Tintagel*: the rapturous colouring of exultant choruses of horns and trumpets, and the dark menacing choirs of trombones, decorating his scores with traceries of flute arabesques and the gentle flutter of woodwind. And in *November Woods, Summer Music, Nympholept* and *The Happy Forest* he lashes the orchestra to a fury with the incisive biting attack of the strings, or floods the mysterious forests of his imagination with sunshine in passages warmly iridescent with harps and divided strings. And in the Overtures—*Overture to a Picaresque Comedy, Rogue's Comedy Overture, Work in Progress*—he paints with the garish colours of trumpet, oboe, tuba, bassoon and xylophone and evokes an atmosphere of brilliant ceremonial and pageantry touched with sardonic humour. But he is not always Wagnerian. There are numerous delicately scored passages in the orchestral works where he reduces his forces to a minimum and the texture to a gossamer-like fabric of exquisite colour. This is noticeable in the symphonies; and, perhaps to accommodate the less aggressive voice of the soloist, in the Cello Concerto. In the latter work the recapitulation of the soloist's opening material is scored for three flutes, three solo violins and basses to which Bax adds violas and cellos (*divisi*) and a muted trumpet. And there is a remarkable passage in the central Nocturne in which the soloist is accompanied by three solo double basses.

Bax seldom uses classical string tone as orchestral basis, preferring to spread the strings widely, in *divisi*, or to deploy them in a texture of pointillistic light laced with the sharp colours of the higher woodwind or soaring, in octaves (with flute parts also in octaves) in swooping patterns over great swinging rhythms in the brass and lower woodwind, or against static points or *ostinati* in the brass. Although he asks on occasion for unusual or neglected instruments—the baritone oboe or hecklephone, the sarrusophone, bass flute and bass clarinet, the anvil, piano or organ—he often achieves strange effects by a cunning disposition of his orchestral resources by opposing differences of register and tone colour. Many themes take their character from the orchestration —notably those given to the brass, especially trombones, and the clarinet writing in the fifth Symphony is important in the actual development of the work and seems part of the emotional conception. He writes with virtuosity for the violas and for harp, of which he generally uses two, both playing different patterns.

With the brass he evokes ceremonial brilliance or a kind of sullen grandeur. He uses muted brass to great effect, especially in such passages as that for muted tuba in the fifth Symphony.

The first work of the eight Balfour Gardiner concerts to be given at Queen's Hall on 13th March 1912 was *Enchanted Summer*, a setting for chorus and orchestra of verses from Act 2, scene 2 of Shelley's *Prometheus*. Within this important composition several major features of his style begin to be noticeable.

Ex.7 'Enchanted Summer' (Shelley)

This is the Bax of *Nympholept* and of *Spring Fire* and *Winter Legends*. There is another fingerprint which is of considerable significance (see Ex. 12). This pattern of a rising broken figuration based on the chord of the diminished 7th occurs frequently in Bax. The two interlocked tritones of the diminished 7th occur frequently in this kind of pattern. The significance of this harmony which requires a note from outside the chord itself to draw it in a specific tonal direction is deeply bound up with Bax's psychological make-up. In an essay on Roman Vlad in *Music Review* (May 1961, p. 126) the composer Ronald Stevenson says of the diminished 7th: 'Its ambivalent enharmonic nature and structural symmetry contribute as much to the music's form as to its emotional content. . . .' The pattern is, in embryo, a basic ground plan of the arc which is present in the curve of Bax's symphonic progress (see Ex. 12 on p. 120), but the significance of the harmony is psychological as much as intellectual, the diminished 7th seeming, in its capacity for modulatory freedom, to personify Bax's search for that 'ultima Thule' to which his entire symphonic direction points.

Bax's attitude to form was neither unusual, loose nor rudimentary. His own personal application, not of the conventions of sonata structure but of its logic, is at the heart of his symphonic thinking. The large-scale operation of formal balance in the symphonies and symphonic works can be traced to the melodic structure—the scaffolding as it were which is infilled with the mortar of harmony. It is the outline, the logic of the melodic flight, with its inherent harmonic progression that the ear grasps, however much Bax may decorate the texture. The flow of musical idea (Delius insisted that a sense of flow was the main thing) is governed not only by the capacity and the direction of the melody and its span, but by the rhythm and the tonal points which are made in its unfolding.

Bax the poet was conscious of the intricacies of rhythm in poetry and equally conscious of the difference between speech rhythm and instrumental rhythm. The natural rhythm of English music tends to be lyrical and rhapsodic. Violent rhythmic gestures seem to intrude, to be imposed from without, representing bursts of unaccustomed energy whose force is quickly spent and which relapse almost immediately into the quiet flow when the passion has passed. Bax's rhythmic drive is virile and masculine, strongly asserted in four-square patterns (unlike the hypnotic triple time found so often in Delius). Its strength is earthy, often granitic, pounded out in heavy *ostinato* and pedal point. Its affinities are with Sibelius rather than with either the warlike tread of Holst in 'the bringer of War', or the grotesque scratchings of hob-goblins in Vaughan Williams's Sixth.

Bax's rhythms are complex, and throughout the ostensibly *scherzo*-like quasi-*vivace* passages, one is conscious of a larger beat, a more fundamental rhythm which belongs to the kind of time scale as broad as that of *En Saga* and *Tapiola*. Lighter movements, like that of the *Picaresque Comedy Overture*, are capricious and vivacious, rather than true *vivace* or *presto*.

The triple rhythm in Bax is almost always orgiastic—ecstatic rather than rhythmic. It is most often expressed in waltz time (a relic of the nineteenth century and of Strauss, and also seen in Scott's 'Pierrot Gai' and Bowen's 'A Romp', a kind of Beardsley-esque romanticism that is neurotic in origin) with something of a nightmarish or delirious quality. This dance element, too, is basically a two-beat rhythm, the first accents of each two bars (of three-four) being taken together to produce a kind of broader underpulse to the triple rhythm.

In the tonal plan, as in the melodic structure, Bax follows a logical and probably instinctive need, rather than an elaborate pattern. In the symphonies (apart from the first, and in the second there is already ambivalence) keys are not stated. Departures from conventional procedures are occasioned not by a desire for novelty but by sheer psychological necessity, by the splendour of his ideas and the profusion of his invention. Both prologue and epilogue—the one exposing sometimes mood, sometimes material, often both, the other unifying and refining—have their own logic.

The tone poems and other single-movement works are cast almost without exception in a modified ternary form—A B A, from which B emerges, generally *ff* or *fff*, and in augmentation, and as Bax matures it grows apparent, particularly in the movements of the symphonies, that final development leads to the fusion of AB, which *e duobus unum* is a reflection of the man.

With the exception of *The Garden of Fand*, where the formal structure is loosely governed by the exigencies of a vague programme, this principle operates to some extent throughout Bax's work. In this triadic idea lies not only curious strength, but a further underlying connection with Celtic ideology whose triple deities, like the Christian Trinity, are resolved in unity. In the tale of Deirdre, the three sons of Uisnech have a common life, and in Celtic religion, as in other religions, the triple deity, such as the three Morrighans, is common. Many movements of Bax's music fall into this kind of threefold unity, as in the Overture Elegy and Rondo, the threefold form of the Violin Concerto's first movement, and the last movement of the sixth Symphony.

There are, however, a number of compositions, particularly the piano works, whose formal structure is based upon a kind of incessant variation which, seen in embryo in all the development and recapitulation sections (for he seldom repeats literally) is rather like improvisation in nature.

The chamber compositions have a formal logic of their own which is dictated by the nature of the material. The Piano Quintet and the first two String Quartets fall into a more or less straightforward three-movement form, the third String Quartet into four. The Piano Quartet, *In Memoriam* and the *Lyrical Interlude* are cast as single movements, the Nonet and Clarinet Sonata in two movements. And of the three Violin

Sonatas the first is in four linked movements, the second in three, also linked, and the third in two.

In the Symphonies Bax adopts what amounts to a compromise between the classical symphonic architecture of exposition, development and recapitulation, with its orderly tonal plan, and an organic cyclic form developed over the first five symphonies under considerable pressure—not only from the tonal stresses of the symphonic form but from the conflicting demands of the two aspects of the exposition material, both of which argue powerfully for dominance. The inevitable result of this conflict is the final fusion of the two aspects which gradually coalesce, from the second to the fifth Symphony, in the recapitulation sections. This is an expansion of the ternary idea which admirably suits Bax and still leaves him with considerable room for scenic design and philosophical argument. In the first Symphony the form is clear as long as one bears in mind that any such terms as A, B, C and D, used to denote subject material, have already begun to show kinship, and that over the seven they will all be expressed in terms of A and B—and finally AB. In the first Symphony Bax allows the 'romantic' E flat major to fall back into the minor. He does not repeat the process at the conclusion of the work, although with a degree of ambivalence he allows the dark nature of the material to override the G natural of the major chord.

The second is more complex. The vague bitonality of the Introduction crystallizes, in the *Allegro moderato*, to E minor, the F natural pedal of the Introduction falling a semitone. The second subject rises a semitone (as in the first Symphony) and the development is chiefly concerned with E major. The return to the minor at the end of the movement is less forceful.

And at the end of the Symphony, after the insistent G major/minor is interrupted by a repeat of the tonally ambivalent introductory music, he resolves the work, also bitonally, in F and C, as if in response to both aspects of the primary material.

The B flat of the third Symphony's first subject exposition becomes the dominant of the second subject's E flat major which is again harshly interrupted by the summons of the opening motive of the symphony. And in the third also, the exposition and development sections begin to fade at the edges and lose their identity, and also throughout the development of the B material, the primary A runs like an undercurrent in the bass, before erupting violently at the end of the movement. But the tendency of all Bax's primary material to fall—

even the aggressive rising patterns usually reach a note only a semitone distant (an octave or two above) from that on which they commence, with resolution to the unison in the sixth and seventh Symphonies—and the secondary to rise, is beginning to interconnect, and in the final C major of the Epilogue they reach their common logical conclusion.

In the fourth Bax is less tormented by the primary subject matter since it is conceived in much more genial terms. Its exposition and development are partly combined in E flat major while it is the turn of the second subject to revert to the minor, and in the development section Bax devotes his attentions to fragments only of the first subject. The development of the second subject is curtailed by a *poco animato* dovetailing of both subjects, which brings about a very festive climax in the home key. The second movement opens in E major, with the 'Romance' theme in A flat—and a central climax in G major, which is recalled in the E flat major Epilogue.

It is virtually impossible, except with the ear which has its own logic, to parcel out the sections of the fifth Symphony into exposition, development and recapitulation. In the very first bars, both aspects of the material appear darkly, and with the progress of the music we are led, through climax after climax, to the Epilogic consummation— further strengthened by the overall progression from C sharp minor to D flat major.

The tightly knit first movement of the sixth Symphony, like the first, is a result less of Bax's desire to follow any kind of formula than of the nature of the material. And in the sixth and seventh Symphonies, the process of fusion, which finally reconciles the two types of subject material in the Epilogue's Theme and Variations, is pursued to its ultimate conclusion.

9 Tone-Poems, chamber music, vocal, choral and piano works

'I am the master of my measureless dreams.'

From 'Flames and Dreams' (MS), Dermot O'Byrne.

Although Bax wrote prolifically in almost every field of music (except opera), his reputation has long rested on a handful of orchestral pieces which have become well known. As early as 1903 he began the first of a series of tone-poems which were to establish, at least to the general public, the nature of his gifts and, as I suggested earlier, to set upon his expression those apparent limits that in large measure accounted for his later neglect. Of these *The Garden of Fand, Tintagel* and *November Woods* quickly established themselves and rightly earned the composer acclaim. Their principal constituent is a mixture of impressionism and romanticism, evoking the poetic conception with a virtuosic technique comparable with, and often superior to, that of Strauss. The result is not mere scene-painting but a distillation of the poetic image in terms that are not, in spite of some delineation of visual image (notably the sea), objective nor yet subjective—but have to do with the very nature of the image itself. *The Garden of Fand* opens with an enchanted Atlantic, and *Tintagel* with the waves that sparkle beneath the cliff but, while these outward settings remain unchanged, Bax suggests in the music, with solo arabesques wheeling like birds upon the air, sneering muted brass, chorusing horns and deeply probing bass figures, what is for him the reality behind this outward scene—the seductions of Fand the enchantress and the panoply of Mark, Arthur, Iseult and Tristan—just as in Machen and John Cowper Powys we are made powerfully aware of things unseen. And in *November Woods* the same imagery begets an emotional experience that cannot be described in literary terms.

The early tone-poems, with the exception of *In the Faery Hills*, have remained in manuscript. *Into the Twilight* was premièred by Beecham in April 1909, and *Christmas Eve in the Mountains* included in the Balfour Gardiner concerts in 1914. *Nympholept, Spring Fire* and *Cathleen ni Houlihan*[1] had to wait until the nineteen-seventies for performance

---

[1] Bax's first major orchestral work, *Cathleen*, shows an assured sense of style. There are many indications of the mature Bax: in the harp writing, the falling string and

November Words.

(under the auspices of the Bax Society), and *A Song of Life and Love, A Song of War and Victory* and *Rosc Catha* (the MS score of the last only has survived) remain unperformed.

The form which Bax adopted for these 'mood-evocations' (the term was first used by Edwin Evans but was current among Bax's fellow students) was basically ternary with the recapitulation of the principal material embodying the triumphant emergence of the secondary material in the penultimate climax, before the final bars establish the first, or unite both. This simple framework Bax retained not only in the tone-poetical piano pieces but in many of the sonata-form works, including the symphonies.

Bax wrote over thirty chamber works, some of fairly large dimensions such as the Nonet, the Concerto for flute, harp, oboe and strings[1] and *Threnody and Scherzo* for bassoon, harp and string sextet.

There are many complex scores such as the big three-movement Piano Quintet, but a convenient starting point for any newcomer to this music might well be the first String Quartet (1918).

This is a cheerfully extrovert work, and its gracious lines and pleasing harmonies must silence the criticism that has often been directed at Bax's chamber music. Few could fail to be won over by the lyrical opening with its jaunty walking tune. (Ex. 8.)

The richly contrived counterpoint of the second String Quartet is, however, less immediately approachable. An uncompromising and formidable work, it opens in a rugged mood with contrapuntal dialogue between cello and viola. Yet amongst the complex developments of this there is a wealth of fine melodic writing which contrasts with the more sombre liturgical moments. The geniality of the first Quartet and the seriousness of the second are blended in the third String Quartet which is also much larger in scale. The opening movement has a vigorously striding melody throwing the liturgical *Lento* into relief. The plaintive chromatic droop of this second movement is marked again in the ensuing *Scherzo* (with a trio of dreamy abandon), whose grotesque caricature has something nightmarish about it. But

---

brass figures, and in the Celtic curve of the central melody (which is echoed in the third Symphony). Its haunting nostalgia is not so much post-Wagnerian as that which, a decade later, found expression in the music of the Georgians, Butterworth, Ireland and Gurney.

[1] Originally written as a Sonata for flute and harp for Count Benckendorff, the work was re-scored in this form in April 1936 and is in three movements.

Ex. 8 String Quartet No. 1 in G

the gaiety is restored in the final movement whose brisk themes, echoing those of the opening, unite the work.

Bax's three Violin Sonatas, like the Piano Sonatas, fall into two groups. The first two, in mood and expression, are sensuous and ornate, the third more austere and scored more economically. The melodic material of the first Sonata dictates the form of the work and has, beneath its glowing tune, a hint of melancholy. The two outer movements, which share the same material, are separated by a barbaric dance.

The second Violin Sonata is an important work which, like the first Piano Sonata, embodies the 'germ' motif that Bax was later to develop in the symphonies. Like the second Piano Sonata and second Symphony, the sonata has an atmosphere of brooding melancholy stemming here from the 'drooping' melody of the first few bars—a motif that recurs in *November Woods* and elsewhere. Much of the material was also conceived in the velvety nights of the Ukraine spring and the solo line is much decorated with quasi-oriental arabesques. There are four linked movements, the first of which entitled 'Fantasy' opens with a slow and gloomy introduction which exposes both mood and material. The 'rough and fierce' *Allegro* which follows seems to portray a disquiet of spirit that throws the central melody, a nostalgic song-in-exile in the piano over a persistent flattened 7th which undermines the tonic key, into sharp and poignant relief. The truncated resumption of the first motif leads, without a break, into a fast waltz. There is no gaiety, however, in this shadowy and spectral dance (entitled 'The Grey Dancer in the Twilight') around whose cadaverous version of the song-in-exile the empty 5ths of the dark fiddler seem to hover. The music sinks to a troubled quiet as the motif of the opening reappears over a long and hypnotic arpeggio interlude which leads into a sultry nocturne-like slow movement. Its languorous spell is woven into a kaleidoscopic texture of shifting harmonies over which the violin spins an elaborately decorated song. The ensuing *Allegro feroce*— a dramatic variant of the first movement material—is interrupted by the enmeshing web of the interlude whose spell, however, is quickly broken and the *Allegro feroce* is resumed in a mood of demonic frenzy. The conflict is finally resolved in a serenely tranquil epilogue.

The third of the sonatas, whose first movement evolves around a wayward Celtic song, is more direct in its approach, and resembles the fourth Piano Sonata in the clear and precise scoring. The second movement, with an atmosphere of cruel ferocity, comes to a wild and ecstatic climax.

Bax wrote three works for cello and piano: a sonata, largest in scale and breadth of vision, whose energetic first movement is followed by a nocturnal sea-scape and the unholy proceedings of the final *Molto vivace*; a sonatina, extrovert and approachable, whose second movement, again a kind of northerly sea-scape, has a hypnotic quality banished by the ebullient and triumphant *Moderato*; and the *Legend* Sonata whose clattering rhythms and tangy harmonies suggest an even more northerly setting. Its final *Rondo* flowers into a powerful thrusting theme of heroic proportions.

The most immediately attractive of the larger scale chamber compositions is the Nonet, written for the Bradford Triennial Chamber Music Festival of 1931 and first performed on 8th March of that year. Like the first String Quartet it is an engaging score blossoming from the opening muted viola triplet figure, and, like the Ravel Introduction and Allegro (which it resembles in mood), gives prominence to the role of the harp.

In the *Threnody and Scherzo*, scored for harp and string sextet as well as bassoon, it is the bassoon that gives the score its character, and the sombre mournful melody of the opening dominates the whole first movement. The *Scherzo* has a gay chattering quality, but soon becomes tense and brittle and ends on a note of menace. Similarly the Octet for horn, piano and string sextet, written for Aubrey Brain and Harriet Cohen, derives its character from the principal solo instrument, the horn. Amongst other combinations such as the Quintet for harp and strings, the Elegiac Trio for flute, viola and harp (by no means as evanescent a work as the combination might suggest), and the engaging Oboe Quintet, there are more complex works such as the String Quintet and the Sonata for viola and harp, this latter a virtuosic *tour-de-force*. It is perhaps strange that out of such a catalogue few, if any, of Bax's chamber compositions have achieved the popularity that would establish them in the concert repertory.

If the chamber works have been unjustly neglected, Bax's songs have been virtually ignored. Yet all his songs are well written, some of them are exquisitely beautiful and all of them show inclinations that cannot be seen in any of his contemporaries. His choice of texts is significant. In the early songs (before 1911) he chooses Fiona MacLeod, the Pre-Raphaelites and (perhaps under Clifford's influence) Ruckert, Dehmel and Jacobsen. With the single exception of 'Go, Lovely Rose' he has not set those minor lyricists to which so many English composers of the time turned for texts. Nor (except for 'O Mistress Mine') did he set Shakespeare—nor the Elizabethans, nor the Georgians. The English folk-song influence, so apparent in the English art-song genre, is quite absent in Bax. And when any kind of folk element is present, it is generally Irish or Northern, present in touches of colour in the piano part, or expressed in a burst of song that does not always fit happily into the rest of the piece. Only later, in the Three Irish Songs to words of Padraic Colum, does the melodic element begin to dominate. Other influences in the earlier songs tend to turn the melodic line inwards upon itself (as in 'The White Peace' (MacLeod) at the word 'plain'). And in the very earliest an obsession with the setting cramps and inhibits the melody.[1] In or around 1910 Bax collected together (for possible publication) the best of these early songs including the only setting of Yeats,[2] and the solitary instance of a setting of his own words:

Ex.9 'A Roundel' (Dermot O'Byrne)

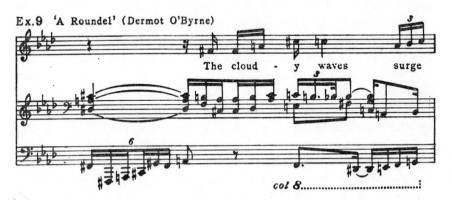

The cloud - y waves surge

on - ward to the land.

In this setting of 'When we are lost' ('A Roundel', Dermot O'Byrne, words from a manuscript in the author's possession) significant passages occur that, in their coalescence of vision between poet and composer,

[1] It is not unlikely that Bax thought of many of the accompaniments in orchestral terms, as several of his songs were later scored.

[2] 'The Fiddler of Dooney', Dresden, 1907. Bax often remarked on his disinclination to set Yeats and it is remarkable that in spite of a discrepancy in dates 'The Enchanted Fiddle' is the self-same song, with words ostensibly anonymous yet which have all the hallmarks of Dermot O'Byrne.

act like a kind of Rosetta Stone in the identification of images that recur in later works.

The early 'Ideala' later appeared as the piano piece *Nereid*, and 'A Lyke Wake Dirge' was later orchestrated. In 1919 Chester published an important collection of seven songs that has for long been considered representative and which brought him a wider public. Three ('The White Peace', 'A Milking Sian' and 'Shieling Song') are settings of Fiona MacLeod, tinged with an oppressive Celticism that has become Bax's best known yet least significant mood. The two Irish songs in the set, 'To Ireland' (J. H. Cousins) and 'The Enchanted Fiddle' (Anon., but see footnote 2 on p. 99), are less important than the later settings of Colum, Synge and Campbell. The two remaining songs are much more interesting.

'A Christmas Carol' (fifteenth century) does not quite come off, although there is a hint of richness in the ornamented Alleluias. But at the phrase 'res miranda' one feels an impulse stronger than the dusty piety of formal orisons. The setting of Chaucer's 'Your eyen two wol slay me sodenly' is later in date (1914), and shows a development in the assurance of its harmony and contrapuntal strength. It is to 'A Christmas Carol' what *Mater Ora Filium* is to the other carol pieces. Conspicuous is the 'alleluia' pattern of the motet, and of *Nympholept*, and the form is more tightly knit than the verse-variation form of the earlier songs. It is a soliloquy on love (like the first and best of the Traditional Songs of France, 1920), which forms an interesting contrast with Warlock's 'Sleep'.

The later settings of Colum, Campbell and Synge (Five Irish Songs, 1922) are probably his best. Certainly 'I heard a piper piping', with its simple yet almost orchestrally effective piano part, is the most popular and best known of all his songs. The other Campbell setting, 'As I came over the grey grey hills', is at the other end of the scale—big, heroic and full of rich colour. (See Ex. 10.)

'Beg Innish' (Synge) is full of a raucous, bawdy humour, the Irish Bax at his best. It is a dance, characteristically larger than life, with the jig played, as if by the devil himself, on 'silken strings would draw a dance from girls are lame or shy'. 'The Pigeons' and 'Across the Door' are in contrast to this, and full of rich expressive colour of chromatic harmony which matches Colum's words.

If the music of Vaughan Williams reveals the agnostic, and even occasionally the passive atheist, Bax's music, full of doubts, perplexities and joyous affirmation reveals in those very perplexities the human

predicament in the twentieth century. His Quaker ancestry and his nonconformist upbringing, both shed for more esoteric-seeming paths, might, had he voyaged less far, have led him ultimately to the haven of the Roman communion. But he had little use for the trappings of conventional religion, although his music speaks eloquently of some great spiritual experience, which he himself described as ecstatic, and which appears in the music most often as a kind of pantheism.

This was by no means agnosticism—and only atheism if one seeks to express it in words. In the music, it is the expression of a human spirit in its quest for spiritual knowledge, momentarily more powerful, if less sustained, than *The Dream of Gerontius*. Faced with the ambiguities of life and the vastness of Nature, Bax is at once joyous and fearful, doubting and affirmative, despairing and exultant, and he clings to those forces which have most nearly the attributes of omnipotence and permanence—the elements of Nature. As a man his philosophy was less tortuous: 'With all Arnold's outward realism and agnosticism pertaining to religion he had a peculiar love for anything mystical, or deeply religious. And although he seldom revealed it, when he did so he was as simple and believing as a child.'[1]

While the most cogent expressions of this spirituality are found in the symphonies, the most overt indications are to be seen in the choral works, where the quasi-religious texts themselves dictate the terms in which the mood is to be expressed. And here in *Mater Ora Filium, This Worlde's Joie* and parts of *St Patrick's Breastplate*, as in the symphonies, when the spiritual experience is deepest—whether it be of good or evil—the mood is one of fierce joy or terrible splendour.

The religious element in the semi-secular carol pieces—'Of a Rose I Sing a Song', 'The Boar's Head' and 'Now is the time of Christymas' —is a curious blend of reverence and gaiety, jocular, raucous and profoundly mystical by turns.

With this earthy kind of spirituality Bax was quite at ease, and the musical possibilities of the form—the blend of song and dance—attracted him as a composer far more readily than the conventional religious forms, the hymn tune and the anthem, in which he was ill at ease.[2] The solemn opening of 'The Boar's Head' is soon banished by the principal tune of the carol with its rhythmic background, suggestive of

---

[1] Tilly Fleischman, 'Some reminiscences of Arnold Bax' (unpublished).

[2] It is worth noting that the *Magnificat* (1949) is in fact a rewriting of the early song of the same title 'after a picture by D. G. Rossetti' with a self-conscious alteration in the first phrase of the melodic line.

the village waits. To the voices Bax adds flute and piano, in 'Now is the time of Christymas'; and harp, cello and double bass in 'Of a Rose I Sing a Song', a ravishingly beautiful setting of fifteenth-century words. The shapely expressive song of the opening tenor voice is treated, quasi-variation style, in increasingly complex patterns in each verse, depicting the six branches of the rosebeam of which the fourth, whose branch 'sprang into Hell', is a snarling evocation of medieval colour. The dominant motif of the last verse, however, is 'send us good life and long', although the work ends with an eight-part Amen of some complexity (perhaps rather out of keeping with the simple form of the carol).

The remaining choral works, *The Morning Watch* and *St Patrick's Breastplate*, belong more nearly to the choral tradition of the festivals. The influence of Byrd and the Tudors which had so flooded *Mater Ora Filium* is here mingled with, and to some extent diluted by, that of Elgar. And as a result the antiphonal clashes of the Amens are grandiose rather than Gothic.

The Morning Watch is a setting of Vaughan's words:

O Joys! Infinite Sweetness!
With what flowers and shoots of glory
My soul breaks and buds.

whose pantheistic 'symphony of nature' appealed to Bax. The long orchestral introduction is based on a rising figure full of somewhat portentous hints of the forthcoming choral entry. A majestic and powerful climax ushers in the Elgarian 'Prayer is the world in tune' which Bax sets in orthodox festival fashion, yet with a nobility that is well worthy of that tradition. *St Patrick's Breastplate* (1923), a setting of words from the Irish/Gaelic hymn 'Luireach Naoimh Padraig', is a more convincing work and its burning power, although not always avoiding conventionality, strikes a note of catholic sincerity. The devotional aura of the words is treated by Bax in a mood of mystical fervour, a mood he perhaps felt most strongly in Ireland.

The music of the opening invocation is powerful and strong: 'I bind to myself in Tara this day', and it is characteristic of the whole work. With the evocation of the seraphim and the angelic hosts the music rises to ecstatic heights begetting a trusting simplicity in the words 'resurrection unto reward'. The invocation to the elements brings flashes of the real Bax, followed by a meltingly beautiful passage of prayer for wisdom and understanding. Amens and avowals of the universality of Christ lead, with an imaginative stroke in the sopranos, into the final *Allegro con brio*, whose climactic Amens end with the 'Salus tua Domine' and here one feels Bax really puts his heart into it.

Few English composers have succeeded in expressing a characteristically English idiom in adequate keyboard terms. Neither Elgar, Holst, Delius nor Vaughan Williams has contributed anything very significant to the literature.[1] I once asked Cyril Scott the reason for this. His answer, that to write good piano music one must be both a good composer and a good pianist, may not be quite the over-simplification that it appears. For the reason for the neglect of the piano by so many English composers is probably one of circumstance rather than of psychological peculiarity. That many should choose, in the light of the choral tradition firmly upheld at the provincial festivals, a more eloquent medium than the piano was a direct result of the influence of the Royal College and of Stanford and Parry. Those who studied with Corder and Matthay, or were influenced by their teaching, were taught to look more closely to Liszt and Chopin rather than to Bach, Handel and Brahms.[2] Bax's love of Chopin and Liszt was reflected in his handling of the keyboard. The lyrical element in his music, the delicately poised cantilena with its falling cadence,[3] its undercurrent of shifting harmonies often given the texture of water-colour with the sustaining pedal, is Chopinesque—and to this Bax adds the contrasting brilliance and power of Liszt. Much of his piano writing, especially in the four sonatas, is complex and difficult. It was often through the medium of the piano that he conceived the orchestral sonorities of the

[1] Dale's Sonata, Cyril Scott's Opus 66, the *Nature Poems* of Goossens, and John Ireland's Sonata (though Ireland is a special case) are isolated examples.

[2] There was something in the make-up of the R.A.M. professors that had an affinity with that wildness that is the natural plumage of the great Lisztian virtuoso artist—something that contrasts strongly with the very English decorum of the Royal College. It is this 'bohemian' element that distinguishes, by its unique fire and flashes of scarcely controlled temperament associated with the vagaries of genius, the piano music of Liszt and Chopin from that of Bach, Schumann and Brahms.

[3] There is a curious parallel here with John Field, also a singer and poet, a wanderer and nomad, an Irishman whose travels took him finally to Russia. Gerald Abraham, in his book *Borodin* (Reeves, 1927) writes: 'Critics may be led to trace a false genealogy as in the assumption that the mantle of Field fell upon Chopin, whereas, as a matter of fact, it has only quite recently found a legitimate wearer in Arnold Bax.'

large-scale compositions. Yet the result of a good performance is never obscure or difficult.

Bax's piano music may not seem particularly English. There is a wealth of chromatic detail and a luxuriance of effect that is too florid, too sensuous. The diatonic impulse is buried beneath languorous arabesque which is oriental in inflection. And, where the main melodic line emerges, its character is more often noticeably Irish or Russian. *Mediterranean* evokes the exotic, while the early *A Romance* hints at Scriabin. (Ex. 11.)

Yet the kind of eclecticism found in Bax is itself English and this is reflected in all his work—as well as in the more obviously English instances such as *Morning Song—Maytime in Sussex* (for piano and orchestra), and the later occasional music with its affinities with the ceremonial music of Elgar and Walton (and with the 'Agincourt Song' and 'Men of Harlech'). Bax's Englishness is stylistic rather than thematic, and recognizable in the same way that we recognize the Frenchman in Fauré. Less obviously 'Georgian' than Ireland, Bax is closer to the music of Elgar, Eric Coates and the cosmopolitan Delius.

With the exception of the sonatas and the Toccata Bax's piano music is expressly tone-poetical and impressionistic. *Nereid* is a graceful aquatint whose characteristic 'water' theme rocks easily on its fluid undercurrent. *A Mountain Mood*, *A Country Tune* and *A Hill Tune*, each in a kind of variation form, are rarefied and ethereal, like the mountain air from which they emerge, hovering on the breeze before being borne away. *Whirligig* is kaleidoscopic rather than nebulous. *The Princess's Rose-Garden* is an elaborate and complicated Nocturne, *Apple Blossom Time* a freshly aerial nature impression, and *Sleepyhead*, the only composition he dedicated to his wife, a subtle wash of harmonic colour as hypnotic and dazzling in its iridescence as *L'Après-midi d'un Faune*. All these are fanciful, poetic, and the thread of their evolution is drawn as naturally and as fragrantly as the growth of a flower.

All is not light and air, however. There are dark and sombre pieces like those tragic landscapes *Winter Waters* and *Dream in Exile*, with their score directions 'dull' 'muffled' 'sullen' and 'sighing'. There is, too, a robust and clattering vitality in such pieces as *In a Vodka Shop*.

In spite of their frankly programmatic and tone-poetical nature, Bax's compositions for the piano are rather nearer to the Fairy Tales of Medtner than to the Preludes of Debussy. The implication of Medtner's generic title suggests the ballad rather than strict narrative —events being presented in superimposition with fanciful, even

Ex. 11 'A Romance'

Very moderate tempo
Dreamy and passionate

fantastic, overtones. There is a hint of the heroic. In *What the Minstrel Told Us* the substance of the tale is divulged only by its emotions. Like all true heroic ballads it is sad, beautiful and virtuosic. The tale is framed by a slow and stately introduction and concluding epilogue that depicts the chords played by the kerne or seannachie—the bardic minstrel as distinct from the player who accompanied the dance. The strange, sad song of the melody is given out unaccompanied, in heroic fashion, then deliciously coloured in chromatic harmony, recalling some ancient rune, a race-memory half forgotten. But the tale is passionate and stormy. The casting of such ideas in keyboard terms bristles with problems. These problems Bax surmounts even more readily in the music for two pianos: *Red Autumn, The Devil that Tempted St Anthony, The Poisoned Fountain* and the Sonata for Two Pianos.

Between 1910 and 1934 Bax wrote four piano sonatas—each of considerable dimensions, richly scored, tempestuous and magical by turns, and of some technical difficulty.[1] It is paradoxical that in the richer medium of the two-piano score, which Bax may have found more congenial for the expression of his kind of pianistic colour, the ideas themselves have less depth and intensity than in the sonatas for solo piano.

All four were first performed by Harriet Cohen and two (the second and third) are dedicated to her. The first and second are in one single movement and owe much to the piano music of Liszt, although the matter in each is much stimulated by Russian influence.[2]

In spite of the discursive nature of the material of these first two sonatas Bax contrives by a sure grasp of harmony to knit the emotional activity into a compulsive logic. And however much we may be tempted to invest the musical ideas with image or character, this logic remains a purely musical one. This apparent discursiveness is to some extent the result of Bax's tendency to avoid recapitulation as such, while the

[1] Bax seems to have made few concessions in these works to the small hands of their principal exponent, Harriet Cohen. She could not strike a 9th in either hand and could only cope with the interval in the right hand by placing the fingers separately.
[2] Another composer strongly influenced by Liszt and by Northern influences in his piano sonatas, also four in number, was Edward MacDowell. There are several striking similarities between the Bax sonatas and those of MacDowell—MacDowell entitled his *Tragica, Eroica, Norse* and *Keltic*—titles which might well apply to the Bax sonatas. The quasi-orchestral trills, the heroic six-four chords (often cloaked in Bax by decorative accretions), the characteristic theme (MacDowell 1 p15 bars 5–6; Bax Ex. 4(a)) are common to both. In the final pages of the *Eroica* the great unspread chords resemble those of Bax and there are similarities in the opening of the *Eroica's* third movement and the second movement of Bax's third sonata. Even the figuration in the penultimate pages of the MacDowell is strongly recalled in the closing pages of Bax's fourth sonata. But a very much more striking resemblance between the two composers is to be found in the *Sonata Tragica*—at the thirty-first bar of the fourth movement, where MacDowell employs a rising figure G sharp, D, B almost identical with the opening of the slow movement of Bax's First Symphony, a bass rise of D, A flat, D, F, and C flat, with only a slight variation in the rhythm.

exposition spills over with material that is, properly speaking, development. In the first Sonata the recapitulation is brief, half the length in
performance of the exposition, and leaves the final word to the sub-
stantial fifty-three bar Coda.

The first Sonata is in first movement form and was written in the
Ukraine in the summer of 1910. It was begun in a mood that alternated
between adolescent despair from the disillusions of unrequited love,
and exultation in the sensuous beauty of the landscape. The Sonata is
impelled by the fierce poignancy of the opening F sharp minor subject
with its underlying 7ths, whose brazen and glittering climax leads to
a bridge passage, a sighing motif of fifteen bars hung over a pedal F
sharp which provides the dominant of the B major second subject. Its
climax is impassioned, anticipating the E flat major/minor theme of
the second Sonata, but like so many of Bax's climaxes it cannot bear
for long the intensity of emotion and begins to disintegrate almost at
once in a chromatic breaking up of the harmonic pattern. This resolves
at once upon the other second subject motive, a quasi-liturgical four-
note chant that may well have had some pictorial significance (like the
gigantic Coda) for the composer. A sombre march-like fragment of the
first subject leads into the development section, which suggested to
Harriet Cohen 'the illimitable distances of the Russian plain'.[1] From
this point a huge momentum is built up, the uncertainty of mood being
implied in the tonal plan. At first the subject material is heard in
octaves in the bass in the key of A minor, but a brief *martellato* half-
climax is followed by increasing emotional tension which leads to the
despairing urgency of the recapitulation. The F sharp tonality is now
firmly established in all three motives, the minor of the first subject
being finally transfigured in the brilliance of the Coda, whose march-
like triumph and huge processional pageantry is punctuated by the
din of the Easter bells in some of the finest pages of piano music ever
written by an English composer.

The second of the four sonatas Bax describes as 'in G', suggesting,
as in the second Symphony, the ambivalence of its moods. It is also
cast in one movement with epic-heroic subject material. But the one-
movement form is more complicated than that of the first Sonata and
seems to fall, like a great arch, around the 'very still and concentrated'
Lento section, whose brooding quiet contains all the warring elements
of the outer passages. The uneasy tension of this *Lento* section is transfigured in a magical Epilogue into a mood of peace that suggests either

[1] Quoted by Julian Herbage in *British Music of Our Time*, Pelican, 1946.

the ultimate victory of the darker of the two contestants for supremacy
or, perhaps more cogently, that the two factions are aspects of a single
whole, a feeling that is borne out by other experience of Bax's music.
It is difficult to avoid ascribing the characters of good and evil to the
two aspects of the main subject material or not to follow their conflict
as if they were actual protagonists. The blurred tonality of the opening,
with its dark clashing of two keys a semitone apart, ends quite conclusively in the major of the home key. This *tenebroso* opening conceals,
in its murky depths, much of the ensuing material. From this dark
context of a tremolo C minor a rising chordal progression, ostensibly
in B minor, indicates a shifting of tonality towards the *eroico* G major.
The first thematic element to emerge, which reveals the germ of the
major/minor coalescence of the drooping oriental pattern that occurs
in the first Symphony and in the first and second Sonatas for violin,
has once again its C minor tonality challenged. The second aspect of
this primary material is a menacing Baxian theme, 'wailing' and
serpent-like. At the conclusion of this the whole material is lifted a
major 3rd higher out of its darkness into the glittering sunlight of G
major. This heroic march does not survive long the baleful breath of
the dragon. The brief development section begins in a Mixolydian E
minor with a whispering four-note descent pattern, a very Russian
motive that seems to combine the two elements of the exposition.
Attempts to unify these elements end with the return, now in diminished 7th chords, of the primary motive. This leads into the central
Lento, the F sharp of the preceding bars being carried into the new
context of E flat major as the Lydian sharp 4th of C minor, which
tonality still persists as an evil shadow in the background. A brief
vivace skirmish intervenes before the material is re-asserted *trionfale* now
strongly in the major, the C sharp now D flat (the 7th).

From this point Bax seems to retrace his steps in an imperfect or
distorted mirror-image. The introductory material is heard again with
the 'menacing' theme now beginning a strange transformation (here
marked 'like a tuba'). The tonal clash now seems even more powerful
and the *molto largamente* reappearance of the heroic theme (brazen and
glittering) leads very quickly to a precipitate descent once more into
the darkness in which the slow central theme is heard. In the solemn
processional of the final pages the major/minor dichotomy is finally
ironed out in an extended *molto tranquillo* epilogue ending unequivocally
in G major, an ending recalling once again the final progressions of
Delius's *A Village Romeo and Juliet* and the Symphonic Variations.

III

The third of Bax's four sonatas was completed in 1925, just before the third Symphony, and shows the waning of the direct influence of Liszt—at least in the piano writing. The attempt to grapple with the problems of texture, not altogether successfully, and the agonies of transition between the second and third Symphonies is also apparent. And in the Sonata the picture-postcard atmosphere of the early Russian pieces has quite gone, and the Irish/Celtic aspect, in spite of the rather sugary middle section, has become quite assimilated into what is now clearly a personal and distinctive style.

The key of the first movement is G sharp minor, the second G major (with a central E flat major) and the final movement makes an unequivocal return (except for the key signature) to the opening key of G sharp minor. There are close interrelationships between all aspects of the material which obviously has a common source. The Sonata opens, *Allegro moderato*, with the G sharp minor tonality underpinned by a figure built on the subdominant C sharp, the Lydian colour partly obscured by the registration.

The first theme, cloaked in thick chords, rises upwards through a kind of half-light to a *martellato* outburst, and a continual process of development, thrice repeated, is evolved from this opening, and out of these first seven pages all the music of the Sonata derives. The wayward second subject points clearly to the Celtic imagery of the second movement. A *lento lontano* echo of the first subject and a sepulchral shadow of the lyrical material precedes the return of the first subject, now in E minor, much developed and with the sharp tang of an Irish dance. The surging climax is now extended in a curious and characteristic Baxian pattern of unrelated and unresolved dominant 7ths, 9ths and 13ths that seems inseparably linked in Bax's work with the pull and wash of tides on far shores. Its barbaric savagery is underlined by harsh and discordant jangles and a brilliant sheen of arpeggios.

The return of the first subject embedded in its G sharp minor is beset by the whirling of these patterns, but the recapitulation is brief and the music sinks back into the mood of the beginning. The darkness that enshrouds the harmony is reflected in the final chord of G sharp minor with a bottom A natural, a tonal ambiguity that, though employed for practical reasons, may well be considered as contributory to the strange reverberations that Bax's final chords often have—a kind of savage crash—for Bax repeats the device, without the compulsion of practicality, in the conclusion of the fourth Sonata. He also concludes the third Sonata's finale with a bottom G. Other solutions to the purely

Alfred Ridley Bax

Charlotte Ellen (Lea) Bax

July 1894 (Arnold and Aubrey in blazers)

Arnold in highland costume

A group at Ivybank (Arnold extreme left, Clifford standing centre, Evelyn sitting on arm of cousin Hilda's chair)

Arnold at the piano, Ivybank

Glencolumcille

The Old Broughtonians
Left to right, back row:
Ralph Straus, Cecil Palmer,
Eric Gillett, Armstrong Gibbs,
J. C. Squire, A. D. Peters.
Middle row: Arnold Bax,
Clifford Bax, R. H. Lowe,
Keith Henderson.
Front: P. Knox-Shaw and
H. C. Prew.

Arnold Bax—

Bax, Moeran and Mrs
Fleischman at Kinsale

Harriet Cohen

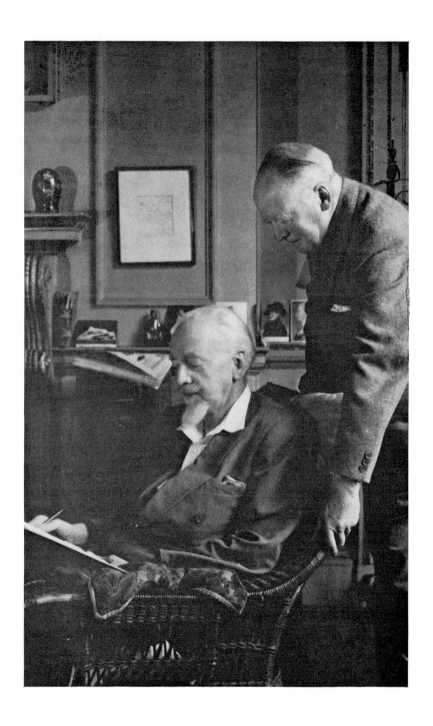

Arnold and Clifford in Albany

Sir Arnold Bax

practical problem of the missing G sharp at the end of the keyboard are available and it is reasonable to assume that Bax was here using the sound musically. For many of his score directions indicate just this kind of sound—'dull', 'muffled', etc.

With the remote echo of the G sharp minor chord the second movement droops to G major and exposes a melody, Celtic in character, derived from the second phrase of the first subject's *Andante con moto*. Again, like the melodies of *Tintagel*, it is a line spun out by a continuous process of variation, not folky, neither love song nor lament, neither lament nor rune, but perhaps pure nature music. For with the rising tonic dominant flat 7th in the bass against decorative chords Bax clearly suggests the music that has always seemed in his work to relate to the sea. And as if to clinch this, Bax now uncovers, in E flat, a kind of song-type melody like the song of Fand, whose passionate climax is drowned in a great wash of colour overtaken by a chromatically decorated version of the opening theme of the movement. The surge of this, concealing the wrack-like swaying undulations of the final movement's theme, is marked by the composer *pp molto smorzando* (as much pedal as possible).[1] And at the conclusion of the movement, a wraith-like echo of the central 'song' theme is heard (reminiscent of the closing bars of *Fand*), before it too is lost, banished in the windy sunlight.

The third movement opens in the key of G sharp minor, with a toccata-like pattern of whirling semiquavers—a variant of the opening of the Sonata, still *smorzando*, but with something of a restless feeling that once again suggests the sea. The rising bass theme is there, too, in the depths. The swirling eddies die away, the water is suddenly still. The piano writing in the last few pages has become thinner in texture, foreshadowing the clarity of the fourth Sonata. The resumption of the toccata figure leads back to the opening mood and the Sonata ends with a procession of strange modal chords.

The fourth Sonata, a more muscular work than its predecessors, is also in three movements. But the texture is crystal clear, the thematic material less wayward and the sound more brittle. Exposition, development and recapitulation are condensed into a mould almost classical in its economy and directness. The tonal architecture is also classical

[1] Bax gives only sparing pedal indications but liked liberal use of the pedal in performance. Balfour Gardiner, who had a way of bestowing the epithet 'old' as one of both affection and derision, was once heard to remark, 'There's old Arnold improvising away with the pedal down all the time', a practice which often preceded creative work.

in outline. Modal colour (the Lydian sharp 4th and Mixolydian flat 7th) permeates all three movements, recalling perhaps Grieg, and is certainly Nordic in feeling.

The plangent climax of the first movement makes full use of the percussive sonorities of the piano and suggests at the same time the brilliance of the incisive tones of the brass (a kind of synthesis of the first and second subject material) but is far removed from the romantic ending of the first sonata. The first subject material is exposed without preamble and consists of two patterns, a troll-like motive rising from the bass, and an inverted pedal point B natural with a pattern in 10ths that bears a weird resemblance to *Finlandia*.

From these two rather gnomic figures much of the Sonata evolves. The exposition of the first subject lasts for a mere thirty-eight bars when the D major second subject appears. It never succeeds, however, in shaking off the first subject. The troll-like figure snarls at the heels of the *largamente* reprise of the second subject and ushers in the development section. Its main theme (the first shadow of its final *allegro maestoso* appearance at the end of the work) is recognized by its lyrical and impulsive upward 6th, under which the troll-like figure is heard, darkly, in *ostinato*, insistent and almost hypnotic. The brief recapitulation is rounded off by a martial Coda.

The second movement is perhaps one of Bax's finest for the piano. Marked 'very delicate throughout', its song-like melody is spun out over a long syncopated pedal G sharp. Even if, as Tilly Fleischman suggested, the melody strongly resembles the Irish song, 'Has sorrow thy young days shaded', the harmonic colour here tends to sound more Russian than Irish. The whole movement is distant like a faery song, crystal clear. But in spite of this mood the gnomic first subject is still present at the end of the exposition. A new development of more of the first subject material is laid out over modally clashing parallel 3rds. It is an interlude, quiet and rather sad, in spite of the unobtrusive waltz rhythm. With the aggressive opening *allegro* fanfare of the third movement this mood is banished. There is something almost heraldic here that suggests mythical beasts rather than real ones, and there is savagery. Through the harsh chording the thematic material first developed in the first movement with its clashing 2nds and modal friction begins to assert its supremacy.

And in spite of every attempt by the darker forces that oppose it, nothing can hold back the joyous *allegro maestoso*. *Trionfale* it is echoed, and with a brief half-flourish of the opening fanfare the Sonata ends.

Part Three

10 Symphonies 1-3

'Never have I heard such music,
In the course of all my lifetime,
As is played by Väinämöinen,
Joyous and primeval minstrel.'

Kalevala, Runo XLI (trans. W. F. Kirby).

Bax seemed most clearly destined to achieve greatness in music of a tone-poetical nature. He was perhaps the ideal counterpart in music of the writers of the Irish/Celtic movement, to whose elegies and heroic sagas he was so strongly attracted. He was able to make the astonishing pronouncement that the poetry of Yeats meant more to him than 'all the music of the centuries'. *The Garden of Fand* and *November Woods* had proved him a master both of orchestral technique and of the creation of atmosphere such as surrounds places with legendary associations. It might have seemed most natural if he had, like Sibelius in those works whose origin was the *Kalevala*, recalled musically in a cycle of tone-poems the tales of Deirdre and of Cuchullain, of Diarmait and Grainne. But although Bax reacted to those formative influences primarily as a poet, he was a composer, a trained musician with an assured grasp of technique, and his thought processes were those of a musician.

There is a marked dividing line between the two halves of his creative personality as expressed in Arnold Bax and Dermot O'Byrne. And the only element both have in common is that of 'imagery'—the language in the poems and tales, and the 'Celtic' tunes of the music. The force that motivated him appears, however, on the surface, to have been directed to that other self, where, as Dermot O'Byrne, it was given a direct, sometimes emotional, expression in a peculiarly narrow nationalism.

It would be naïve to suppose that because Bax's vision was directed to the pursuit of what, in the harsh and realistic twenties, could only be called 'dreams', he was totally unaffected by the catalytic influence of war. Even if, outwardly, the tragic deaths of Padraig Pearce and Thomas McDonagh in the bloody business of Easter 1916 touched him more closely, the physical confrontation of total war was more real to him than the ideologies which prompted it.

Bax's symphonies belong to a period between the wars which has a special artistic character all its own. It was a time of enormous creative vigour, when immense energies were directed less to the pursuit of beauty than to the facing of facts—not only to the freedom and progress in whose name so many lives had been given and taken, but to the transformation and the destruction of the established order.

In music the prophets of light and of darkness, Sibelius and Mahler, had gone before, and in 1934 Ernest Newman could write a mournful epitaph in the *Sunday Times* (17.6.34): 'With the death of Delius[1] there has died a world the like of which it will be a long time before mankind can create for itself again. It may be, as some think, that we are in the first hour of a new dawn in music—but that hour is grey and chilly . . .' The splitting of the atom in 1919 was more symbolic of the irreversibility of the movement towards freedom than was the upward leap of Elgar's 'spirit of delight'. And at no time in English musical history had there been such a need for formal strength.

It may seem strange that Bax, the romantic *par excellence*, and a composer supposedly addicted to overstatement, should have elected to write so often within the requirements of the sonata principle. For one of the greatest problems of the romantic composer is that of the incompatibility of the romantic idea and the classical form inherent in the symphony. The earlier romantics such as Chopin, Schumann and to some extent Liszt thought naturally in small forms, cast in the symmetry of dance movements or in song-like paragraphs which carried within them their own natural architecture. Extremes of emotion are only physically possible for very short periods of time and are followed by exhaustion or at least quiescence. If this hurdle has been straddled with varying degrees of success by every composer since Beethoven, it is an indisputable fact that musical England in the Romantic and late Romantic era was not the breeding ground for symphonists. The niceties of classical symphonic decorum and the rather weak nationalism that had begun to appear were uneasy bed-fellows.

By 1921 musical England was quite content to accept Elgar as the last and mightiest of a symphonic line, which, had it really existed, might have led to our now having a very different view of music altogether in this country. But it did not exist—except, and then most gloriously, in Elgar himself. The peculiar qualities of Elgar that fitted

[1] Elgar had died in February.

him, in 1908, for the composition of the first major English symphony,[1] a work which inspired not only international respect but the public acclaim that accounted for over a hundred performances within its first year, were conspicuously melodic. His ability to handle his melodic material, to infuse it with life that existed apart from its significance on paper, and to manipulate it over long periods of time without having to resort to the clichés of convention to disguise the seams, and at the same time to sound completely English, suddenly thrust England back into the symphonic tradition of Europe, upon whose fringes the English symphonists had long lingered under the shadows of Brahms, Mendelssohn, Tchaikovsky and Dvořák. The influence of such a figure upon younger composers was bound to be considerable. And if we do not always recognize it, it is perhaps only because of the breakneck speed with which developments have followed one another since Elgar in this whirlwind century.

Elgar's symphonic music invited respect, but it did not invite emulation. Paradoxically such influential and commanding figures seldom gather imitators around them in schools. Elgar was individual and aloof. But that 'spirit of delight' which prompted the ecstatic outburst of the second Symphony's first movement was both the culmination and the turning point of a symphonic tradition in English music that had virtually sprung fully armed into the musical scene. Here is the epitome of the romantic movement in English music illuminated for us by the rest of the poem[2] from which his 'motto' derives.

The paradox of Nature—the eternal and the ephemeral, the rocks and the water, the hills and their changing colour—this was the pantheistic order that could survive the chaos of war. Bax's knowledge and understanding of the act of creation, though he gave it no voice in any kind of literary manifesto, was perhaps more profound than that of any of his colleagues.

His imagination, borne on the surefootedness of a phenomenal technique, ranged far and freely. The strength of his purpose, and the superhuman energy of his mature creative processes are, in the seven symphonies, controlled by a powerful musical intellect. But it is an intellect which, even in its most Promethean moments, is prey to human doubts and fears. This power which he calls forth in the

[1] Richter went further, and declared it 'the greatest symphony of modern times by the greatest composer' (adding 'and not only in this country').

[2] Shelley, 'Song' ('Rarely, rarely comest thou, Spirit of Delight!').

unearthly incantations (of the interlocked tritones—the *diabolus in musica*—of the diminished 7th chord) of the opening pages of the first Symphony was a power with which he was forced to grapple, almost as if it were an entity existing outside himself, full of menace and dire threat. He denied that the first was a 'war' symphony. Its awesome portents relate only momentarily to the actuality of war. Like Vaughan Williams in his fourth (which is dedicated to him), **Bax** felt intuitively the rending of the fabric of the world and the impending dissolution of created things, but at the same time recognized the imperishable nature of the human spirit whose voyage amongst the stars Clifford sensed with a kind of awe.

Bax had dredged deeply. Not even Sibelius had conjured up such inimical forces from the grim fastnesses of *Tapiola*. This is not evil in the religious sense. It is the antithetic juxtaposition of negative and positive—of dark and light—the extension of the basic principles of the two aspects of life, the male and female counterparts of the *id*, and thus ultimately the dichotomy of his own inner personality, symbolically presented, at the very outset, in the major/minor clash with which the first symphony opens.

Bax's symphonic design was intuitive. Edwin Evans later opined that the direction he then took was undeclared even to himself, and the facts that surround the emergence of the first Symphony bear this out.

After the poetic fancies of *The Garden of Fand* and the elegiac ending of the Viola Sonata, the harshness of the symphony fell with brutal violence on the ears of the Queen's Hall audience on 2nd December 1922. Bax's seemingly abrupt change of direction had, however, been forecast—in the first and second Sonatas for piano, in *Winter Waters*, and even in the priapic shadows behind the cavorting wood spirits in *The Happy Forest*. For the primary symphonic material with which Bax deals in the first Symphony, and develops in subsequent works, is found, in its earliest form, in the first Piano Sonata, a work which was the outcome of considerable emotional stress. And significantly, though it is part of both first and second subject material, it is found in the first six bars (in the upper line of the theme, G sharp, A, F sharp, E sharp) and at the *allegro passionato* statement of the second subject derived from this. This thematic device, with its major/minor ambivalence and drooping semitone, is re-echoed even more strongly in the second Violin Sonata, where, from its appearance in the first two bars, it dominates the entire work. It is further elaborated, with the addition of a tail-like 'descent' pattern of four consecutive notes, in the second of the sonatas for piano. It reappears in *November Woods*, almost in the same guise, and from then on becomes a kind of personal fingerprint. But in the first Symphony the mask is ripped off and the terrible darkness of these primary forces is revealed.[1]

The violent energy of this work was to power not only the first Symphony but the whole seven. The entire first Symphony, like its opening germ theme (Ex. 13a) which is symbolic, heaves itself, saurian-like, from the gloom of the primeval slime, with a fearsome challenge, only to sink back—a monolithic erection whose root goes deep, but whose opening gesture led Bax onward, through twenty more movements, to the ultimate vision of the close of the sixth and the final seventh. It is quite apparent from the final passages of the first that resolution of the conflict was beyond the scope of one work. The musical idea was truly symphonic but its relevance and design were not properly apparent until the completion of the third in February 1929.

And even then the consummation was only partial. For it remained for the fifth and, more finally, the sixth to show that the most positive expression of both primary and secondary material (the first subject theme groups and the second subject central, so-called Celtic, more lyrical subject matter) had the same origin in the exposition of each work, and, in the overall pattern of the seven, deep in the prototype of the first Symphony.

So closely identified do the primary and secondary materials become that their ultimate fusion is essential and logical. Both are creative manifestations of Bax's spiritual force. The two facets of the same basic germ are seen darkly and obscurely veiled—and reflected in a clear and transparent light—and it is not difficult to see the revelation of the brutish opening of the first in the epilogue of the fifth.

The symphonies are in this sense cyclic. But the cycle is circum-ambulatory rather than repetitive. The basic material, amorphous or not, is seen from a cosmic viewpoint as its centre is viewed in changing lights from varying angles by the composer, as if he were in some vehicle revolving in space around the sphere of his inspiration. This cyclic

[1] After the first Manchester performance of the first Symphony Neville Cardus, with sensitive perception, wrote that the work seemed not to be composed but '. . . erected out of some amorphous basic material—and then subtilised by as keen a musical intelligence as any known at the present time. Bax is a case of a sophisticated mind dealing with primitive material.'

Ex. 12

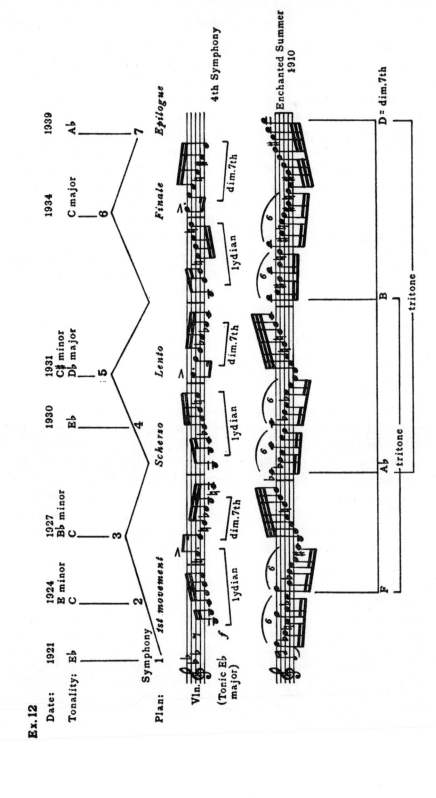

element also seems capable of another interpretation, and one for which there is considerable internal evidence in the music itself. There is a demonstrable unity, not only in thematic stuff but in physiological content. The development from the postulates of the first Symphony to the logical arguments of the fifth and the conclusions of the sixth and seventh could be made explicit in a graph. It is then realized that, however complex the detail, the outline is simple. The overall framework of the seven is a matter of some importance. We have scarcely yet had a chance to grasp this, since dearth of both performance and recording has obscured the larger view. But this overall plan could scarcely have been designed, since the composer was carried by the sheer force of his inspiration at least one-third of the way along his symphonic course before he himself had any clear idea of his own direction. The graph, very roughly approximating to Bax's symphonic progress (in much the same way as we might trace Orion from the relative positions of Betelgeuse and Rigel), is outlined in Bax's own work by a curious rise and fall pattern progressing upwards, often pointing the rising minor 3rds of the diminished 7th, and finally expending itself, like the great wave of which it might be symbolic, in a final thrust on the strand of some remote and magical island (see Ex. 12). From this intuitive logic Bax's symphonic plan takes unusual strength, further underlined by the unity of thematic material and the strong dependence upon conflict and coalescence of recognizable key and tonality. Classical symphonic procedures depend upon this conflict and coalescence of tonality where the two keys of the exposition are united in the recapitulation as both subjects reappear in the tonic, leaving the development section for the exploratory material suggested to the composer by the initial idea and expanding the 'view' by penetrating vistas of tonal country foreign to the key of the work. Bax departs only slightly from this, but so keen is his harmonic sense and his feeling for cadence that he seems often to have wandered far from the tonal centre, blurring the tonality with decorative appoggiaturas, or by unusual texture, or even by employing over long periods a fluid undercurrent of unresolved chords.

In *Musical Opinion* (December 1922) Havergal Brian wrote of Bax's first Symphony: 'He has that wonderful faculty for uninterrupted continuous thinking without which works on a large scale are impossible. One sometimes gets the impression that this self-absorption and power of concentration will lead to obscure paths and darkness—in *Tintagel* for instance . . .' How far does Bax demonstrate symphonic thinking within each work and within the actual material of the symphony?

The first Symphony is primarily concerned with a single idea, albeit of a dual nature, embodied in the first five bars of the work. To this grim exposition the central lyrical matter acts not as a foil but as a complement underlining the powerful nature of the material from which the music is hewn. It offers no escape, no solution.

The final *largamente* of the first movement is an intensification, and an extension, but neither development proper, nor recapitulation. This passage is succeeded by a complex reorganization of material that postpones the denouement to the final bars of the whole symphony; but implicit within that secondary material is the power ultimately to control, if not to overcome. But it is not until the end of the third Symphony that this element attains any kind of sovereignty, an uncertain precedence that is pursued through fifth and sixth into the limbo of the seventh.

Thus within the compass of one work is seen the *ultima Thule*, a brief glimpse it may be, towards which Bax's symphonic drive is taking him. The epithet *trionfale* which heralds the final march of the first Symphony, in the minor of the home key of E flat, does not make for a happy ending. For this is no fairy tale but grim reality. So decisive is the victory that the secondary material is, at this stage, quite forgotten.

The entire second Symphony is given over to the further conflict between the two forces, now on a wider field of battle, but with a less well-defined outcome. The final *niente*, after the huge upthrusts of the primary material, is not peace but utter exhaustion. The logic of the second Symphony, in spite of its seeming discursiveness, is inexorable —demonstrable to the ear, although less easily so to the eye. No composer in this country has had such strange phantasmagoric dreams. If on its own it is momentarily the most beautiful of all the seven, for the same reason, and because of its deep and complex associations with its neighbours, it misses abiding greatness, at least until all seven are heard. With the third Symphony—and it is perhaps significant that Bax found it necessary to escape at this juncture to western Inverness-shire—Bax seemed about to reach the summit towards which he had been driving in the preceding two. Characteristically, however, once that peak had been climbed there appeared another beyond, more remote and distant, more inaccessible.

The keynote of the third is still aspiration and not achievement. Together the three are a very human record. The Epilogue of the third is a coming to terms with life, imbued with hope and with resignation not untroubled by the still present murmurings of the turbulence of the first movement which it might seem momentarily to have subdued.

Throughout the first movement of the third Bax is concerned to control the generative motive that, seen initially veiled in dark and shifting mists, rises to the orgiastic heights of the *largamente* climax (marked by a stroke on the anvil) and driven by a power that he often finds difficult to control. The contrast of the slow movement consists of the cessation of the strife of the first movement and of the third, to whose Epilogue this central movement points. Yet the principal subject of the second movement shows that it is not a release from the problems of the first but another aspect of the same material. If this is subjective, then it reflects something deep within the man, more elemental than his own nature. If it is objective—and Bax seems to treat it as such—then it is a primal force that gives these works their existence. For Bax is concerned, in spite of his dreams, with reality. There is nothing of the 'artist-as-hero' in these works. The quasi-programmatic 'legend', that might seem to be the inspiration of the movement, exists only in the music. (Bax himself denied any kind of programme in this particular movement.) For here, as in the slow movement of the first Symphony, Bax (like Chopin and Medtner in smaller forms) uses formal outlines to imply a programme that is never explicit. Here it is predominantly sea-music; but not in relation to the heroic strivings of mankind, or as background to a solitary figure 'on the beach at night alone'. It is the sea of *La Mer*—an element at once awful and beautiful in which there is both awareness and oblivion, both joy and sorrow. It is devoid of passion or emotion, yet seems to exist only to be revealed in the moody eyes of man, as if it existed in its timelessness and inscrutability only to represent the macrocosm in which the microcosm of man's spirit can live. It is the eternal environment. It is like those massive pedal points upon which some immense universe seems to hang in the music of Sibelius. Here for the first time we see the vastness of Bax's time scale which seems to hold the music on a steady course through the seething crucible of the preceding seven movements—a vastness which is unquestionably symphonic.

With the completion of the scoring of the final bars of the Epilogue of the third Symphony in February 1929 Bax summed up, as far as he had then gone, the music of all three symphonies.

And at this particular point in his life several important influences were to affect his direction. The problem of his symphonic design was uppermost in his mind. And between the third Symphony and the fifth (the latter scored during the winter of 1931–2) Bax completed several works which show quite clearly the indecision that these influences aroused in him: *Winter Legends*, two Northern Ballads (with a third in 1934),[1] the Nonet, *The Tale the Pine Trees Knew*, the fourth Symphony and the *Overture to a Picaresque Comedy*. Bax himself felt that continuity between the third and fifth Symphonies was more demonstrable in *Winter Legends* than in the fourth Symphony, and yet there is no doubt in retrospect that the respite of the fourth was to be a necessary part of the symphonic 'arc'. The energies that had prompted the first Symphony had by no means been exhausted. It seems more likely that, having written *Winter Legends* strongly inspired by Sibelius (he completed the score in a very short time), Bax felt that his natural direction had in some way changed—and his indecision is reflected in this work (as a part of the symphonic series) rather than in the fourth Symphony. It remained unpublished.

After the insubstantial triumphs of the march that concluded the fourth Symphony (and in the fourth Bax had admitted the idea of programme by averring that the opening represented for him a rough sea at flood tide on a breezy sunny day) he turned to the problems that the absolution of the third had neither eased nor banished. But the harsh edge of the conflict had gone, and the breadth of vision and the grim belief in a final inescapable consummation to which we are led in the concluding pages of the fifth look forward beyond the end of the music to the culmination of the sixth. The dire assault of the dark powers is resumed in the sixth with chilling ferocity. But this onslaught, powerful though it may be, is shorter in duration and in this same work the ultimate climax is reached. The glimpse of perennial summer in the slow movement (where the Scotch 'snap' recalls Delius's song 'Hy Brasil') precedes the enormous build-up of the strange triptychal finale, whose climax ushers in an unearthly benediction, untouched now by the ravages of time or conflict. And here, in the supreme moment in all Bax's symphonic music, the primary material (the diabolical *scherzo* pattern) is quite transformed into the

---

[1] It may well appear, when the Northern Ballads are better known, that their intimate relationship with the symphonies, notably fifth and sixth, will show them to be attempts to find this new direction, for they have thematic material in common with both these symphonies.

Epilogue in the forlorn majesty of Bax's other-worldly goal. Nothing can follow this movement, to which all Bax's symphonic reasoning points. The seventh Symphony, with tensions resolved and all conflict gone, ends with the Theme and Variations, posing no problems and leaving no loose ends. Bax's vision clouds over and the symphonic testament closes.

As if the strength of this overall pattern were not enough Bax has linked the seven together by a complex unity of primary material (see Ex. 13). (I have chosen primary material since the character of much of the secondary material, lyrical in nature, would quite naturally exhibit relationships in common personal melodic characteristics rather than as unity of idea.) This is not conscious intellectual artifice but again intuitive—a subtilizing of that same amorphous material from which the first is born.

The evolution of Bax's musical language has been a distinctly personal process. Many influences—musical, literary and sensual—have played their part. But the final distillation is Bax's and his alone. No other composer could have conceived the strange melodic twists of *Winter Legends*, nor envisaged those strange pages that are found in the symphonies (see published score: fig. 15 in the Trio of the sixth).

The conspicuously melodic features of his musical style are at once responsible for the problems of successful symphonic organization and also the unifying element that, more than any conscious architectonic process, makes for the coherence and musical logic of the symphonies. The most characteristic elements of Bax's melodic speech are incorporated in a feeling of flow that of itself generates an expectancy which carries the music over the potential stumbling block of the folk-like melody. And Bax's acute harmonic sense is largely responsible here for taking the strain at moments where it seems he has sung his way into a melodic *cul-de-sac*—which he magically opens by harmonic means. The slow movement of the fifth abounds in instances of this sure harmonic judgment.

But with a sureness of touch Bax leaves his melodic line when it has reached full flight and in most imminent danger of collapse (since it seems it has nowhere else to go). He leaves his line open-ended, not *unendlich* as in Wagner, but with a final cadential expansion into the harmonic ether that might lead anywhere. It is open-ended, soaring, Scriabinesque, penetrating new and strange realms of sound and imagination. This harmonic sense and his orchestral texture both play a large part in the development of his melodic material.

Ex. 13   PRIMARY MATERIAL.

SYMPHONY No. 1

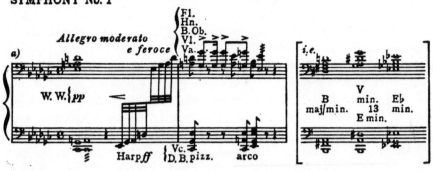

SYMPHONY No. 2

b)

SYMPHONY No. 3

c)

SYMPHONY No. 4

d)

COMPLEMENTARY PRIMARY MATERIAL

LITURGICAL

BASS RISE

Neither pattern appears conclusively in 4th Symphony.

WINTER LEGENDS

e)

PIANO

SYMPHONY No. 5

f)

2 Clar. in A

Vln.

SYMPHONY No. 6

g)

B. Clar.
CA. Clar.
Ob.
Hn.

Tuba
Bn.
V.C.
D.B.

SYMPHONY No. 7

h)

3 Clar. Bb

In. the last three symphonies this material is unified:

Bax does not work backwards from the full melodic 'theme' in a process of dissection and reassembly. Nor does he, like Sibelius, amass fragmentary exposition material and weld it into a whole (although it is true that most of the symphonic material proliferates out of a germ source, and indeed the germ source in the first bars of the first Symphony; and in the fifth we have to wait until the final climax before all else slips into place—but this latter is a psychological thing rather than a technical device). In the fifth, in that final moment of time, all is made clear, the whole scaffolding is seen in its totality, and it is as if we experienced the whole symphony in an instant of revelation that seems the essence of all very great music. The melodic nexus of Bax's work, often thus highlighted in the work itself, is both cause and effect, present in embryo in the germ (seen initially as in the third through a veil) and still present, but in spirit, in the final Epilogue. Bax does not look forward, developing his material, but drives urgently towards it, in spite of many sidelong glances, finally looking backward in the Epilogue over the course along which he has been led by the urgency of his conception.

Each symphony seems to forge, in a crucible of its own intense conflagration, a basically lyrical element, seen first darkly crystallizing under the stress of forces whose power cannot always yield to orthodox symphonic procedures. This element emerges, in each successive work, more and more refined and tempered until, in the last movement of the seventh, it becomes the purely musical device of the Theme and Variations. It is when Bax is driven hardest by his inspiration (in the first movement of first and sixth Symphonies) that he is most successful with the problems of form. In both these movements the exposition and development are stretched tight over the framework of sonata form, with the second subject linked more closely to the primary material and less flowery in expression, restless, urgent and driven by the power of the opening surge. These movements are more muscular with fewer of the distractions that the musical imagery constantly presents to Bax's crowded imagination.

Basically the symphonies rely upon simple ternary form A–B–A, where B represents the second subject material. This is similar to his approach in the tone-poems, and reference to these will show that the focal point lies in the B context, and that more often than not Bax allows this B material to reappear in a kind of summing-up process that provides the fusion of both A and B material, foreshadowing the function of the Epilogue. Although Bax is often accused of going on and never knowing where to stop, this is further evidence of the struggle for supremacy between the two aspects of his musical personality. It is his nature to produce the B material at the end, joyful and jubilant, often in augmentation and *largamente*, but also his nature that the A material is too strong to allow this unreservedly—and the result is a fusion of the two elements.

Bax's seven symphonies were written during that period (1921–39) between two world wars which, in English music, produced also Vaughan Williams's third and fourth, and Moeran's Symphony in G minor. After the war, Vaughan Williams's fifth and sixth took him out of Bax's orbit into the new post-war world—and Moeran wrote only the one. But with the *London* (1914—the revised version of which dates from May 1920—whose strident first subject made an impact as forceful as that of Bax's first) and with the uncompromising fourth, and with the cloud-hung and windswept G minor Symphony of Moeran, Bax felt on common ground.

Probably the strongest single influence upon British symphonic thinking at this period was Sibelius, whose music had been played in England under Bantock (in 1905) and under Henry Wood. It was an influence that had a profound effect—and Bax was by no means unmoved. He was deeply impressed by *En Saga*—and even more affected by *Tapiola*:

> I went with Arnold Bax to Queens Hall to hear the first performance in London of the symphonic poem 'Tapiola', conducted by the late lamented Leslie Heward. Half way through I turned to look at Arnold and tears were pouring down his face. Years later he was to tell me that he and Cecil Gray had decided that, if Sibelius had written nothing else, this work would place him amongst the immortals for all time.[1]

That Bax was quick to absorb every emotional experience into his work is apparent as much in the tone-poems as in the symphonies. It was the musico/poetical idea[2] in Sibelius to which Bax reacted, rather

---

[1] Harriet Cohen, *A Bundle of Time*, p. 65. Bax's reaction to such music was in fact emotional. Harriet Cohen once told me that, during a performance of the fifth Symphony, she had turned to Bax and told him that the passage in the final movement (2 bars before fig. 30) reminded her of 'sleepy polar bears turning in the far northern snows' and how this idea had affected him in the same way, reducing him to tears.

[2] Although Bax was frequently driven by the power of his inspiration when idea and expression fuse into one, at less inspired moments (and no composer works constantly under such creative pressure) the first stirrings of his creative impulse were poetical.

than the musical material or the symphonic argument, in neither of
which does Bax resemble Sibelius more than momentarily.

The earliest directions in Bax's symphonic thinking derive quite
clearly from Liszt and the post-Lisztian romantics—from Raff (cf.
Spring Fire) and from Rimsky-Korsakov and the Russians (*Antar* opens
with a theme which Bax seems to echo in the fifth Symphony, and the
famous *Apache* motive of Borodin's second is recalled in the fanfare-like
motive in Bax's second).

Bax also had a great admiration for the symphonies of Glazounov.
The bleak Russian-liturgical opening of Glazounov's second is very
close to Bax—and in the Trio of the last movement of his sixth Bax
quotes this theme, in very similar dress. Glazounov's visits to London
were infrequent and too early to have brought him within the orbit of
Bax the symphonist—but thanks to Edwin Evans (with whom
Glazounov was on friendly terms) and to Wood, Glazounov's music
was well known, and at the time greatly admired.

It was not mere chance that prompted Bax to translate the opening of
the first Symphony into orchestral terms coloured by the snarling tones
of hecklephone and sarrusophone. For the exposition of the work reveals
the primary material within the first dozen bars as dark and baleful in
character. I have already suggested that this work contains the elements
whose violent interaction is to provide the cosmic energy that propels
the entire corpus of his symphonic thought. And in the opening bars
this primary material, A, its shadowed fabric shot through with
flashes of necromantic brilliance as if to suggest a darkly regal nature,
appears as the source or germ of which each successive work is a
development. Bax describes the Symphony as being 'in E flat' without
adding major or minor, and after preparing in the opening chord (on
lower woodwind and harp, the tonality shrouded by the gong's sullen
vibrations) what might seem to be the dominant 7th B major/minor
introduction to the sharp key of E (with which tonality the second
subject is concerned) he plunges immediately and catastrophically into
the darkness of E flat minor (see Ex. 13(a)). With this sudden snarl
Bax establishes a mood of grim portent that the secondary lyrical
material can lighten only momentarily. And from this point the listener's ear is engaged by a cogently expressed and dramatic chain of
ideas, the logic of which is carried beyond the first Symphony. The
first forty-seven bars of the work embody not only this primal germ
motive but a triple incantation (Ex. 13(a¹)), each time increasing in

intensity and rising in pitch, whose liturgical invocations suggest the hellish priest at whose bidding the first subject proper is raised from the primeval darkness into which it sinks back after a *largamente* climax. This formidable mood extends throughout the short bridge passage before the second subject appears in the wintry light of E major (in first violins), a *moderato espressivo* theme (not unlike that of Corder's Elegy for twenty-four violins) which seems at first sight to be the means of slackening the tension. But a brief *poco rubato* passage with strings and woodwind answering each other antiphonally establishes not only the first point of rest in the movement, but the first moment in which the fusion of the two subject materials begins, and from which are developed the huge climaxes of the fifth Symphony.

With this taut and cogent exposition, the strongly underlined sonata form of the movement, and the arch-like central slow movement with its overall tonal plan E flat—A/C—E flat, the strength of Bax's idea is apparent. On both points at which this (*poco rubato*) motive appears, as on two great pillars, Bax hangs the fabric of the first movement. The development section, whose trenchant Holstian rhythm is itself an expansion of the basic drive inherent in the germ, reaches a *vivace* climax which is largely concerned with the descending figure (derived possibly from *Tristan*) that at the beginning forms a kind of tail to the first subject. This motive is an integral part of the subject matter and points to at least one conclusion in the Epilogue of the third Symphony, and later to the slow movements of the sixth and seventh.

The development section continues with the second subject material, distorted, *poco staccato*, in bassoon, flute, cor anglais and clarinets, whose climax points again downwards in the descending steps of the diminished 7th (rising by similar means in the slow movement). The recapitulation is brief and the emphasis has shifted. The liturgical invocation, *moderato feroce*, again conjures up the elemental first subject, but with the reappearance of the second subject delicately scored for flute and horn solos, harp and strings, the second point of rest is reached. The relationship between this and the fifth Symphony is even more clear as the rhythm is eased back and the time scale is broadened as if, from this vantage point, Bax looks forward over the path he must yet travel to the misty havens that, dimly seen, are the goal of all his symphonic endeavour. The brief coda presents the germ, in diminution and in augmentation, in E minor, and the vision again clouds over.

In the tale 'Ancient Dominions' (*Children of the Hills*, pp. 100–35)

Dermot O'Byrne relates the story of a weird nocturnal excursion in the moonlit incandescence of a May night in Donegal:

> Further out the Atlantic dreamed impenetrably, an enormous grey allurement, tender and terrible. Suddenly the full strangeness of this night's mood came upon me almost with the directness of a physical sensation. The sea, the moon, the pallid jewelled glimmer of the sleeping hills and the phantasmal appearances of homely and commonplace objects near at hand all seemed to shadow forth some mystery soon to be revealed either to my bodily eyes or supersensual perception (p. 107).

With growing apprehension of uncanny doings the teller of the tale stumbles on the entrance to a vast underground cavern in whose awesome bowels the dark tides of the Atlantic provide the backcloth to a strange unearthly ritual to the sea-god of the ancient Irish:

> And then suddenly over this threshold of vision a presence passed. For an instant I saw again the wave-crowded mouth of the cavern and the green light in which it was bathed invaded by something vast and dominating, whether breath or light or shadow I could not tell, but I knew that all those men and women below me were again kneeling with veiled heads, their brows almost to the ground, that all were shaken by some obscure ecstasy of terror and joy. Then over myself it swept like a sun-smitten storm and my soul seemed pierced through with shafts of blinding green light and to vibrate and rock in an awful and delirious rapture as though cradled within the soul of the sea (p. 125).

The second movement of the Symphony, marked *Lento solenne*, seems to deal with such an encounter. From the first bar, muted horns, trumpet, harps, timpani, side drums with slackened snares and sul pont strings evoke an atmosphere of druidical mystery.

Out of this deep throbbing a menacing bass figure rises (Ex. 13(a²)) the diminished 7th with the tritone, a reversal of the figure that descended in the first movement—that might easily evoke the sea. With terrible solemnity muted trombones and tuba utter a powerful invocation, whose dark Celtic twist suggests to the imagination the blowing of some ceremonial conch shell. This strange ritualistic music, with its macabre trombone writing, its brassy *pesante* climaxes, its massive rhythm strongly asserted, now throws up, as if at the consummation of the rite, a liturgical motive—that of the first movement broadened into a kind of plain chant—which is echoed, like an organ, on woodwind and brass, and in which the four-note 'descent' pattern appears as a kind of 'Amen'. The invocation, to whatever black deity Bax envisages, is heard again, more intense and more powerful, under whose brazen incantations the trombone and tuba intone a *cantabile* figure derived from the first movement, and again foreshadowing the fifth Symphony. The darkness returns, the black waters rise once more, and the vision fades from sight.

The *Allegro maestoso* third movement opens with the liturgical figure (Ex. 13(a¹)) now in the dominant B flat, which ushers in a variant of the thematic material of the second movement, now capricious, marked *Allegro vivace ma non troppo presto*, and in the home key. From this a grotesque figure on cor anglais, trumpet and viola (which foreshadows the opening theme of the third Symphony) emerges and leads to the syncopated reappearance of the primary material of the work, whose halting rhythm seems to accentuate its dark origins. Horns and cor anglais underline the relationship of the two subjects of the work, A and B. But glimpses of the ultimate resolution are soon whisked away by the propulsive energy of the climax, which, with the hammer blows of the 'tail' motive, firmly establish the *trionfale* march rhythm in which the first subject material is reasserted in a kind of demonic paean —a coda of immense strength whose triumph and final E flat major leave an impression not of light, but of the subjugation of everything by this brutish material.

Having established the three-movement form in the first Symphony, Bax did not elect to vary his symphonic structure in the symphonies that followed. Each subsequent work was to be laid out, like the first, in three movements. But creative necessity—and the nature of the superfluity of material—set him problems. His thematic material, in spite of the apparent tonal nucleus around which it resolves melodically, emerges throughout the symphonies as plastic and linear, characterized by cadential movement rather than by intervallic tension. The 'germ' themes in the first two symphonies (and those of the second Violin Sonata and first Piano Sonata from which they derive) in spite of the apparent symbolism of their vertical (harmonic) make-up in the con-trolled tension of the interval of a semitone, are characterized by the inherent possibilities of linear shape and development. The primary material of the first droops, and that of the second rises—and the developments that emerge therefrom give the two symphonies very distinctive characters despite the common source of melodic material. Bax soon found it necessary to prepare the way for the full flowering of this material by some kind of prologue, and to round it off by similar means in some kind of peroration that did not constitute, but was consequent upon, the climax. And these Introductions and Epilogues thereafter became the means of setting mood, of exposing the raw material of his argument, and of translating it to the spiritual plane. In the first Symphony the Introduction is important to present the primary material in its most elementary form and there is no need for an Epilogue as the final March overpowers the thematic progress. But in the second (whose Introduction fulfils a similar function, but on a bigger scale) Bax felt the necessity of rounding off the argument and releasing the tensions that the *molto largamente* climax of the movement had generated. And in this work he was to allow the enormous upheaval to settle and the tensions to evaporate *niente* in a kind of shadow Epilogue. Out of this nothingness the thin thread of the lonely bassoon line, which opens the third, picks its way unhappily like Yeats's osprey, into the *Allegro moderato* of the first movement proper.

From this point Bax, although retaining the three-movement form, allows the material to overflow as his creative purpose directs, combining the absent *scherzo*'s capricious impishness with the darker primary material to which it belongs in some of the finale themes. Only in the sixth does he depart from this, developing the final movement of the triple form into a further triptychal subdivision of *Scherzo*, Trio and Epilogue—but the finale of the sixth is, after all, something special; and the seventh reverts to the usual three-movement pattern.

Without any kind of exorcism in the baleful last movement of the first Symphony, the second seems about to plunge us deeper into the darkness. Bax describes the Symphony as 'oppressive and catastrophic' and gives the key (which is omitted from the title of the ensuing works) as E minor and C. But though the complexities of the symphony are formidable, the score is full of passages of strange cold beauty whose enigmatic cadences are islands of desolate peace amongst the stormy music of the more agitated passages. Bax suggests further that, in the trilogy of the first three symphonies, which have a common emotional origin, the second pursues the arguments of the first into deeper, more introspective fields of thought—and certainly much that happens in the second seems to take place deep beneath the surface, as if the music existed on two levels or had analogous connections with the sea. But it is at the same time perhaps the most beautiful of all the seven, and if the vistas on which it seems to open are not yet flooded with the sunlight that warms the fifth, they are none the less very beautiful. Its moments of beauty are, however, permeated with sadness, that 'grey wandering osprey', and truly Celtic in their cold purity. Bax suggests that the inner conflicts waged in the first and now intensified in the second are subjective, born deep within his own being—but there is nothing subjective about those moments in this work where his inner vision is illuminated by flashes of bewitching loveliness. If these moments are once again static, perceived only in absolute cessation of movement, they are special moments of inspiration which few enough composers in the twentieth century have been able to share.

The second Symphony was completed during the winter of 1924–5 at Geneva where Harriet Cohen had gone for treatment for the illness that shadowed her whole life, and is dedicated to Koussevitsky, who first performed it in Boston, Mass., on 13th December 1929. It was not given in England until 20th May 1930 when Eugène Goossens conducted it at Queen's Hall.

Like the first, the Symphony seems, in spite of the proliferation of its material, to have emerged in Bax's mind as an entity, grown from the sixty bars of Introduction in which the germinal material is stated, though in less embryonic form than in the first. The primary material is heard as four closely related ideas forming, like the Apocalyptic horsemen, out of the oppressive and menacing atmosphere of the opening. In the first of these primary motives, underpinned by a bass G natural, the lower strings, bassoons and harp clash darkly in G minor with the A flat of the trombones (Ex. 13(b)). The pedal falls to C sharp (smothered by a soft trill on the gong) and a *declamato* fanfare-like motive is heard, with tritone colour, on cor anglais and bassoon (Ex. 13(b¹)). This is linked by the third motive, a cadential bass rise (Ex. 13(b²)) to the fourth, an answering pronouncement in flutes and trumpets.

With these and the icy blast of a rising string figure Bax generates a controlled expectancy. With the *Allegro moderato* comes a welcome forward movement—a war-dance theme derived from the second primary motive, grotesque, vaguely disquieting but not really menacing, an impression confirmed, as the music progresses, by the skeletal sound of the xylophone which joins in the proceedings. This propulsion, how-ever, is soon checked by decorative accretions to the rhythm, and the music, rising on the diminished 3rds of C, E, flat and G flat, achieves an almost ceremonial brilliance before a *molto largamente* climax, with the dance theme in gross augmentation, clears the air for the F major appearance of the second subject in flute and cello which is itself derived from the primary material (an inversion of the opening minor third motive—the final bar of the theme could also be said to be formed from the first motive of the Introduction). The link between this and the first, third and fifth symphonies is part of the symphonic fabric, the great proliferating song whose chief characteristic is the eloquent falling and rising line, full of poignancy and tenderness, with its final lift. The moment of tranquillity achieved in the cadence—one of those 'special moments' in Bax's music—is held, lulled by the alluring enticements of a variant of the fourth motive, in flutes and solo clarinet, like the spirits of those immortals who ride above the enchanted waves in Fand. The illusion is shattered by the summons of the first motive, and with the first of two development sections, the rhythm of the *Allegro moderato* is re-established. A *poco largamente* climax in the sudden light of E major re-introduces the first subject, much embroidered and spun out, and an ecstatic note is heard in the music, with *molto vivace* triple time and xylophone colour. But an interrupted cadence and a spectral trio of muted trombones turn the development towards the second subject material now flooded with the washy green of sea-light and in the key of E major. Solo flute, horn and oboe wistfully echo the fourth motive of the Introduction which is now transformed. Suddenly the mood switches and in only twenty-nine bars the tightly compressed recapitulation section ends the movement with a modal cadence on E minor.

Bax has always been able to work a potent magic in his slow movements. And nowhere is this magic more powerful than in the slow movement of the second Symphony. For the first time in the symphonies Bax is able to suspend the antagonism of the opposing forces for more than a few bars, and to look longingly, and with something of the final serenity, at the far desirable havens. The music is deeply felt rather than idyllic—and unmatched for sheer beauty anywhere else in Bax where he enters this unhandselled world, despite the dire reminder at the climax of the movement of that darkness out of which he has come. Although it is musically an integral part of the symphonic structure, this evocative movement must inevitably reflect that inner vision that is the essence of Bax's poetic vision. In this sense it is tone-poetical, but without any kind of delineation. It evokes mood, like the central movements of both first and third, but its imagery is undefined—atmospheric yet not veiled, fluid, yet darkly thirled to earth by the figures that underpin the rise and fall of the music. Its setting is again the sea, and like the tone-poems of Sibelius it evokes the spirit of the element, rather than the element itself. Yet paradoxically, as in all Bax's work, we know part of the music to be human experience, while part can only be known intuitively. Between the first and second movement (an immense plagal cadence leading to the B major of the *Andante*) Bax has wrought a kind of sea-change permeated with that same sea-magic that colours the openings of *Fand* and *Tintagel*. On this enchanted seascape, with its shifting rhythms and alternating triads, its drooping horn call and the important augmented octave rise in the bass (from the third of the Introduction's primary motives), Bax sets one of his loveliest melodies:

Ex.14 2nd Symphony (slow movement)

This magnificent tune, open-ended on the dominant, leads to the swaying movement of the opening (now in A flat/F) and to a *poco meno mosso* section coloured by the flat 7th. Over the undulating patterns of the opening, an arabesque-like liturgical figure is heard on flute and oboe. A short bridge passage (in solo violin—a very Straussian touch), echoing the melody of the first part of the movement, links all this to a new section in A minor whose principal characteristic, an octave rise, provides the development of the melody, is related to the second primary motive and, as it develops, seems to look forward to the Epilogue of the third Symphony, with the promise of peace. Around this new theme contrapuntal movement begins to generate the energy that, after a strange haunting little motive in solo clarinet (the first notes of whose phrases form the chime-like pattern which concludes the opening statement of the first primary motive at the very beginning of the work), brings a C major climax, full of affirmation and reminiscent of *Die Meistersinger* in the string writing. The gradual increase of tension from this point leads to a further *poco largamente* climax where the composer's vision falters, to expose dramatically the dark and menacing primary motive (Ex. 13(b)) in brass. With the passing of this moment, fraught with nameless menace, the return of the eloquent song is highly charged with emotion, richly decorated with harmonic colour. And to this, now imbued with a note of tragedy and sorrow, the *poco meno mosso* octave rise pattern forms a poignant coda, drenched in harp and celesta sound, and haunted by the augmented octave pattern on trumpets.

The *Allegro feroce* third movement is preceded by a ten-bar Introduction, starkly underlining the third of the primary motives, whose augmented octave figure, coupled with the other aspects of the primary material, Bax allows to dominate the ensuing pages. For the greater part of the movement this energy is developed into a satanic march whose *feroce* gestures (with the horn parts marked 'coarsely blown') and dotted rhythmic pulse are checked only momentarily by thirty-four bars in which this is developed lyrically by clarinet, a theme which seems to be trying to rise above the conflict, seeking resolution. But none is found, and the promising development is lost in an almost literal repetition (very unusual for Bax) of fourteen bars of the introduction to the first movement. This revelation of the basic material is crowned by a *molto marcato* delivery, now with savage triumph, of the second primary motive against an inverted pedal G on strings. The tension of this is unbearable, and resolution comes not with quietness but with a sudden and violent *largamente* delivery of the third primary motive (the augmented octave, now C, F sharp, D flat) like a huge thunderstorm, the full organ throwing its weight into the music. With this enormous expenditure of power Bax allows the tension to evaporate in a long drooping passage underpinned by a pedal C, as if in a kind of epitaph to the preceding five movements. In the piano score manuscript Bax originally sketched this denouement, like the conclusion of the First, as a march (*Tempo di marcia*) but discarded this in favour of the infinitely more powerful slower tempo of the published version. The first of the primary motives reappears on solo violin, completely transformed, and is echoed quietly by the fanfare of the second motive. With the augmented octave pattern, the music drifts into silence—a silence out of which the lonely bassoon climbs in the opening bars of the third Symphony.

Bax had not been totally engrossed with the compulsion to complete the first cycle of his symphonic progress. He had finished the Romantic Overture for small orchestra, dedicated to Delius, for performance at the Harrogate Festival. And in the same year, 1923, he had also written a long Cello Sonata for Beatrice Harrison (using some of the material from the abortive *Spring Fire*), the perky oboe quintet for Leon Goossens and a dark sombre movement for piano quartet,[1] which he later orchestrated as 'Saga Fragment' and which Harriet

---

[1] 'A savage little work much admired by Bartók' (Harriet Cohen, *A Bundle of Time*, p. 228).

Cohen first performed at Queen's Hall with Constant Lambert and later in Edinburgh under Tovey.

But the implacable fury of the first and second Symphonies had not abated, and with sketches of a third Symphony Bax looked for some haven of escape from the city to complete the work which was now forming in his mind and which was in some measure to resolve, however temporarily, the conflicts of the earlier symphonies.

A family holiday in 1902 had taken the Baxes to Scotland. When in the late spring of 1905 Bax returned from Connemara to England and found Clifford had set out on a journey around the world (see *Inland Far*, p. 59) he left London to explore again the rocky coasts of western Scotland. The road to the isles had always fascinated him and with the long and lovely Highland Line through Inverness-shire, he took the train to Mallaig, spending August there, and later sailing to Lewis and Harris. The wild scenery filled him with the same joy as had the coastline of Ireland, and although in the intervening years he had found Glencolumcille in Donegal, he thought again of Inverness-shire in the autumn of 1928 as he completed the third Symphony. With the half-finished sketches he set out once more for the west coast of Scotland— to Morar where he settled for several months in the local hotel.

It is probably only a romantic notion that the poet or musician confronted with the rough nobility and grandeur of the Scottish hills must turn in a kind of creative frenzy to his pad or score. The creative process, in music at any rate, is not like that, but a slow gestation aided by prolonged experience of the environment and nourished by memory. But these coasts and hills have something else of great importance to the musician above all: that quality of silence, a deep, almost tangible stillness that seems to embalm, in the low westering sunlight, the land and seascape. It is not a muffling silence, but is crystal clear, pointed by the natural sounds with which it contrasts, and which are somehow heard within it.

The casual visitor to Morar, any winter from 1928 until the war, might have seen in the hotel lounge a quiet dark-suited figure, reserved yet not unapproachable, a gentleman farmer perhaps or a retired country doctor, seated in thought or in puzzled concentration over a crossword puzzle. Even had the figure confronted an orchestral score it is unlikely that Bax would have been recognized, except perhaps as he might have been recognized in Glencolumcille—as a friend.

Pre-eminently a depicter of Nature's moods, and extremely susceptible to his environment, Bax found in Morar a refuge where he could realize the powerful musical imagery that makes up not only the third Symphony, but many of his later scores, which bear the final legend 'Morar' and the date. Here the white sands fringe the sea, brass-burnished by the sun, or veiled beneath the towering storm clouds that march out of the west, or hidden in the swirling curtains of the rain. And in the faery ocean, like enchanted fortresses, rise the islands of Rhum, Eigg and Skye, romantic bulwarks of Hy Brasil edged with the sun, an earnest of the shimmering lands of Tir Nan Og invisible below the horizon.

And as Western Eire, with its legends and heroes nourished the composer of *The Garden of Fand*, so was Morar the cradle of Bax the symphonist. It was significant not only that Bax now turned north, but also that he should do so as a symphonist and in the winter months of the year. For the extremes of Nature's moods are reflected in the music, and in his symphonic character. Here at Morar he found the peace that was to infuse the Epilogue of the third Symphony. Here he found that self-identification with the forces from which the music is forged, the interlocking energies that hold the music of the seven together, and give it both tremendous power and ineffable calm.

The third Symphony, in spite of the force with which the opening theme is thrust upward at the climax, has less of the sternness of which the first two are made. Shrouded in silence through which the solo bassoon threads a melody that seems to ask

What aged war wouldst thou awake in me
Thou subtle world-old bitter Celtic voice? [1]

the opening is veiled in dark mists that are tinged with a forlorn sadness rather than with menace, as those mists that hide and blur the definition of the final pages conceal the mountain tops.

Bax saw the third Symphony, at the time at any rate, as a resolution of the stresses which had driven first and second, and the serenity of the Epilogue seems to suggest that peace had been won. But at bottom it is an uneasy peace which was quickly succeeded by the anguished cry of the opening of *Winter Legends*. But at least the resolution was nearer than when he had begun. He marks the opening bassoon solo *dolce* (Ex. 13(c)), and this, with the high register of the instrument, produces a strange sound whose unhappy mood is reflected in the

[1] 'On pipe-music heard in a London street', in *Seafoam and Firelight, Orpheus* series No. 2, p. 28.

vagaries of the rhythm. At the tenth bar the first clarinet joins in, followed by the second (with harp chording), flute and oboe (with an important variant), trumpet and horns—a web of sound which begins to clarify, still vaguely defined, with the first crystallization of a rhythmic pulse (a cor anglais figure derived from the opening) from which the *allegro moderato* stems some bars later.

This figure, in bass strings, is the background to a characteristic liturgical pronouncement (Ex. 13(c¹)), given out by trumpets and trombones, clarinets and bassoons, which represents the corollary of the first figure, forming out of the nebulous opening with portentous solemnity.

As if in response to this, the energy that was implied in the cor anglais figure is released, within five bars to establish without a break the dynamic pulse of the *allegro*, and the vague tonality, after a brief F sharp minor, is abruptly switched to B flat minor.

The full exposition of the first subject begins with the germ theme in strings, now totally awakened in character, whose impulsive rhythm is heralded by a *marcato* figure in the bass which again thrusts upward in triumph at the end of the movement.

With the rhythmic impulse firmly established, Bax allows this material, with derived counter-subjects which are whisked away almost as they appear, to generate the first big climax. At its height the incisive upward thrusts of the bass figure and the liturgical motive, now in the brass, give way to a kind of disintegration of the fabric of the music within a few bars. As the pulse sinks back to *piu lento*, the primary material is heard, first as an elongated shadow and then in an elegiac transitional passage scored for five solo violins which concludes on a pedal B flat.

In complete contrast to this stormy opening, the *lento moderato* exposition of the second subject material (quite clearly a derivation of the first) begins with a warm reflective muted string passage, richly ornamented, and a pleading figure in horns. From this a solo horn entering on what Bernard Shore describes as a 'horribly dangerous top note',[1] points to the tranquil moments of the second movement.

But with the opening three notes—A, B flat, D flat—of the germ theme, first on timpani, then delivered on full orchestra, the mood of tenderness is dispelled, and the development section begins. The opening theme is now given to the violas and as before the strands of

[1] *Sixteen Symphonies*, Longmans, 1949.

the pattern, with the added delicate notes of celesta, begin to re-assemble and the *allegro moderato* rhythm is re-established. The urgency of this rhythm becomes even greater than before, and with gradually increasing intensity Bax builds up the impressive climax, marked by the sonorous clang of the anvil, and the theme is now blared forth defiantly. This climax, in which the first theme is set against a descending passage in strings anticipating the Epilogue, once again presents Bax with the perennial problem in his symphonies of how much supremacy this primary element must be allowed. The exultant baying of the horns, the huge swaying movement of the basses support the tension; but in the end it all becomes unbearable, and Bax is obliged to re-introduce the second subject material. But this is now shredded with the agonies of doubt—a mood underlined by the liturgical incantation and the eight-bar figure of clarinets.

With renewed ferocity the energy boils up within only a few bars, and with one of the countersubjects in the exposition—the snarling bass figure (Ex. 13(c²))—triumphing, the movement ends.

The slow movement opens like the first with another solo instrument, the horn. But the mood is very different. Gone are the mists and the darkness—all is light and air, as if some celestial sunrise had discovered a pristine world gradually illuminated by the first fingering beams of the morning.

The material is again two-fold, related thematically to the material of the first movement, but Bax now fills us with wonder at the transformation. The slow fanfare-like call of the horn solo is echoed by solo viola, muted and blurred as if laden with tears, in the midst of a chorus of quiet strings. From this twofold exposition Bax draws the panorama of the slow movement. As the distance clears, the sun picks out the far horizon in melting modulatory changes, trumpet echoing the horn in a clear D major. The seascape, for such it soon appears, dances in the shimmering light of celesta, flutes and clarinets. As solo trumpet develops the first motive the tonal colour droops to B flat and the opening viola solo melody (now in first violins) leads to an expansive development and to F major. Delicate traceries of flute arabesque now encircle the fanfare tune (in divided strings) and the climax proves to be a kind of inversion of itself, with strings, trumpets, horns and woodwind alternately striving for mastery. The long pedal G, however, finally resolves upon the closing C major tonality where the peace which settles, although marred by the experience, has that elegiac quality that the opening seemed to prophesy.

With a brusque gesture, the third movement banishes the reflective mood of the slow movement with a series of *vigoroso* chords (the liturgical theme of the first movement) and a characteristic war dance given to clarinets and violas.

With a cello bass suggestive of the double tonic this dance theme, malevolent but with a restrained kind of violence, is succeeded by the opening chordal pattern like the viola theme from the second movement. This is joined, with a touch of wry humour in tuba, by a singing theme in first violins whose peroration, an *accelerando* build-up and a savage snarl of triumph from the horns, ends in brassy triumph, the dance theme now in trumpets.

A *piu mosso* section follows and, in a mood of increasing expectancy, the opening chordal theme appears in a syncopated variant, over which the oboes and clarinets introduce a related melody, with a strangely sardonic twist, which is echoed by chorusing horns. This lyrical material is allowed to flourish until the advent of a reflective figure on solo cor anglais, punctuating the development of the opening themes. But within a few bars the chordal theme resumes its rhythm, the war dance returns, and a climax in broad augmentation brings these proceedings to a head; and suddenly an enormous calm is felt, subduing the demonic energy that had built up as if with a spell, as the beginning of the Epilogue is reached.

Time, which seemed in the slow movement to stand still, now moves with slow but inevitable tread. Over the chordal bass a long drooping theme (on oboes and clarinets) speaks of the transience of all beauty, and the impenetrability of time. A beckoning theme, full of unearthly command, seems to motion the listener into this strange unearthly world, but in response, under the ethereal chords of harp and violins, a shadow of the primary motive utters a dark warning. A solo violin, like some ascending soul, is heard. The final cadence is led by the horn, and the Epilogue closes with a reminder of the primary motive still present, but for the moment quiescent.

11 Symphonies 4-7

'. . . and at the moment, some strange melodious bird took up its song, and sang, not an ordinary bird-song, with constant repetitions of the same melody, but what sounded like a continuous strain, in which one thought was expressed, deepening in intensity as [it] evolved in progress. It sounded like a welcome already overshadowed with the coming farewell. As in all sweetest music, a tinge of sadness was in every note. Nor do we know how much of the pleasures even of life we owe to the intermingled sorrows. Joy cannot unfold the deepest truths, although deepest truth must be deepest joy. Cometh white-robed Sorrow, stooping and wan, and flingeth wide the doors she may not enter. Almost we linger with Sorrow for very love.'

George MacDonald, *Phantastes*.

With three symphonies to his credit Bax was a force to be reckoned with in British music. In 1931 he was awarded the gold medal of the Royal Philharmonic Society and on this occasion Barbirolli conducted the Royal Philharmonic Orchestra in a performance of the second Symphony as a tribute.

But in spite of the apparent resolution of the Epilogue of the third Symphony, the dark shadows that had lain over the first two works were not to be dispelled so easily. And it was part of the quandary in which Bax now found himself that he recognized that the opposing and conflicting forces that had battled in the course of these works were in fact one element, part of his own nature of opposites, remaining with him unexorcized to trouble his spirit. With the inner compulsion that was to express itself in the increasingly austere music of the later symphonies grew the nomadic impulse that drove him from the city and further and further from society. Unable to settle, he had visited in 1923 Capri, Rapallo, Pompeii and Constantinople—and now he turned towards Iceland and Finland. With the ending of the overt drama of the first three symphonies and in a mood of reaction to the cathartic outburst of these works Bax felt unburdened of the immediate stresses. But the serenity apparent in the last works of his life was a long way off and, in spite of the sensuous beauty of the opening movement of the Nonet (scored in January 1930), a desperate kind of energy had now to be worked out. The *Overture Elegy and Rondo* and the *Picaresque Comedy Overture* are the first signs of this—in both of these there is a feverish gaiety. This vigorous activity, which was to spill over into the fourth Symphony, had, however, little of the demonic drive that so far had powered the symphonic writing.

In 1928 Bax heard *Tapiola* for the first time, an experience which made a deep and enduring impression. Significantly it was *Tapiola*, with its gaunt and chilly landscapes ruled by the great gods of the Finnish northland, rather than Sibelius's symphonies that turned Bax's gaze northward. He had heard a great deal of Sibelius, to whom so many writers looked for the musical salvation of the twentieth century. Both Cecil Gray and Constant Lambert had written as if Sibelius alone linked the past with the unborn future. And Bax no less than other musical minds of the day found himself naturally drawn to this music whose terrain was so congenial to him.

It may well appear to future students of Bax that the influence of Sibelius on his work was not the saving grace that it appeared to be at this point. For its greatest impact came upon Bax at precisely the time when he was least equipped to deal with and assimilate it as he had so readily done with the less musically powerful influences that had gone into the make-up of his character. Exhausted by the titanic exertions of the first three symphonies, and conscious that his symphonic course was only partly charted, he seized upon the compass of Sibelius's music and turned his eyes to the North. As the poetry of Yeats had led him to the environment which had inspired the poet, so *Tapiola* directed his steps to the gaunt and forbidding land of northern Finland. The impact of Sibelius, at least initially, was certainly comparable to that of Yeats and acted less as an influence as such than as a kind of release valve. But this was also a musical influence, expressed in language to which Bax, and not now Dermot O'Byrne, was quicker to react. The direct influence of Sibelius is, I think, the real reason for the indecision which Bax felt in the transition between third and fifth Symphonies—or perhaps even more specifically between third and sixth—for the fifth symphony embodies its ultimate results. With this, probably the most powerful influence of the time (other than that of Stravinsky), Bax the symphonist had to come to terms.

Bax had some misgivings about the third Piano Sonata, and some indication of his indecision as to the direction he might now take is given in a number of scores on which he worked between 1925 and 1931.

Apart from the *Overture Elegy and Rondo* and the *Comedy Overture* (the latter was completed in Morar in October 1930), the *Northern Ballads* (and *Cortèges*, written in Switzerland in 1924) show the beginnings of this new direction that was to follow the third Symphony and of which *Winter Legends* was the culminating point.

Bax's indecision is reflected in the *Northern Ballads*, the first of which was completed on 26th October 1927 (although the short score is headed with the Roman figure III), and which was subsequently entitled No. 1 in November of the same year. The so-called second was not completed until the winter of 1933–4, again at Morar. These scores, with the exception of that headed III, might have heralded a new symphonic direction, overlapping the first series of three symphonies which was concluded in 1929.

The *Northern Ballad* No. 1 (dedicated to Basil Cameron and unperformed until April 1961) showed more clearly the strange amalgam of musical impulses felt by Bax. The work opens with a decisive horn figure which arises from the germinal opening of the first Symphony. A *marcato* bass in *pizzicato* strings indicates the possible development, but before these march-like elements can be properly established into a rhythm a *vivace* development of this introductory material appears, (marked *feroce*) displaying a very pronounced resemblance to the last movement material of the fifth Symphony (linking it with the demonic character of the second).

The central material of the Ballad consists of a rather mournful little tune in a Scotch 'snap' rhythm (which reappears in the *Lento* of the sixth). After this, some brassy fanfares re-introduce the *Tempo di marcia* and the development of this is extended into a folk melody which, with its trudging open-air forthrightness of the kind associated with Percy Grainger, seems to suggest that Bax's assimilation of recognizably Irish characteristics did not preclude an instinctive awareness of other folk music types (such melodies appear elsewhere in Bax—in the Clarinet Sonata, and the Legend Sonata for cello and piano). A fleeting and almost tragic glimpse of the Scottish theme ends the work, which peters out with the final *sfz* bang.

The *Northern Ballad* marked III (and given in short score no other title than the numeral—it was not orchestrated) is dark and uncompromising, bleakly liturgical in mood with the plangent theme of the sixth Symphony, or a foreshadowing of it, in 4ths on three trumpets and harp. A *dolce cantabile* contrast to this primary material is also very liturgical in character and with its development Bax seemed to get into difficulties (part of the manuscript score is crossed out). This central material is much less warm than is usual in Bax's central themes, and if Sibelius's influence is already at work, then the difficulties of containing Bax's often demonic energies by huge granitic strength as Sibelius had done so successfully in *En Saga, Tapiola* and the fourth Symphony, proved too problematical to resolve in the kind of terms Bax had been dealing with in these Ballads.

The Ballad No. 2, though not completed until early 1934, deals much more satisfactorily with the re-orientation that the music of Sibelius had produced in Bax. The music of the entire score grows with a natural progression (although the characteristic hiatus—a few string chords in this instance—between the first section's dark-hued, wintry churning of the chromatic scale, and the second section's almost vernal melodies in flute and clarinet (cf. third Symphony) is still present to shape the form) and although it sounds very Sibelian in content it does not attempt that kind of organic growth that, as if the very themes were living entities growing from the germ, and almost endowed with separate, probing vitality, makes the fourth Symphony of Sibelius such a fascinating work.

The third Symphony was completed in February 1929 and Bax returned from Morar to London. But by the time the fourth had begun to shape itself in his mind a new and very important score had been completed in a period of concentrated creative activity that occupied the three months from October to December of the ensuing winter. This new work, a massive symphonic concerto scored for piano and orchestra, Bax entitled *Winter Legends*—not specially to underline a programmatic basis in the music but rather to reinforce the true nature of those elements which had proved most vital in the conception of this work. Although he went on almost at once to write the fourth and fifth Symphonies and, the culmination of this driving creative inspiration, the sixth, this new score (like the Symphonic Variations destined to remain a hidden masterpiece) probably represents the peak of his achievement.

It is symphonic in scope, full of majestic grandeur and idyllic poetry, but is at the same time one of his most powerfully organized works. And although the relief afforded by the lighter fourth Symphony appears, in retrospect, as a very necessary part of Bax's overall symphonic design, *Winter Legends* is a logical development of those influences that in the third Symphony had begun to come to the surface. The principal element in *Winter Legends*, set in a bleakly beautiful orchestral landscape, is one of tender passion, developed from the quasi-heroic opening material—a mood born of the romantic agonies of all the music he had already written, and which was now uppermost in his nature. This (Ex. 15) and the enormous final Epilogue relate the work to the earlier Symphonic Variations. Once again the solo instrument, though carrying the burden of the material, is treated in a concertante fashion. In spite of the difficulties of the virtuosic piano part, it is participant rather than protagonist, the piano writing being an integral part of the massive score.

Although this work is undoubtedly the first fruit of that new direction opened to Bax by his first experiences of the music of Sibelius, the music owes probably much more to Harriet Cohen for whom, like the Symphonic Variations, the work was written. Bax had originally dedicated the score to Sibelius, but shortly after this dedication was deleted and Harriet Cohen's name substituted. The work was then given to her for performance. Her joy with the music was unbounded:

> It was about this time that there germinated in his mind the idea for the great symphonic concerto *Winter Legends* which was to be the joy and pride among the collection of pieces that were written for me in so many countries . . .[1]
>
> Chronologically and emotionally the concerto was another Symphony in Arnold's mind—'my No. 4 really', he would say, and it was to lead inevitably to the great fifth Symphony which was dedicated to Sibelius. 'In these two works', he said, 'I have gone Northern!'
>
> One of the first to realise this was Sibelius himself: he adored this music. In those last twilight hours I spent with him at Järvenpää, some ten months before his death, I played him snatches of *Winter Legends*. 'Bax is my son in music,' he said.[2]

Neither the Symphonic Variations nor *Winter Legends* were offered to the publishers—and speculation as to the reasons for this only reinforces the true nature of the music. For both works were written for Harriet Cohen, and her personality is very much an integral part of the music. It cannot escape comment that, in the central movement of the symphony which finally appeared as the fourth, Bax chose to incorporate the early piano composition *A Romance* (Ex. 11), a nostalgic love poem which he had also written for her.

Bax's relationship with this strong and dominant personality was a complex one. Physically attracted by her youth and her dark, fragile beauty, he was drawn also by a curious strength of interpretative power in her playing of his music—and by her realization of that cold ferocity which rose so often to the surface in his work. The vital energies and sustained mental and physical effort needed for the granitic music of the Concerto was counterbalanced in Harriet Cohen (though in different proportions than in Bax) by a wayward and capricious

[1] *A Bundle of Time*, p. 152.   [2] ibid., pp. 181–2.

element in her nature—that feminine sensitivity and northern ancestry which informed her playing and understanding of Bax's piano music. Those elements in his own being and their proportions one to the other were complemented in Harriet Cohen.

The manuscript scores of both these compositions were given to her and during her lifetime no other pianist played either.

The title *Winter Legends* is appropriate, implying as it does both legendary and seasonal connotations. Both these elements are very much a part of Bax's musical personality, but there is little actual programmatic significance in this enormously complex score, other than an indication of the mood in which the listener ought to approach the music. The two elements are closely interlinked, but in the same way as in John Ireland's 'Mai Dun' and 'The Forgotten Rite' in which the tumulus and earthwork provide the focus for the almost tangible manifestation of associations that never take concrete form and are sensed rather than seen. The natural element in *Winter Legends* is a vast northern Pohjola, its inhabitants great dignitaries of natural myth, the personification of lakes, rocks and trees rather than human heroes. And in spite of much wintry proceedings Bax's landscape is flecked with sunlight glittering on lonely waters, and filtering through traceries of leaves. Sibelius's reaction to the work, which he was never to hear performed, is interesting. Like the symphonies, the concerto uses Bax's own brand of cyclic material, and resemblances to the music of Sibelius are in fact slight (those of tone colour and even of melodic pattern occur in almost every Bax score). But its setting naturally appealed to Sibelius, not one to be flattered by mere imitation, and his admiration was that of one great artist for the work of another.

Winter Legends is in three movements, with Introduction and Epilogue, and the thematic material of the work—which recurs in all three movements—is built around the nostalgic waywardness of the central piano solo (Ex. 15) (which appears first of all as the heroic principal subject of the first movement) and flowers, as in the Symphonic Variations, into a sensually beautiful Epilogue.

The work opens with a thirty-nine bar introduction. The side drum, which foreshadows the syncopated rhythm of the *Allegro* (a pattern which also appears in many guises throughout the work), leads into a surging piano figure whose climax is a statement, on strings and upper wind, of the agonized first theme of the work (Ex. 13(e)) a highly ornamented chromatic descent pattern, followed by a complementary beckoning figure on solo viola.

The mood of this Introduction is wintry enough, and the rhythmic chordal 'liturgical' figure (Ex. 13(e¹)) which opens the *Allegro* with its strange syncopated pattering, evokes the natural background against which the heroic principal theme of the piano is set. A dark rising figure (Ex. 13(e²)) (on bass clarinet, bassoon, tuba, cello and basses)— also ubiquitous—pre-echoes the piano's main entry with the subject. This subject is the dual participant in both primary and secondary roles through out the whole work. It is immediately seized upon by flute and oboe over a piano arpeggio, and the intensity develops to a new rhythmic pattern rapped out *energico* by the orchestra derived from this material. A decorative and wintry section works out the material at the conclusion of which, with a nostalgic echo on the horn, the piano reflects on the theme:

Ex. 15

This mood is broken at length by the return of the opening material whose insistent rhythms and driving energy bring about a huge climax in which the first subject and the opening figure compete for supremacy. A brief coda-like figure in the piano (prophetic of the second movement) develops again into a powerful rhythmic build-up and the movement ends *maestoso*, with the *largamente* return of the opening figure, now in the major.

The central movement is marked *Lento*, and derives all its material from the first movement.

Bax, in spite of his love for Chopin and John Field, wrote no piece of music that could truthfully be described as a Nocturne (with the single exception of the slow movement of the Cello Concerto to which he gave this title[1]). Certainly there are plenty of half lights, twilit groves and shadowy waters; and there are also the sunbursts of early dawn—in *Spring Fire* and elsewhere. But only O'Byrne the poet speaks of the night—and then with a kind of dread (in, for instance, 'The Valley of the Bells') as if it were synonymous with death. It is as if for Bax the romantic hours of night veiled the earth and hid in the oblivion of sleep the driving life force that generated his creative work. But the slow movement of *Winter Legends* has all the attributes of a Baxian nocturne—evoking that land whose winter brings with it the long hours of darkness in whose shadow the landscape takes on a new and strange colour, almost nightmarish in its ghostly luminescence.

Nothing else can describe the witchery of this music, recalling the slow movements of Bartók's concertos which, also nocturnal, are vitally alive and vibrant with sound.

The opening bars are delicately scored for two bassoons and strings, a remote and austerely beautiful sound from which the piano appears with a version of the coda figure (from first movement), a wistful and wayward theme which seems to crystallize in music the soft, shivering movements in the darkness of the landscape. This is developed at some length before the liturgical rhythmic figure (first heard at the opening of the *Allegro* in the first movement), now elusive and dream-like, disturbs the mood. Dark threatening bursts of sound, with tympani *ostinati* and *martellato* piano octaves, frame the central material, a chorale-like tune which concludes with an incredibly lovely horn solo

[1] The slow movement of the Cello Concerto has no parallel in Bax's music—either in mood or in subject matter. It is perhaps the most modern-sounding of all Bax's music, and the strange cold beauty is nearer in spirit to that period of late romanticism that produced the 'Gurrelieder'.

(with references to the *Lento* of the third Symphony). The texture thickens as if the night had deepened, and the dream-like liturgical figure again introduces the opening material to round off the movement.

The third movement, *Molto Moderato*, forms a magnificent climax to the Concerto—ending, like the Symphonic Variations, in a long idyllic Epilogue with the solo piano taking precedence.

A bare fifth (A and E) in strings and a decorative piano figuration evoke a rising figure on tuba and on bassoons, with the liturgical motive (Ex. 13 (e^1)) in woodwind and horns.

This is the prelude to a grotesque march-like theme in piano (again characterized by a rising 5th) which forms the principal subject. After this is hammered out by the orchestra the tempo quickly changes to an *allegro molto*—two in a bar—for the development of the subject, a clattering theme in solo piano (the characteristic descent 'tail' pattern of the symphonies). Beneath the glittering piano writing Bax allows wraith-like shadows of the first theme of the work to develop, and the tempo slackens to expose the idyllic song that is to become the subject of the Epilogue, the rising fifth now falling and with a triplet tail figure attached. The next section is warm and rich, like the later *Morning Song*, in the sounds of nature. But once more there is an abrupt switch to *allegro vivace*, with the march theme, a dialogue between the solo and the orchestra, hammered out into a strange procession of chords. An enormous climax begins, with the development material prominent, and the idyllic theme in the piano gradually evolving to the complete form which it takes at the beginning of the Epilogue.

This long and idyllic piano solo, so characteristic of Bax, is the equivalent of the 'Triumph' of the Symphonic Variations, and at the conclusion of the work the heroic first subject (Ex. 15), now calm and tranquil, is echoed by the solo horn's dying call through a filigree of piano arabesque.

In *Winter Legends* and the fourth Symphony Bax explored the two avenues open to him. One might expect the fourth of any series of seven to take some kind of new direction, and in the Bax symphonies the trilogy of the first three made this imperative. Both *Winter Legends* and the fourth Symphony follow naturally on the Epilogue of the third —the concerto exploring those elements which had throughout the first three symphonies begun to exert an ever more dominant influence in Bax's personality; and the fourth Symphony shrugging off the inner tensions and turning outwards to a lighter, more extrovert mood.

In both scores the central point of the work, quite apart from the obvious function of the slow movement, is to be found in the B context, whose hard-won supremacy in the final pages of the third, though not unchallenged, had weighted heavily the balance in Bax's future development that was to culminate in the glorious final moments of the sixth. It would not perhaps be surprising if, at the same time, the fourth of the series were to seem pivotal in the series of seven, and if we take the mathematically obvious point, there is something symbolic about Bax's choice of fulcrum. For at the heart of the slow movement of the fourth symphony Bax uses the music of the earlier piano piece *A Romance* (a piece written for Harriet Cohen showing quite clearly a relationship with Scriabin) to fulfil exactly the same purpose that motivates the scores of both *Winter Legends* and the earlier Symphonic Variations.

After the fourth Symphony, a new note of affirmation sounded amidst the festivities of the fourth's final movement is more and more strongly felt in the Epilogues of the fifth, the sixth and in the final Theme and Variations of the seventh.

The introductory passages become more compressed, the primary material striving more urgently for supremacy. The action becomes more violent, the conflict more open. Each symphony, like the roughly boisterous opening of the fourth, begins with a decisive rhythmic figure (the fifth grimly throbbing, the sixth a menacing *ostinato* and the seventh filled with a repressed joy—each contrasting with the rudimentary snarling figures that open both first and second and with the dark gropings of the third).

Each Introduction, after the fourth, is cut off by a pause—G.P.—and the basic tonality moves out of the darkness into the light. It is interesting to compare the triumphal march which concludes the fourth symphony with that which brought the first to a terrifying close. Both are in E flat major (although the first ends bleakly enough), and both are festive.

But the pageantry of the fourth is far removed from the savagery of the first, as if the page of history had turned and had substituted dragoons and yeomen for the cudgel-bearing Picts. To this festive conclusion—dark on the one hand and glittering on the other—the opening material of the symphonies points.

The opening of the fourth Symphony and the final bars affirm quite unambiguously the E flat major triad, and all the material of the work points dramatically upwards. It begins briskly with an alternating broken chordal pattern (the flattened 3rd is present but unaccented) in viola, cello and clarinet, whose accents are vigorous but not ferocious. Bax himself acknowledged a programme by admitting that this opening reflected the sea at flood-tide on a breezy and sunny day. A 'tail' pattern and a swaying rise and fall lead to the exultant climax in brass from which the first subject appears—an immediate development of the initial figure with an aggressive directness (not unlike the theme in the last movement of Dvořák's *New World*), a rhythm which is at once threatened by a triplet figure.

As so often in Bax, exposition must inevitably include some development, and as the Holstian beat is re-established the first subject begins its elongation and compression to a *poco ritenuto*, when the dominant 7th of E flat takes us to an inflected C major. A skeletal development of the opening pages ensues and, with a brusque gesture from the horns, the 'tail' becomes the subject of attention.

With the return of the *moderato, pesante e ritmico*, and the change of accent to three-four, the first subject is churned about in woodwind as if blown by the gusty winds. The time signature reverts to two-four and, as the 'tail' rhythm peters out, an oboe introduces the second subject in C minor—a *Schéhérazade*-like song, with the clarinet accompaniment descending in chromatic steps, and with an Irish twist in the phrase following.

At the conclusion of this second subject material the transition to the development of the first subject is dovetailed by a generative pattern built from the second subject, plaintive figures in the woodwind and the undulating wave-like pattern (which reappears in the fifth Symphony) over which ghostly muted trumpets, heard through a kind of haze, lead to a climax which seems about to re-introduce the first subject. The *Allegretto semplice* which follows, marked 'calm and idyllic', finds the first subject in a Delian mood of playful warmth, like flickering sunlight.

The *tempo giusto* climax is quickly rounded off as the 'tail' figure prepares for the further development of the second subject, cloaked in Grieg-like harmonies and given out by the strings. This Bax cleverly turns, with material from the end of the exposition, into a coda—and the opening music of the symphony is resumed in a recapitulative coda where all the foregoing material joins in an exultant final chorus.

The *Lento moderato*, in E major, is less warm than many of Bax's slow movements, as if the breezy freshness of the opening had brought with it clouds to mask the sun. The chromatic 'droop' (tonic/flat 7th) provides once again a kind of undulating background for the first theme, on woodwind, a rather melancholy Celtic song. The trumpet solo which follows this gives a hint of the central melody, with a touch of poignancy that the first theme's reappearance on strings underlines. This is to become the theme of the slow movement of the sixth Symphony but is not yet quite mature enough. The huge waves which follow this exposition (like the two waves in *Tintagel*) are powerful, born deep in mid ocean and driving into man's orbit with great thrusting and swelling crests. These waves take on the shape of the tune, as if a visionary Undine had arisen out of the sea. Pre-echoing the seventh Symphony, with a 'seagull'-like pattern in flute solo and harp, the central section takes the languid theme of *A Romance* in viola and cor anglais, now in A flat, a phrase of which (E, C flat, B) turns to G major providing the affirmation that follows the vision.

At the conclusion of all this comes a fragment of the second subject of the first movement, now in 4ths. Solo violin, celesta and bass clarinet decorate this as fragments of other subjects and memories are woven into the music, and the movement ends with a Delian touch of nostalgia.

The *Allegro* final movement is brisk and busy, with overt and purposeful developments of the first movement. A busy chattering woodwind rhythm overlays the festive rising 5th theme in the depths of the orchestra, then nearer, on horns, as if a host of Neptune's creatures were riding the waves and approaching the shore. This seems about to come to a climax when, with a sudden abrupt change of mood, a staccato march rhythm in solo trumpet paints the outlying figures of the approaching carnival, satyrs and pouting cherubs, romping and gambolling in syncopation. With a change to F major the whole cavalcade sweeps forward with a new progressive theme on horns that surges with forward movement. The capricious and satyr-like parts of the procession, with bitonal clashes in trumpets and trombones, broaden to B major and in five-four time. And now the final march theme begins to take shape. The *allegro scherzando*, in a Lydian E flat major, begins the final section. Echoes of the opening are heard and the Epilogue (although not so marked) is a *Marcia trionfale*.

In the winter of 1931 Bax went once again to Morar to score the fifth Symphony. From there he returned to London early in April 1932 and set off with Balfour Gardiner to join Harriet Cohen in Stockholm.

Harriet had been a friend of Sibelius for many years. (Challenged once with her presence in his house at Järvenpää, Sibelius, who was reputed to dislike 'mere' executants, had exclaimed, 'Ah, but she is my daughter!') Bax had already met Sibelius—once as a young man, at an evening at Kalisch's music club in 1909 when he described him, in *Farewell, My Youth*:

> ... the earlier Sibelius gave one the notion that he had never laughed in his life, and never could. That strong taut frame, those cold steel-blue eyes, and hard-lipped mouth, were those of a Viking raider, insensible to scruple, tenderness or humour of any sort. An arresting, formidable-looking fellow, born of dark rock and northern forest, yet somehow only half the size of the capricious old Colossus of today.[1]

From Stockholm the trio set off by steamer for Åbo and thence to Helsinki. And with Helsinki as centre they made several trips into the wild Finnish countryside—to Imatra with its wild and dashing falls—touring by car round the lakes and through the forests of Karelia, and the Savo province, delighting in the lakes and forests and fields of wheat. They visited Ladoga and the island on the lake, Valamo, to the monastery on which they were ferried by boat. Back in Helsinki Harriet took Arnold to meet Sibelius again, at a well-known restaurant. This meeting lasted twenty-four hours, prolonged by ardent discussion punctuated by refreshment (during which Bax, overcome by the effects of the whisky, fell asleep) and during which Bax and Sibelius became close friends. Sibelius had a very high regard for Bax's music (he accepted the honorary presidency of the Bax Society after Bax's death), and to Sibelius Bax offered the dedication of the recently completed fifth Symphony.

The strong bond of sympathy between the two composers was scarcely surprising. Bax found in the country of Finland the essence of the kind of music he was beginning to write in the symphonies and in the fifth he appears to come closest to Sibelius. But in spite of obvious similarities between this work and, for instance, the fifth Symphony of Sibelius, there is no real relationship in their symphonic procedures.

Bax's material is unlike that of Sibelius. It is thematic rather than motivic and, although Bax in the Epilogue brings off a huge expansion of the initial 'germ' theme, it is not strictly speaking a synthesis of previously exposed material but an organic proliferation. Bax's entire symphony grows like a living entity from the pregnant opening figure by a process of thematic expansion—a romantic procedure—while

---

[1] *Farewell, My Youth*, p. 61. Bax suggests that the later meeting with Sibelius took place in 1936. But Miss Cohen was quite adamant that it was in the spring of 1932.

Sibelius creates a physical architectonic structure which is closer to classical procedures.

Bax lacked the extreme discipline that Sibelius had learnt in his fourth Symphony. He was capable of intense concentration, and no extraneous material finds its way into either fifth or sixth Symphonies— but the flowering of the fifth's final movement encompasses far more than the plunging themes in the Sibelius. Much of the forward movement in Bax, which is continually interrupted by passages which seem to obstruct and hinder the flow, owes its propulsive nature to his sense of harmonic progress and line, hanging the fabric over slowly moving points of interrupted cadence and undermining each cadence with ambivalent chords that keep the movement liquid. But in the end the undercurrents begin to merge and the logic of the exposition becomes plain only in the final recapitulation in the Epilogue.

Although there are many references to Sibelius in Bax's work (the quotation from *Tapiola* in the sixth Symphony, for example) the direct influence of the Finnish composer is less easily traced in Bax than it is in E. J. Moeran (in the slow movement, and final chords of the G minor Symphony). The apparent resemblance between the opening of the Bax fifth and the opening of the slow movement of the Sibelius does not bear scrutiny after the first few bars.

Bax's fifth Symphony is perhaps the most difficult of all to analyse, although it is by no means difficult to comprehend. It is rich in invention, and yet the flowering of ideas is strictly controlled. Indeed, unity of purpose and idea is its strongest characteristic. It gives the impression of having been composed, like the first 'all of a piece', not in the blazing heat of inspiration but as if the composer, working on it over a period of time, did not let go of anything or distract himself with anything else until the final bar had been written. All the material, of which there appears a very great deal, evolves from the opening, but since this thematic material is closely interwoven, it becomes difficult to find clear patterns of exposition and development within the movement. The work is much more closely knit than a glance at the score would indicate.

By the logic of harmony, the progress of the symphony is quite clearly indicated, and the 'big' moments (published score, pp. 36–7, 59–62, 84–5, 116 and 140) are infinitely satisfying to the ear.

Certainly the fragments of material that are evolved in the course of the work are not consolidated until the end, but the embryo of the work is complete in itself, like a cell or nucleus, and not a series of fragments which are later joined. The fragmentary nature of the material is an emotional fragmentation rather than a musical one. And the logic of the music is addressed to the ear and not to the eye.

The Introduction to the first movement falls into two sections. In the first a sombre clarinet figure (Ex. 13(f)), in short rising and falling minor 3rds, forms a kind of arch over the first twenty bars, built upon the darkly pulsating pedal E (and scored for timpani, bass drum and divided basses—a very melancholy sound) through which the entire ground of the symphony can be seen, stretching into the infinite distances. This panorama is icebound—stark but by no means featureless—and as the 3rds expand into 6ths (without the granitic *ostinato* pedal) the wan sunlight of the north throws shadows on the bleak landscape. The clarinet colouring of the opening has already an important formal significance, for Bax seems to suggest the dark and powerful spiritual forces that inhabit this hostile country of the mind, as they enter into antiphonal colloquy with the strings in a foreshadowing of the slow movement and of the theme that dominates the symphony's conclusion.

A wave-like motive in clarinets, the dark antithesis of the same pattern in the fourth Symphony, leads to the second section of the Introduction. The pedal E reappears in horns, but with quickened pulse and with the increase in tension a *poco marcato* cello (and bassoon) 'rise' pattern begins to stir. A swaying string passage which becomes important in the development (and a turgid echo in brass as the pedal note drops to the C sharp of the *Allegro*) leads to a brief halt, the music poised on the brink of the first subject.

The *Allegro con fuoco* begins in C sharp minor, with an aggressive clashing theme Ex. 13(f) (and its tail-like pendant) whose alternating C and C sharp (developing at the triumphant recapitulation into the characteristic major/minor clash) and lumpish rhythm give the impression of brute strength. But this time its supremacy is short-lived. An *Allegro giusto* diminution of the opening clarinet figure appears first in strings in G minor then in woodwind and horns, under which a 'sway' figure foreshadows the mood and form of the second subject. The close relationship between this and the opening material shapes the whole of the first movement—and here there begins that coalescence of primary and secondary material, in some way analogous to the fusion of Celtic and Nordic elements in his expression, which makes this particular movement differ from the first four symphonies. So closely interrelated do these two aspects become that first subject and second subject as such almost lose their identity.

Further development of the first subject material is cut off by an interrupted cadence on the dominant 7th of A—on which the following seventy bars hang like a shadowy Epilogue (with the final theme in a kind of nostalgic inversion beneath fluttering in clarinets). This, bearing the seeds of its own decay, forlornly tries to prolong the mood, even exulting, but comes at last with the tonic A to the despairing drooping figure in clarinets and the second subject proper in the strings. After a few bars of rather Delian musing on this, Bax allows the tonic to drop suddenly to C sharp for the development of the first subject.

The development section is not limited only to the first subject—and after several pages of barbaric ferocity, in the course of which the first subject is used as an accompanimental figure to support the great driving string themes that thrust the music forward, a variant of the second subject appears as a kind of folk-dance with the opening figure of the symphony compressed into the whirling patterns of the music.

The recapitulation of the first subject is in an heroic C sharp major, its tail strongly asserted in trumpet, leading the tune to a *jubilante* conclusion, the trumpets echoing the mood of fierce joy. But realization of the transient nature of this mood brings the composer quickly back to the melancholy of the second subject, poignant in horns and strings. The clarinet figure of the introduction returns, darkened with bassoon colour, and with a final cry of resignation and anguish in strings the music dies away.

After the momentous spiritual experience implicit in the *Lento solenne* of the first, the slow movements of the next three symphonies afforded some relief from the opening movement in melodies of characteristically Celtic hue. In the fifth Symphony, however, Bax returns to the mood and to the subject matter of the first Symphony's opening movement. It is, in spite of a central moment of affirmation, a strange dark experience, and provides the initiation ritual for the gorgeous ceremonial of the Epilogue. Its panoply is regal, and over a harp figure and high B flat minor string chord the trumpets set the stage.

The theme appears in divided violas, cellos and basses, a solemn plainchant with its antiphonal response in woodwind and horn. This Bax develops contrapuntally towards a dominant 7th of E flat when the theme takes on a more lyrical aspect in cor anglais. The relationship with the central movement of the first Symphony is again underlined in bass clarinet and, as strings take up the theme, the peak of the movement, an impulsive upward gesture, is reached and passed. A muted tuba, like some acolyte of hell, intones the theme and is answered by gong and the brazen rejoinder of brass. But the moment has passed, and with an almost weary resumption of the theme in cello and cor anglais the movement ends.

The third movement begins with the same liturgical theme now on a less spiritual plane and roughly in its final form. Eight bars of this introduction precede the *Allegro*, which begins in C sharp minor with an *ostinato* figure in trombone, timpani and cello. Over this is heard, like a flock of excited penguins, a chattering version of the primary material, punctuated by brusque interjections in horns and viola. Hard on the heels of this comes a subsidiary theme in trombones (developed from the swaying theme of the first movement, in inversion). With no cessation of the rhythmic drive this is echoed in horns. But the syncopated interjections now give way to an exultant *ostinato* figure in trombone and tuba as the climax is reached. The key changes to D minor and with this *ostinato* figure in bassoon and cello the chattering theme is taken up by strings. This is gradually transformed into the liturgical theme adumbrated in the introductory bars, around which the *ostinato* figure dances with joyous glee. But its hour of triumph has not yet come, and with the clucking of the woodwind and little twisting figures in piccolo the rhythmic pulse dies away.

The next section is marked *Lento* and is a kind of pre-Epilogue. Whatever its formal significance in the movement, there is no question of its psychological impact. Over a drooping chromatic figure the horns and cor anglais are given a version of the theme which seems to mark a half-way stage in its development, as if in the pursuit of the infinite the composer raises his head to view his progress. It is slow and trudging, and assailed by all kinds of doubts. Its pendant, a strange concertina-like succession of chords (built upon the same kind of harmonic pattern that underlies the seven—cf. Ex. 12), is echoed again, with the pattern in broken chords in clarinets which Miss Cohen described as 'sleepy polar bears turning in the snow' (see p. 131, note 1). The chattering theme is again resumed but its recapitulation is shortlived. A *maestoso* chord on full orchestra re-introduces the liturgical theme, and against it, in the violins, is set the spectre of the second subject motive from the first movement. With both primary and secondary material interlocked at the climax the transition is made to the Epilogue.

The *ostinato* figure that had so joyously erupted during the movement now subsides to a quiet D flat major, the furthest remove from the opening C sharp.

The great sombre theme of the Epilogue (Ex. 13(f¹)), heard first in clarinet with a benedictory Amen in horn, is like a solemn hymn—a stately processional that, gaining in intensity, with a fervent avowal of faith, is interrupted by *con brio* episodes (in which the agitated rhythms of earlier passages are straightened out) before being blazed triumphantly forth in the brass.

The Epilogue is crowned by a huge fanfare in which the *Allegro* theme and all the music of the entire symphony are welded in a triumphant conclusion.

By the time the fifth Symphony was in rehearsal (for Beecham's Courtauld/Sargent concert on 15th January 1924) Bax had already begun work on the sixth and had gone as usual to Morar to complete the score. Returning to the C sharp major/minor harmonic terrain of the fifth, Bax opens the sixth Symphony with a pounding *ostinato* figure, Ex. 13(g) (a foreshortened version of that which underlies the melody in the Epilogue of the fifth) marked *pesante*, its catastrophic granitic beat driving the fifty-five bar long introduction to a ferocious climax. This grim prelude to the onslaught of a new and more powerful assailant is more icy than any of the snow-laden pages of the fifth, its chilling atmosphere penetrated by the eldritch cries of the woodwind who give out the principal subject, Ex. 13(g) (the final 'snap' of which is to prove important in the slow movement). This is at once elaborated with hammer-like triplet figures and is taken up by divided strings, a hollow and eerie sound. Over a rock-like pedal C sharp which maintains its strong pull throughout, the theme is further developed, urged on by the powerful surges in trombones. The excitement of the *ostinato* is stepped up and the tension increases in a climactic rise. This enormous build-up is thrown into stark relief by the sudden dramatic silence of the G.P. Between the Introduction and the beginning of the *Allegro*, a unison B–C sharp–B leads to a dramatic chord of F major. This awesome delivery is repeated with a plunge first to E flat and then a slithering descent to a Mixolydian C minor.

With the *ostinato* figure in diminution in viola and cello the principal theme, now in its *Allegro* form, can be seen as an elaborate version of the *ostinato* bass, suggesting that it has the same kind of primal origin as the theme of the first Symphony. The whole of the exposition drives along at a furious pace, whipped by jagged figures in strings and woodwind, to which the timpani and side drum add their weight with hammering triplets. Over this hellish cacophony the strings extend the theme to a great shrieking climax where the tension disintegrates and the music calms to allow the flutes and horns to state the second subject. The key changes to E flat major, but after the onslaught of the opening the second subject is only a pale gleam of very wintry sunlight. Its beauty is elegiac and its culmination a Tristanesque droop. Its ancestry in the principal theme is clear and its rather fragile loveliness achieves only a momentary caress from the strings. The horns, in melancholy 3rds, try to keep the subject going but the exposition peters out with the deathly rattle of tenor drum.

The development section seems to herald a more springlike atmosphere. Fragments of the *ostinato* and the principal theme are followed by a pattering motive in oboes, flutes and clarinets. But, supplanting the relentless rhythm of the opening over a throbbing pedal A flat, the theme emerges darkly in bass clarinet and bassoon, with a snarling growl from the brass and with more wintry writing for strings. The music begins to approach an even more devastating climax into which Bax flings all the forces at his command—the snapping of horns and trombones, the spectral rattle of the percussion, and the whirling string figures—through which the trumpets howl the main figure.

The reappearance of the second subject is given to the solo trombone, a melancholy sound, which oboe echoes. The strings again underline the elegiac nature of the second subject and at the conclusion of this a new variant of the opening theme appears, dance-like in woodwind, in C major/minor. With snatches of the second subject ringing out vainly in the brass this dance-like figure seems about to lead somewhere but, after a few more bars, the movement is abruptly terminated.

Although only in his early fifties in 1934, at the time of the composition of the sixth Symphony, Bax had already reached the summit of his creative power. The sixth Symphony's final two movements afford conclusive evidence not only that he was then at the height of his power but also that it was a peak from which there could only be descent. For in the slow movement—certainly the most beautiful piece of orchestral writing since Delius (and strange that Delius should that year have died)—Bax takes a last lingering look at the loveliness of life and his natural environment. All the figures of the movement fall, with an intensely romantic nostalgia.

And in the final movement, after the demonic exultation of the *Scherzo* and the *molto largamente* paean of the liturgical figure, Bax shifts the tonality upwards and by so doing enters another sphere—a domain of the spirit. And with the return of the subject in the Epilogue, the whole conflict of the symphonies is resolved and he is at last at peace.

With the slow movement in E minor and G the wintry proceedings of the opening give place to the nostalgic fragrance of an all too brief Arctic summer, illuminated with the cold brilliance that only sun on snow can give. With a brief but important reference to the central movement of the fourth Symphony in the flutes, the first theme, born from the elegies of the first movement's second subject, is given to the first violins. Bax prolongs this beautiful melody for some thirty bars with a nostalgic 'droop' figure (foreshadowing the 'snap' of the second theme of the movement) whose triadic summons and Grieg-like harmonies form a kind of epilogue to the melody. The theme is now taken by bassoon and viola and set in an orchestral haze of murmuring flutes, *sospirando* strings and the glittering sparkle of harp and celesta. The 'drooping' coda-like figure is followed by a brief viola recitative and out of the 'droop' pattern the trumpet, supported by trombone, tuba and horn, forms a melancholy little dance, whose Scots 'snap' was heard in the first theme of the symphony. At the suggestion of the strings the mood lifts to a warm E flat major, with the 'snap' tune in oboe. But it is of too fragile a nature to last long, and with echoes in solo trumpet and horns, the fragment (from fourth Symphony) heard at the opening begins a coda. This, however, is extended with an exquisitely rhapsodic line in strings and a brief climax seems about to lead to something new.

A transitory version of the theme leads to another climactic point, but Bax turns his face from this in a series of semiquaver broken chord patterns derived from the snap figure. The tonality now reverts to E minor and the principal theme returns. But the spring-like fragrance has gone. With a throbbing *ostinato* rhythm in trombones, timpani and tenor drum, and drooping Wagnerian phrases in second violin and clarinets, the theme makes its way slowly, like some vast cortège, briefly lit by the flickering glimmer of the second subject, towards the procession of falling 9ths (in G major), which seem to mark the slow but yet too swift tread of time. The strings, with the flute fragment from the opening now spun out into a threnody of great solemnity, bring the movement to a close.

Bax begins the final movement with a solo instrument as he had done in the first and second movements of the third Symphony. Here, the clarinet's opening theme, underlining the tonal shift from the preceding movement, begins G–C (Ex. 13(g^1)). But in contrast to the opening of the third Symphony the theme is now in epilogic form—with the 4th sharpened, the 3rd characteristically ambiguous (though the flattened 3rd and sharpened 4th are a Baxian fingerprint indicating the drooping semitonal upper 3rd of the triad as in the fourth Symphony). This clarinet theme, full of a rather remote majesty, is spun out by variation of its two-bar cell. At the twelfth bar the other clarinets, harp and horns join in (harp distorting the processional 9ths from the *Lento*) and with a quiet C major chord the theme is given to the strings, with the falling tonic-flat 7th in basses undercutting the tonality. With the ceremonial of a Requiem this figure pursues its stately course and at its conclusion a very important liturgical figure is stated (Ex. 13(g^2)) by woodwind, as if on some great organ. The cadence is marked by a pattern of rising 3rds on the harp and the introduction ends—merging into the *Scherzo* without a break by means of a clever dovetailing of the rhythm of the liturgical motive, bassoon and viola cutting across the slow measures of the bass strings. An *accelerando*, with chirping wood-wind dominant 7th chords and the return to C major, leads into the *Scherzo*.

The clarinet's opening theme is now given to the bassoon, *poco scherzando*, who with exactly the same pattern of notes, invests it with a mocking sardonic glee. Impish suggestions of the theme are heard in strings which, after some bustling wind patterns and a tympani assertion of the *Scherzo* rhythm, take up the theme.

The liturgical theme also appears (with an irreverent tilt) as the music progresses. A descending chordal pattern of strings begins to straighten out the rhythm—and a climax is built up with rising figures, echoed by the *Scherzo* theme in brass. But as the music reaches its height it breaks off in a very Straussian link passage which leads to the Trio. The strange Russian-sounding theme of the Trio, a skeletal version of the coda of the slow movement, is very delicately orchestrated, and, at the appearance of a sepulchral tail piece to the theme, the orchestration becomes even more intricate. The swaying theme is given to oboe, cor anglais and three trumpets, while the harp, celesta and divided violins, with an unearthly sound, decorate this with a ghostly version of the *Scherzo* theme. The Trio develops, with the outlines of the theme becoming more defined in strings (the cellos reversing the Wagnerian fragment in the slow movement). But shrouded 5ths in bassoon and cello intensify the mood of unreality and lead back to the Trio theme. The solo cello, with a Straussian recitative based on the drooping pattern, concludes the Trio and, *allegretto moderato*, the *Scherzo* returns. Into the resumption of the *Scherzo* material Bax now weaves the strands of a colossal triumph. From this point 'until bar 4 on p. 114 the tempo must be inflexibly rigid', he directs in the score. The rhythm is maintained by a reiterated A flat in the horns as strings and woodwind dance *leggiero*.

With a *marcato ostinato* figure in horns and bass woodwind pounding the relentless rhythm, the strings, *dramatico* and in a high register, sing out a new theme (a quotation of the principal motive of *Tapiola*). The vast climax is built up over 106 bars with the *ostinato* rhythm becoming more and more insistent. Snatches of the theme are thrust up from the bass, brass and horns echoing each other with a hellish glee, until at last with a note of demoniacal triumph the theme is blared out in the brass. This fearsome challenge, however, is met with an even more triumphant blaze of power as the liturgical theme now reveals its true nature against a blazing pedal G, and against whirling flute and piccolo figures. At this revelation the monstrous *Scherzo* theme disappears completely and the liturgical theme rises effortlessly through E major and G major into new realms, leaving irrevocably the domain of the 'demented mould-warp Man'.[1] And in this upper ether the trumpet, *dolcissimo*, cries out the liturgical theme, like the herald of some angelic visitant, the strings descending in four note phrases (B natural to F of the tritone) in a celestial parallel to the procession of 9ths which ended the slow movement. The transition from this peak to the shadow and sunset of the Epilogue, a majestic mirror of the process already undergone in similar patterns in the third Symphony, is something unparalleled in English music.

A falling figure of unbearable sweetness in trumpets sets the stage for the final horn statement of the opening theme, now wreathed in a mysterious light (with the tonic-flat 7th droop of the Symphonic Variations theme in first violin). With the sound of harp dimly in the background Bax divides his strings into a complex tapestry of three solo instruments from each section of the strings, all muted, with two double bass solos.

In the fading glow of this last ethereal sunset (the tenor drum figure, the *Scherzo* theme robbed of all its menace, muted trumpets, and the final elegiac plea of the strings) the spacious Epilogue, its total finality in the empty 5ths of the theme in violas, horns and clarinets, comes to

[1] John Cowper Powys, *Maiden Castle*, Cassell, 1937, p. 230.

a close on a quaver chord of C major—and the horns poignantly voice their final plea (Ex. 13(g^2)).

Although the polarity in Bax's symphonies had now veered from magnetic to true north, he had not forsaken his old love—Ireland. Almost all the last scores were completed at Morar in the quiet serenity of western Inverness-shire, but he returned regularly to Ireland where he acted as external examiner to the universities of Dublin and Cork. However, he went to Ireland now not as Dermot O'Byrne, but as Arnold Bax.[1]

He had met E. J. Moeran shortly after the war. Their mutual interests both in music and in Ireland soon forged a close bond between them. Bax greatly admired Moeran's work—especially the very lovely Violin Concerto. And during Bax's frequent visits to Ireland the two met often and more often than not in Jack Moeran's beloved County Kerry where, at the Lansdowne Arms, they talked, drank and worked, revelling in the wild seascape and the beauty of the Kerry scene.

In post war Dublin, and in Cork too, he had made many friends, amongst them Dr John Larchet, musical director of the Abbey Theatre in Dublin, and Mrs Tilly Fleischman and her family, of Cork. Mrs Fleischman, a pianist of international reputation and a pupil of Stavenhagen, whose son Aloys was Professor of the Music Faculty at Cork University, was deeply impressed by Bax's music. She and her family had been much involved in the growth of musical culture in Cork and had met Bax first in 1928, when he responded to an invitation to adjudicate at the annual Father Mathew Feis in Cork.

With the Fleischman family Bax made firm friends and their championship of his music did much to establish his reputation in an Ireland which, if it thought of him at all, still remembered him as Dermot O'Byrne. On 20th November 1929 Mrs Fleischman gave a recital in Clarence Hall, Cork, with Doreen Thornton (soprano), Sean Neeson (baritone) and her pupil Geraldine Sullivan (piano)—a programme which included *Moy Mell* and *Hardanger*. And in 1934 she gave the first Irish performance of the second Piano Sonata, a work

---

[1] Dermot O'Byrne had not, however, ceased to exist: for as late as 1942 Clifford spoke of just having seen some new tales which he said 'for power of language and variety could scarcely be bettered'. What became of these is not known. I have in my own possession a MS short story entitled 'Cormac Og—A Phantasmagoria' (subtitled 'Told on a stormy night') which is dated Glencolumcille 1911.

which greatly impressed Daniel Corkery (Professor of English at Cork University, and author of *The Hidden Ireland*).

In the company of the Fleischmans and other members of Cork society Bax often travelled around the beautiful west coast of Eire. During these visits he found relaxation from work and spoke very little of his own music. However, while driving one afternoon up the Goat's Pass at Sheepshead with his companions, Bax mentioned an impending broadcast of the fourth Symphony. In haste they drove to the village of Ahakisto, but finding no wireless in the village they went on to a lonely house some way beyond where a local curate lived. As luck would have it the curate was out and one of the party, who was friendly with him, found an open window. Before long the party were indoors and the wireless was turned on. After the performance, to their astonishment, a housekeeper appeared with tea and buns, rather apprehensive but determined to be hospitable! The incident was later related to Henry Wood, who had conducted the symphony, affording him much amusement.[1]

During the five years between the last two symphonies Bax had written comparatively little, as if the huge climax of the sixth had left him emotionally exhausted. In the same year as this symphony he had completed the fourth Piano Sonata for the Irish pianist Charles Lynch —a mature work in which economy of means and an almost austere musical language contrasted strongly with the richness of the earlier piano works. He had also written an Octet for Aubrey Brain (for horn, string sextet and piano) and a Clarinet Sonata in two movements for Hugh Prew (a fellow participant in the Old Broughtonian cricket weeks). And two years later he completed the *Threnody and Scherzo* for bassoon, harp and string sextet which with the Horn Octet received first performance at an L.C.M.C. concert (with Brain, the Griller Quartet, Frederick Riddle, Eugene Cruft, Archie Camden, Maria Korchinska, and Harriet Cohen) on 11th November 1936.

The most important work during these five years was the Violin Concerto, begun in 1937 and completed in March the following year. It was not, however, performed until November 1943, and Bax indicated on more than one occasion that he had deliberately withheld the score until the symphonies had achieved wider recognition. Of Bax's eight works for solo instrument and orchestra only two, those for violin and cello—have been given the name Concerto. Both of these have in fact

[1] This tale was told me by Mrs Tilly Fleischman, who records the full story in her unpublished memoir of Bax.

begged the question implied in the title and the musical material of both has inspired its own very characteristic framework. The other works have been variously styled Phantasy, Concertante or given, like *Winter Legends*, a programmatic description. It is significant that the two works which bear the generic title (the single exception being the Phantasy for viola which, written in 1920 for Lionel Tertis, is essentially a concerto, perhaps even more so than the two so called) are for solo strings, predominantly lyrical voices; while in all the keyboard works with their inevitably richer texture, the voice of the soloist has merged into the more complex colour of the orchestra.

The two concertos, which Bax wrote in his fifties, are both extremely attractive works. Of the two, that for Violin is more immediately appealing and perhaps more characteristic of him. For the incisive tones and poetic range of the instrument serve more adequately the strong contrasts of his nature. He completed the score of the Violin Concerto in 1937 in response to a B.B.C. commission, but, because of the indifferent reception of the symphonies, withheld the work until November 1943 when it was played by the dedicatee Eda Kersey at a concert under Sir Henry Wood for St Cecilia's Day. Asked some time after by Peter Latham about the Violin Concerto's allegiances, the composer expressed the rather curious opinion that it somehow resembled Raff. The romanticism of the work is at all events unashamed. But the musician takes precedence over the poet and the romantic elements are musical and not visual or literary. The fresh and exhilarating sparkle of the concerto came as something of a surprise to those who perhaps justifiably had expected the dreamy luxuriance with which a younger Bax might well have drenched such a score. The unconventional appearance of the first movement, which is cast as a triptych—Overture, Ballad, *Scherzo*—is, like the final movement of the sixth Symphony, something more of an innovation on paper than in performance. The *Scherzo*, which Bax substitutes for the conventional development section, is a recognizable variant of the opening bars. Though its accents hint at an Irish origin it is far less evocative of Ireland than is the Moeran Concerto. And in the same way the brief seeming reference to *Schéhérazade* in the Ballad is characteristic of Bax, rather than evidence of any real Russian element in the music. Standing between the emotional climax of the sixth Symphony and the final works, the seventh Symphony and the last concertos, it is neither Celtic, Irish nor Russian but a fusion of all those elements that had gone to make up Bax's very original personality.

In the *Adagio* he has avoided the temptation to over-colour. The result is a clear-cut, almost Mozartian, slow movement that affords perfect contrast to the rough accents of the outer movements. The vigorous *Allegro*, with its strenuous waltz theme, gives ample indication that Bax was not entirely becalmed on some remote isle—but an 'appreciative inhabitant' of this earth. The Concerto proved a firm favourite. It was played more than a couple of dozen times by Frederick Grinke; Ralph Holmes has also proved an able exponent and Ernest Newman considered it the finest concerto for violin since Elgar's.

In 1935 Bax wrote a fine setting of Vaughan's 'The Morning Watch' for chorus and orchestra for the Three Choirs Festival at Worcester that September.

There were also three short orchestral works: the spirited *Overture to Adventure* (dedicated to Richard Austin), a characteristic work whose main theme echoed perhaps less sombrely the rhythmic motives of *Winter Legends* and the fifth Symphony with a beautiful central section in Mixolydian mode; The *Rogues Comedy Overture* (dedicated to Julius Harrison), a brilliant and extrovert piece of writing whose perky opening theme (reminiscent of 'Hary Janos') is developed into a fantastic march; and *London Pageant*, an occasional 'festive' piece first broadcast under Albert Coates in May 1937.

At the end of any composer's symphonic experience one must look for the answer to the biting questions that had prompted his first steps on such a course. Beethoven underlined the experience in the choral finale of the Ninth (and in the Choral Fantasia where 'on music's mighty pinions' man's aspiring soul rose heavenwards). The plight of the twentieth-century composer is inevitably more acute. Sibelius had seemed (and perhaps only seemed, for the last symphonies still finger the threads that lead back to the comparative safety of the romantic in the nineteenth century) to turn from the problem (in *Tapiola*, for instance) towards the eternity of things older than mankind. Mahler had in mid Europe no access to eternity except one troubled by wars and their aftermath. Bax had emerged from the Epilogue of the fifth Symphony, in spite of its sombre nobility, with the question still unanswered. The conclusion of the second with its almost Mahlerian quiet had forced him towards the massive peace of the Epilogue of the third Symphony. But neither third nor fifth had done more than gaze over the intervening distances towards what was still a horizon.

Bax's pursuit of his ideal, after his early encounter with Yeats and Ireland, was understandable in a youth of nineteen, whose idealism had not yet been chidden by experience. But in 1934, with five symphonies already completed, the 'isles of dream' remained as insubstantial as ever.

He had turned also to the natural world—not for escape nor even for refuge from the imponderables of a dawning age of scientific advance more terrifying than anything that the ancient philosophers could conceive—but because therein, he believed, resided that great creative life force, to which all souls are subjugated, and which, in spite of man's ascendancy, still had the ultimate jurisdiction.

Bax was a lover of life—and the sensualist in him imbibed deeply from the source and fount of that life as he found it in his natural environment. However, the search for that environment and for prolonged experience of these forces of nature was not exclusively sensual but a compelling philosophical requirement of his inner being.

And in the sixth Symphony the tone-poetical imagery of the early works and of the first five symphonies had been distilled. The final pages of the Epilogue show that the ultimate triumph (like that of the Symphonic Variations and of *Winter Legends*) is achieved not by force, but by the attainment of an inner serenity, an at-one-ness with himself and with Nature which was the theme of much of the philosophical content of Clifford's writings.

It is almost symbolic that in 1939, the conclusion of the seventh of his symphonies is resolved in a set of seven variations—the prime number seven having a mystical significance as the perfect number, denoting spiritual completeness.

The seventh and last of Bax's symphonies was completed at Morar in January 1939. The A flat major tonality forms a significant resolution, via the D flat major of the fifth Symphony's conclusion, to the E flat major/minor of the first Symphony.

The mood of the opening *Allegro* is one of tremendous vigour and occupies itself with the development and expansion of a rhythmic clarinet figure stated in the first four bars (Ex. 13(h)). A thirty-two bar introduction (culminating as before in a G.P. break) is dovetailed into the *Allegro* in spite of the break by rapid continuity of material which the introduction not only exposes but partially develops. This fermenting activity, a fragmentary development of the primary material, comes to a brilliant climax[1] (p. 21 of the MS score) built up from the

[1] On listening to this movement it is not difficult to see why Bax was appointed to the post of Master of the King's Musick.

characteristic descent 'tail' figure of the *ostinato* patterns that have upheld the Exposition.

The secondary material is given to cor anglais (and bears a distinct relationship to the eloquent horn melody from Delius's *Paris*) and is in a brief D major, culminating in an anguished appeal in which form it foreshadows the underlying *ostinato* of the transition to the Epilogue.

The ensuing *meno mosso* continues, over a cello ground, the development of the first theme group and extends it towards a broadly augmented delivery of the initial theme of the symphony, whose peroration suggests the complex unity that links the two aspects of the music.

A nightmarish statement, on oboe and bassoon, of one of the principal subjects of the Exposition is transformed by a rising triplet figure into a series of festive climaxes. The transformation of these primary elements marks the beginning of an extended coda-like section. A strange sighing figure, high in the first violins, is followed by the second subject, now full and broadly triumphant. But this intensely romantic moment is not yet the final denouement. A snarl from the brass brings back the first subject, and turns the second into a wraith, before the music sinks back into the depths.

The second movement, *Lento*, opens with a solo cor anglais theme, distantly related to the first movement's second subject, but now introspective in mood. A drooping figure in strings—in 3rds—recalling the opening of the fifth Symphony, provides the material for development into a long and eloquent string melody, full of expressive cantilena. During the course of this, interpolated by the cor anglais figure in inversion, the second subject of the first movement is further developed (now in almost identical form to the Delius melody of *Paris* but with a minor inflection). A rising *ostinato* figure is derived from this, and underlines the climax which culminates in a series of descending chords.

The opening mood is re-established, but after the trumpet's statement of the opening cor anglais figure the drooping string theme is developed by woodwind and horns to introduce the central section of the movement. This is marked 'In legendary mood' but its surging clarinet theme, a further development of the opening material of the whole symphony, has nothing heroic about it. Its E minor suggests the wintry passages of earlier slow movements (a dark reference to the Sibelius Violin Concerto is heard in bass clarinet) and the return of the questioning cor anglais theme—now in strings—ends with a fragmentary echo of the primary theme of the third Symphony. The second 'drooping' figure of the movement returns in strings and brass and is built up to a dark climax from which there is a catastrophic descent. The last few pages are a sombre elegy with the two themes, both in shadow, combined, and resolving C sharp, D sharp, F and E to the chord of C major.

In strong contrast the final movement opens with a resplendent fanfare—more majestic and less apprehensive than that which opens the last movement of the fourth. In these opening bars, the two elements of the work are completely united. Over a drum roll the cellos and basses alone state the theme (Ex. 13(h^1)), a noble liturgical melody of stately proportions, whose solemn processional, following and developing the Epilogue of the fifth Symphony, is coloured by clarinet and harp, as it passes to the strings.

The first variation follows immediately, the theme being given to cello and bassoon with harmonization in horns around which the strings weave some expressive counterpoint. The extension of the final phrase leads to the second variation. Here bass strings and bass woodwind, *marcato*, have the theme decorated by brass and violins, now with more agitated figuration. After the second variation the introductory fanfare reappears, *molto vigoroso*, to establish a bass *ostinato* derived from it, the first phrase of which is seized upon by trumpet. This rhythm persists in clarinets as the third *scherzando* variation brings the theme back, with a minor inflection, in woodwind and strings. The fourth variation, marked *andante*, is nostalgic and lyrical. A solo cello sings an expressive version of the melody answered by horn, and the variation is rounded off by a ghost-like return of the introductory material. The tempo quickens, and the ensuing quasi-fugal variation climaxes in an insistent 'tail' pattern where, in a great clamour of sound, the upward sweeping string figures lead to the sixth variation—a chorale-like elegy for brass, *molto moderato e maestoso*.

The weird half-light that now floods the scene introduces the Epilogue with the theme foreshortened in the bass. A bass clarinet solo amplifies this under an ethereal shadow of the theme on six solo strings. Slowly rising scale passages in harp, strings and finally clarinets reach their culmination in the four-note descent pattern (Ex. 13 'Tail'), marked by trills, on clarinet and oboe—and in the strangely cold and virginal atmosphere of this 'unhandselled world' to which music alone is the access, the seventh Symphony ends—a very final Epilogue.

Epilogue

12 Last compositions and Death

Count me not with those that whine for what is over—
All that once was good is good for evermore;

Clifford Bax, 'Musician', in *Farewell My Muse*.

It was with the Symphonic Variations that Bax was occupied when
Europe was plunged into the war of 1914. When once again, a quarter
of a century later, the skies of Europe were again darkened with a
conflict even more terrible, the seventh and last Symphony was completed. The final mood of the Epilogue recorded not only the end of a
chapter in his own life, but the end of an era. But it was neither a mood
of depression or of false optimism. Arthur Symons's words 'Nation with
nation, land with land' set in 1937 by John Ireland ('These Things
shall be') have a more hollow ring than the detached spirituality of
Bax's last great orchestral epilogue. The seventh Symphony attracted
little attention, and though well enough received in New York, it had
to wait until June 1940 for its first performance in England. Britain
had other things on her mind in 1939 and there was little room for the
allurements of Bax's visionary Hy Brasil as the world fought for what
seemed like survival.

In spite of the outward successes marked by the honorary degrees
conferred upon him by Oxford (1934) and Durham (1935), the award
of the Royal Philharmonic Society's Gold Medal, and the news
(conveyed to him by letter to where he was staying on holiday with
Jack Moeran in Kenmare) of his knighthood, Bax had felt for some
time that communication between himself and the listener had grown
tenuous, and was soon to cease altogether. Gradually withdrawing into
himself, he resolved to leave London. With the new seventh Symphony
in rehearsal in the States, he chose to remain in England. And one
week-end, in the early days of the war, he went for a week-end's rest to
the White Horse Hotel in the tiny village of Storrington, a peaceful
haven on the Sussex Weald, not far from the green crown of Chancton-
bury and near the windmill home of his friend and contemporary John
Ireland.[1] This rural inn became his home for twelve years. And al-

---

[1] Bax and John Ireland, though contemporaries, did not see a great deal of each
other. Though the first symphony was dedicated to Ireland, the older composer felt
uncertain about their musical relationship and had reservations about Bax's music.

though he retained the music-littered rooms in Fellowes Road, Hampstead, he visited London rarely, and then stayed, more often than not, at the home of Harriet Cohen.

Storrington, although without piano or books, had its attractions. Hugh Fitch, the landlord of the White Horse, installed a desk for him in the old billiard room. Not far off, in another converted mill at West Chiltington, lived Cecil Gray, and also near by lived Iso Elinson and his wife Hedwig Stein. Music, however, began to play a less prominent role in his life and he gradually fell into the leisurely life of a country squire, reading (especially detective novels), drinking with the older worthies amongst the locals, playing billiards with his host, acting as president of the village cricket club and, every day, doing the crossword in *The Times*. Mrs Elinson (Hedwig Stein) recalls him then:

> Our first meeting with him was at the house of Sir Robert Mayer in London when Sir Arnold accompanied Dorothy Moulton (Sir Robert's wife) in some of his own songs. He appeared to us rather handsome, with oval-shaped face and a slim figure, and remarkably blue, clear eyes. Later he became a little stout and of a rather ruddy complexion, and his eyes looked shrewdly yet shyly at one—not always focussing in the same way. His walk was shuffling, but full of musicianly onward drive. We met him hundreds of times when doing our shopping at Storrington—he would go to or return from a pub where he used to discuss things with the old locals and his friend Cecil Gray. Sometimes he asked us in for a glass of beer at his hotel. But when encountering him standing at the windy Pulborough station (both parties bound for London) he might be indrawn, like a snail in its shell, and, in the train, quite absorbed in *The Times* crossword puzzles.[1]

With the destruction of the city of London had come tragedy both national and personal. The loss of the Queen's Hall in 1941 and the interruption of the Proms was followed by the destruction, by incendiaries, of Harriet Cohen's home and the loss of many of her most treasured possessions. The manuscript score of the Symphonic Variations was destroyed, but fortunately a full set of orchestral parts was later found in Chappells from which the performances in 1963 (by Patrick Piggott) and 1970 (by Joyce Hatto) were made possible.

The death of his mother in November 1940 dealt him another severe blow. With the move to Storrington a marked change came over Bax and

---

John Longmire's book *John Ireland—Portrait of a friend*, hints that their relationship may have become rather strained (see pp. 104 and 132).
[1] Letter to the author, 23rd March 1961.

in his music. The remaining link with the listener had begun to part and although the last works of his life include several major compositions, there is an undeniable reticence, an intimacy that, stemming from the final pages of the last Symphony, seemed addressed not to the world but to a private ear. Bax gave little outward indication of his feelings. To the inquirer he remarked drily that he had retired, 'like a grocer'. The deep-seated unease with contemporary life reflected in the inner man is not heard in the music. There is no conflict, no disturbing, warring element. All is serenity, and even the vigorous passages give way to an untroubled peace. The calm of *Morning Song—Maytime in Sussex* is typical of this mood. And amid the haunting spring-like fragrance we are left with the strong impression that Bax had come full circle, to the rediscovery of those isles to which he had in the beginning travelled with Niam and Usheen—that land of eternal youth where 'God is joy and joy is God, and all things that have grown sad are wicked'.

O Usheen, mount by me and ride
To shores by the wash of the tremulous tide,
Where men have heaped no burial mounds,
And the days pass by like a wayward tune, . . .[1]

There are plenty of 'wayward tunes' in this late music. And it is this all too rare mood of joyous fresh youth—yet of serenity—that is the abiding characteristic of the best of Bax's last work.

In the early years of the war Sir Henry Walford Davies died, leaving vacant the post of Master of the King's Musick. The position, like that of Poet Laureate, entailed little in the way of onerous duties. As a focal point of national musical tendencies and as a repository of characteristic national culture the post had been filled in the past by such men as Boyce and Elgar. That Bax should have been chosen to fill the vacancy on Walford Davies's death was a unique honour. Yet the mantle of Royal Musician fell awkwardly upon his shoulders. Even the minor rigours of the post were uncongenial to Bax, who disliked publicity and the necessity of adhering to plans or timetables.

Conscious of the honour laid upon him, however, he earnestly endeavoured to fulfil all that was required of him and the office. His discomfort was at times acute, and ceremonial occasions made him

[1] From 'The Wanderings of Oisin' in *The Collected Poems of W. B. Yeats*, Macmillan, 1950.

selfconscious and nervous. His acceptance of the honour was marked by his appearance before the sovereign, then King George VI, in company with the then C.I.G.S., General Sir Alan Brooke. The appointment was not without its critics: 'One cannot help thinking it odd that the creator of this dark universe of primeval gods and satyrs should become the honoured guardian of British musical respectability.'[1]

Several commissions were now laid upon him. Walter Legge, then responsible for organizing concerts for the forces and for war-workers, invited Bax, together with Moeran and Rawsthorne, to compose a short overture suitable for such occasions. Moeran's *Overture to a Masque* and Rawsthorne's *Street Corner Overture* were the companion pieces to Bax's *Work in Progress*. For the documentary *Malta G.C.* Bax wrote his first film score and, as a tribute to the gallant island, the composer was asked to present the score to the Governor, Lord Gort, at a ceremony in London on 19th February 1943. It is significant that the March (which Bax later rewrote for the March for the Coronation— some indication of his flagging energies) instinctively recalls the roots of his nationalism, for in the calm and dignified central theme (which was altered in the MS to conceal the rather obvious reference) Bax reveals a shadow of 'Men of Harlech'.

That same year the tribute paid to the Red Army and the presentation of the Sword of Honour to the city of Stalingrad required of Bax a solemn Fanfare, and the setting of the Poet Laureate's 'To Russia'. Bax had worked with Masefield before—in a pageant for St George and the Dragon, which proved abortive—but he could not stimulate his old love of Russia in more than a very passable setting of the poem.

Two sad occasions drew music from him. The Funeral March from the film score *Malta G.C.* was arranged for organ for the funeral of the Duke of Kent but was played instead, by Sir William Harris with Bax himself in the organ loft, at the funeral of the sovereign.

The death in the summer of 1944 of Sir Henry Wood was a grievous blow to musical Britain and a deep personal loss to Bax, of whose music Sir Henry had been a staunch champion. The commission of a work for performance at the memorial concert on 2nd March 1949 gave him considerable trouble. A kind of triple Concerto for cor anglais, clarinet and horn, with each movement devoted to one of the three instruments, and a joyous finale in which all join, it was an unusual conception and quickly showed that though his avenue of

' Wilfred Mellers, *Studies in Contemporary Music*, Dennis Dobson, 1947.

communication was closing, his powers of invention remained as fertile as ever.

It was completed at Storrington in January 1949. The music is light and unpretentious, each soloist being accompanied by a small orchestra in which brass and woodwind are used sparingly (when trumpets and trombones are added in the first movement, they are marked *pp* and used only to support the bass). The work has a delicacy and fragrance unusual in an artist approaching seventy, and its joyous moods have more relationship with *Spring Fire* than with the symphonies. Nevertheless after the first movement the works falls into the characteristic three-movement pattern of the symphonic works.[1] The first movement is an Elegy for cor anglais, whose decorative melodic line—recalling *In Memoriam*—floats in a summery haze of harp and strings.

The second movement, a *Scherzo*, banishes the sad ceremonial of the opening of the work. The brisk *pizzicato* 'oompah' of the strings and the grotesque buffoonery of the elfish clarinet (whose less lyrical aspects Bax employs to advantage) give the movement a sprightly character. The opening material culminates (as in the later symphonies) in a pause, and the central contrast is provided by a rather sombre little *Allegretto semplice* dance. The third movement in which the solo line, a pastoral, is given to the horn is marked *Lento*. The melodies are less expansive than in similar movements of the symphonies. With a triumphal flourish the last movement begins with a merry fanfare in horns and trumpets, *Allegro ma non troppo brillante*, a mock pageant with an Irish twist in its tail. But, as in the fourth Symphony, this is supplanted by a quietly exuberant theme in triple time, first heard in clarinet against harp, whose joyous bubbling pervades the whole of the movement, and which each of the solo instruments echoes in turn.

A household accident shortly after the war temporarily deprived Harriet Cohen of the use of her right hand and, as a tribute to this gallant artist, Bax began to compose one of his most attractive late works, a Concertante for Piano (L.H.) and orchestra. Again the task was not without its problems. It was nothing like a concerto in the usual sense, and Bax found the limitations of writing for the one hand, and that a small one, very irksome. He confessed that he was very out of practice in writing for the piano at all. The first performance at the Cheltenham Festival on 4th July 1950 was not over-enthusiastically

---

[1] The obvious possibility (in view of his own confession that he had difficulty with this work) that Bax made use of previously sketched material from what might have been another symphony seems, however, unlikely.

received. The accents of the work were out of key with current trends, the music too intimate. The slow movement is, however, one of the warmest and most wistful love poems ever written. The first movement is a tragic lament, and in a letter to John Horgan, the Coroner of Cork, Bax indicated that the inspiration for this movement came from John Brophy's book *Sarah*—the drama of the figures of Robert Emmet and Sarah Curran in 1803. There is a quotation, played by solo violin at the end of the movement, taken from 'She is far from the land'.

The Concertante is barely twenty-five minutes long in performance and is in three movements. The second subject material in the first movement is echoed towards the end of the movement in the solo piano part (with the addition of the violins at bar 8) and the following passage reminiscent of *Winter Legends* indicates not only the nostalgic nature of the music, but also the care with which Bax tackled the problem of writing for one hand.

Ex.16 Concertante for Piano (L.H.) and Orchestra (MS)

The *Variations on the name of Gabriel Fauré* were written at Storrington in August 1949, scored first of all for the piano, but later expanded into a suite for harp and string orchestra and, as such, dedicated to Boyd Neel. The theme, in spite of its contrived nature, is strangely characteristic of this period in Bax's music:

(D)(B) (E)   (G)(D)
G A B R I E L   F A U R É

with the markedly Celtic figure F A U. There are five movements: Idyll (with the theme in strings), Barcarolle (with a rhythmic accompaniment in cellos), a naïve Polka, Storm, and a final *Quodlibet* where the theme appears alone in cello and bass (and is later foreshortened, quasi-*ostinato*, with the flattening of the E (A flat in first violins in the score) of the word Gabriel) in a quiet mockery of the Theme and Variations of the seventh Symphony.

This was Bax's last completed work of any consequence. It was followed by a ten-minute suite for a film about London Museums (about which Bax is reputed to have remarked 'it does not matter what one writes for these entertainments').

With the final serenity of the seventh Symphony Bax felt the spirit of youth, which had all along inspired his search for beauty, had gone and, with flagging energies and the realization that at some stage in his life he had savoured as fully as he would ever do the delights of that fair land of his imagination, he had turned inwards, content with reflection, the old power and the flashing energies faded. Final sketches for other works were left in manuscript.[1]

To escape the minor discomforts of lumbago and gout (which Clifford, crippled in the last years of his life by the same trouble, attributed to 'a port wine drinking ancestor') Bax travelled abroad to the warmer climates of Greece and the Mediterranean. Each year, too, he visited Ireland, where he continued to act as external examiner to the University of Cork and to the National University of Ireland in Dublin, and watched with interest over the fortunes of young Irish composers at the Department of Education's summer schools in music from 1946 to 1949.

With composition he was increasingly ill at ease—doubting his ability to write anything else. In a letter to a Dutch friend he wrote:

> Nearly everyone has written his best work before reaching my age. I feel that I have said all I have to say and it is of no use to repeat myself. The tireless vitality of Vaughan Williams at 77 is astonishing. In this respect there has never been a musician like him except Verdi and Richard Strauss—and Strauss should have stopped long ago. I really have no impulse to compose in these days, and anyhow I have written a devil of a lot in my time.

But ideas still came to him for new compositions. Momentary glimpses of the old magic can be seen, but a failing of the creative abilities—perhaps due less to degeneration than to disinclination, a victim not so much of age as of the age—is also quite apparent.

---

[1] Among them several pieces ostensibly for piano—although in spite of decided indications of pianistic layout, the musical idea seems orchestral—they are entitled *Romanza, Phantasie, Idyll* and *Fantastic March.*

With the commencement of 1953 Bax, in his official capacity, was inevitably deeply involved in the preparations for the coming Coronation of the young Queen Elizabeth. At such a state occasion much is demanded of the Royal Musician. Although already troubled by evidence of failing health, Bax undertook the duties conscientiously, and the strain must have hastened his death.

With the Left Hand Concerto Miss Cohen was greeted abroad with enthusiasm, as she had been received before with *Winter Legends* and the Symphonic Variations. In Ireland, too, more enthusiasm was forthcoming. On 17th October 1950 a concert was given at Phoenix Hall, Dublin, by the Radio Eireann Symphony Orchestra, conducted by Aloys Fleischman, which included the new Concerto, with Miss Cohen as soloist and, at Bax's own suggestion, the third Symphony. At a party after the concert many Dublin celebrities gathered round to meet him, not unmindful, as Lennox Robinson later confessed, of Dermot O'Byrne and the days of 1916. Bax determined, his duties completed, to leave England and public life and to settle in Cork which he had come to love so deeply.

The onerous days of the Coronation passed, he visited his London friends and called (for the last time, as it happened) on his brother Clifford at his chambers in Albany. Increasingly distressed at the neglect of his symphonies, Bax took his leave of Harriet Cohen, who was travelling to the Venice Festival with the Left Hand Concerto, and, promising to meet her later in Cork, he set off for Dublin for the annual examinations.

Although happy to be back in Ireland in September 1953 Bax confided to his Dublin host, Dr Larchet, that he felt tired and unwell and unable to take part in any social gathering. The examination proved sufficiently taxing, and in quietness he awaited Miss Cohen's return with the news of the Concerto.

On 29th September Professor Fleischman joined them and gave a concert of Bax's work, scheduled to coincide with the N.U.I. examinations. The principal work was once again the L.H. Concerto with Miss Cohen as soloist. The final work was *The Garden of Fand*. It was the last music he was ever to hear, and strange that it should have been Fand, with its tale of Cuchullain setting out for the world beyond the seas.

It was now time to travel to Cork for the annual examinations there and, a slight chill preventing Miss Cohen from travelling, Bax and Aloys Fleischman went on alone. At Professor Fleischman's home,

'Glen House' in Ballyvolane, some guests, among them John and Mary Horgan and Seamus Murphy the sculptor and his wife Mairead, had assembled to welcome him.

After the examinations were over it was arranged that they should all meet at the Horgans' home 'Lacaduv' for the evening. Professor Fleischman and his wife Anne were to join them later after a meeting in town. It was customary for the Horgans to arrange an outing by car to some spot in that lovely countryside, expeditions which Bax enjoyed immensely. This was no exception. Earlier that afternoon, at the Old Head of Kinsale, Bax had stood looking out at the seascape before him. The scene was full of colour and Bax, lost in the peace and rapt in contemplation of what for him was the very stuff of his musical imagery, had had to be reminded gently by John Horgan that the house party was waiting their return. Who can tell what thoughts passed through his mind as he gazed at the scene? Only that morning he had opened the box of Turkish Delight which he unfailingly purchased in Cork to take back to England and had shared it amongst the Fleischman children. It was as if he knew he would never return. In a letter to Clifford in London, John Horgan tells of Bax's last hours.

He arrived in Cork last Thursday to examine at Cork University College and stayed with his friend Professor Fleischman. We met him at the house of Professor Fleischman's mother that evening. He was in good spirits but looked very old and tired. I arranged to meet him again on Saturday Oct 3rd to take him for a drive to Kinsale. On Friday he was examining at the University all day and rested that evening. I met him as arranged in Cork on Saturday, about 3 pm, after lunch. My youngest son was with me, and we drove from Cork by Innishannon and the south side of the Bandon river to the Old Head of Kinsale on the coast, which we reached about 5 pm. It was a lovely clear evening with sea, sky and coast looking their best. I said it should inspire him to write another *Tintagel*. We walked up to the lighthouse on top of the Head (only a few yards), and stood for a while looking at the scene before us. We then drove back to Kinsale where we went to look at the old church of St Multose, and then we had dinner at Acton's Hotel. He did not eat much but made no complaints and was quite cheerful. On the way home he told us some amusing stories about Malcolm Sargent and Beecham. He also spoke about Barbirolli, of whom he was very fond, about the Coronation and the Queen. During the drive to Kinsale he kept recalling many of our previous excursions, the details of which he remembered with amazing accuracy. We reached my house about 8.30 pm and after greeting my wife he went into the sitting room and she gave him a drink. He sat down and said very little—then after a few minutes he said, 'I'm feeling very ill: will you take me home.' My car had been taken by my son to fetch some old friends who were coming to our house to meet him, so my wife offered to drive him back to Prof. Fleischman's house in her own small Fiat car. We first rang up Mrs Fleischman to make sure she was in and to ask her to prepare his room. He complained of feeling cold and, as he had no overcoat, I put my overcoat on him and a rug round his feet in the car. My wife drove him as fast as she could to Professor Fleischman's house. He was quite conscious and alert in the car and spoke to her several times. Indeed he was rather annoyed when she suggested that he should stay in bed next day. When he got to the Fleischman's he got out and went upstairs to his room. His face was then blue and he was breathing heavily. Mrs Fleischman, who was a doctor, saw that he was very ill and rang up our leading physician Professor James O'Donovan MD, who came almost at once and gave Arnold an injection, but he was past human aid and died peacefully about 9.30. His last words were muttered in thanks to the doctor. Your sister will probably have told you of the funeral. You may rest assured that everything that could be done was done and that nothing could have prevented the coronary thrombosis from which he died. As Dr O'Donovan certified the cause of death there was no necessity for an inquest or post-mortem examination. We shall be glad to hear from you later on concerning a memorial stone or small monument over his grave, and we feel that this should be carried out by his friend Seamus Murphy, who is a fine artist.

The body was laid out at the Bon Secours mortuary and Miss Cohen (who had arrived from Dublin), Maura O'Connor (the singer) and Mrs Tilly Fleischman went to pay a last homage. Mrs Fleischman was greatly impressed with Sir Arnold's appearance of peace, and asked Seamus Murphy if he could make a death mask. It was too late to do anything then, but on the following morning Seamus Murphy set off to find material for the task. No shop was open and no supplier could be found. At last he approached the Dental Hospital. The man in charge at first hesitated, but on learning the purpose of the sculptor's mission offered him all the plaster he required. He explained that he had always loved Bax's music and was grateful to be of service. It was late that afternoon when the sculptor began, and since the body had already been coffined it was necessary to lift the head slightly. The making of the mask took three hours, and Seamus Murphy later confessed that the sadness of the task had only been alleviated by thinking of the music. The lifting of the body had altered the expression slightly but the effect is one of serenity and bears a remarkable resemblance to Sibelius.

The body is interred in St Finbarr's cemetery in Cork, the city and the land which held so many associations for him. The name of Dermot O'Byrne was not, however, recorded on the simple stone designed by Seamus Murphy.

Much of Bax's belongings, personal effects, books and music were left to Harriet Cohen. She donated a considerable number of these to Cork University on condition that they be housed in a suitable Memorial Room in tribute. This the university authorities agreed to do and the room was opened on 15th October 1955 by Vaughan Williams. An anniversary recital of Bax's music was held next day at the Aula Maxima, given by Harriet Cohen and Maura O'Connor. This was the first of a series of recitals and lectures, taking place each year on or near the anniversary of his death, an event which was endowed by the Bax family.

The Memorial Room itself is of unusual interest. It includes the death mask, the first pages of a translation into Erse of *In The Shadow of the Glen*, a Piano Sonata written at the age of fifteen, three books of Dermot O'Byrne's short stories, two unpublished songs and several manuscripts—a short score of a Symphony in F, a fragment of the music for the opera *Deirdre*, two of the earliest tone-poems inspired by Yeats, *Cathleen ni Houlihan* and *Into the Twilight*—as well as a number of letters.

The year following Bax's death, a number of his closest friends met on 3rd October at the graveside, and as they assembled in tribute to their dead friend John Horgan spoke a short address:

It has been said that those who 'live in the memory of friends are only far away, not dead—dead are those that are forgotten'. With this thought in our minds we have come here today to remember with affection Arnold Bax, who left us just a year ago. He was a fine writer, a distinguished musician, a great composer, but for us he was, above all, a dear and noble friend. Fame and honours, so well earned, did not alter his simple, sincere character. Behind his shy and even humble approach to life there was a delicate and distinguished mind, a sensitive spirit. Born out of his time, a great romantic in an age whose fierce and often discordant realism is reflected in its art, he found here in Ireland the life and atmosphere he loved. Amidst the mountains of Kerry and the glens of Donegal his best work was done. To Ireland he always came for refreshment, rest and peace. How fitting then that his mortal remains should rest in Irish earth under this simple and dignified stone designed and wrought by his friend Seamus Murphy. Remembering him today we may well recall the words of another great romantic:

Here he lies where he longed to be;
Home is the sailor, home from sea,
And the hunter home from the hill.

'And the hunter home from the hill'. Perhaps the words of Robert

Louis Stevenson were more apt than even John Horgan realized. For the hunter of dreams had returned from the hill of dreams to the final reality.[1] Arnold Bax was one of the most complex natures among the English composers of his generation. And since we have come to expect the paradox, he was at the same time one of the most simple.

In the reburgeoning of creative music in England which we call the English Renaissance, Bax played an important and distinguished part. But in the duality of his nature the fire and intensity of his vision demanded that the craftsman take up his tools in the service of the visionary. He wrote no music for his own use, or for the use of others. He occupied no professorial chair, nor organ stool. He taught in no college or institution—nor did he dispense the fruits of his experience to younger colleagues (although, as several musicians of my acquaintance have testified, he was generous with advice and kindly with criticism if called on). Bax was above all a poet.

That he was endowed with a prodigious gift none can doubt. Nor can the rare beauty of his music be denied. Eric Fenby once said of Delius that, in an age when we are not burdened with overmuch beauty, it seemed ungrateful to complain of a surfeit of it in one man. Whether Bax's beauty is in fact truth or evanescent vision is even yet wreathed in the trailing mists of the Celtic twilight. The heavenly and earthly mysteries communicated by the other-worldly visitant to St Columcille were not divulged. We too are left with a final enigma. But Bax does seem to direct us to where these revelations may become clearer.

A defence of the neglect of Bax's music in the forties and fifties is neither necessary nor desirable. Such defence is unlikely to do more than appear at best a special pleading and, at worst, an apologia. The reasons for the neglect are apparent. Apart from technical reasons (such as the complex individuality of his scores, demanding not only the seeming extravagances of triple woodwind, six horns and other expensive items but generous rehearsal time, and the ability to listen intelligently), the visionary land of Eternal Youth has, however

---

[1] There is a strange postscript. The week after Bax's death Harriet Cohen was troubled by two separate occurrences which she later related to me. In the kitchen of her tiny mews flat, whilst preparing supper, she became conscious of an intensely sweet smell, like the scent of decaying flowers, which so alarmed her that she ran out into the mews. A few weeks later she was visited by a friend from Ireland who had come over for the Memorial Service at St Martin-in-the-Fields. The visitor had barely entered the room when she turned deathly white. 'There's Arnold—by the piano,' she said.

temporarily, vanished in the practicalities of a materialistic and technological age. The only true defence is performance[1] without which a clear critical appraisal of his achievement is impossible.

If Bax's work is acclaimed today it is for its individual beauty, its richness of sound and image. Yet one is perversely conscious that, despite this beauty, the true significance of his achievement must lie in the symphonies and those works closely bound up with his symphonic thinking—not for their emotive power, but for the direction of the composer's philosophical reasoning.

It has been suggested several times that his earlier preoccupation with the identity of Dermot O'Byrne diffused much of his creative purpose. However, great discoveries were never made by technology alone—but by the power of the imagination to envisage the unknown and to direct the craftsman's hand. That power Bax had, and perhaps he drew it from that other self which manifested itself in the tales of O'Byrne.

But also in that dual personality was the man of whom Eric Coates could say: 'He was a kindly, lovable companionable person, tolerant of others and loyal to his friends',[2] and Patrick Hadley: 'There was never better quiet company.'[2]

Some time ago I found, among some sketches for the scenario of 'King Kojata', a pencilled page which I think shows something of that other side of his personality, the side that is glimpsed in the occasionally self-conscious prose of *Farewell, My Youth* and that so rarely, if ever, shows itself in the music. It is a sketch for a 'concert programme' in which Bax pokes fun at many of his friends, and includes such items as

Prelude in Asia minor (if only it were)
and
Meditation 'In an Egyptian Mummy Case'
scored for three muted ichneumons, two
tenor ibises, and contra-bulbul   by Granville Bantock

Eclogue for 27 tenor clarinets and
viola de gamba in P sharp   by F. Corder

---

[1] It may nor may not be significant that, in spite of those characteristics of his work that might seem to appeal most to the professional musician best able to appreciate them, Bax's largest following today appears to be arising among those who are not professional musicians.

[2] *Music and Letters*, Vol. 35, No. 1, January 1954.

Soul Rustlings (Three little whiffs
for piano duet—Mild, Medium and
Full strength)   by Tobias Matthay

and ends with a note 'During the evening Mrs Matthay will recite
Chapters XXII to XXXIX of the seventeenth volume of the Act of
Touch'.

It seems doubtful if those who knew him intimately—those restless
spirits of his youth, Godwin Baynes, Maitland Radford, his brother
Clifford (the 'Four Just Men' as Arnold dubbed them (see *Ideas and
People*, Clifford Bax, 1936, pp. 189–206)—ever really knew that inner
self whose soul is riven in the climaxes of the seven symphonies. Even
while wandering in Eire with his friends of later days he revealed little
of himself or of his music. And suddenly, among his companions, he
would become abstracted, withdrawn, as if encountering something of
that visionary experience that makes grim and fascinating reading in
the tales and the scores. For Bax the romantic experience—'within us
the desire becomes an agony to live for a single hour with all the might
of the imagination, to drown our beings in the proud sunlit tumult of
one instant of utter realization even though it consume us utterly'—
flooded that forlorn twilight with a brilliantly clear light. And in that
light we too can look—even momentarily—upon that pristine world.

List of Compositions

Note: A—Avison Edition (Cary); AF—Anglo-French; AHC—Ascherberg; Au—Augener; B—Boosey & Hawkes; E—Enoch; JW—Joseph Williams; JWC—Chester; M/C—Murdoch/Chappell; R—Riorden.

Date of Composition	Title	Scoring	Publisher	Date(s) on MSS[1]
1897–8	Minuet in E minor	Piano	MS	
	Two Hungarian Dances:	Piano	MS	
	Ra's Dance			
	On the Mountains			
	Three Mazurkas	Piano	MS	
	Two Scherzi	Piano	MS	
	Prelude in G major	Piano	MS	
	Nocturne in B major	Piano	MS	
	Minuet in E minor	Piano	MS	
	Sonata (two movements) (Opus 1)	Small Orch.	MS	27.2.98
		Piano		
1899–1900	*Marcia Trionfale*			
	Violin Sonata			
1901–2	Love Song	Song		
	'The Grand Match'			
1903	String Quartet in G	Str. Quartet		
	String Quartet in E minor	Str. Quartet		
	Cathleen Ní Houlihan	Orchestra	MS	

[1] Many of Bax's MSS are deposited in the British Museum under references Add. 50,173–81; 53,735; 54,395; and 54,724–81.

Date of Composition	Title	Scoring	Publisher	Date(s) on MSS
1904	*Fantasy* (Concert Piece)	Viola & Piano		
	A Celtic Song Cycle	Voice & Piano	A JWC	July–Aug. 1904
	'Eilidh my Fawn'			
	'Closing Doors'			
	'Thy Dark eyes to mine'			
	'A Celtic Lullaby'			
	'At the last'			
	Valse de Concert in E flat	Piano	B	
	Trio in One movement (Opus 4)	Piano, Violin and Cello	A JWC	
1905–6	Symphonic Variations	Orchestra		
	'When we are lost' (O'Byrne)	Song		27.1.05
	A Connemara Revel (Irish Overture)	Orchestra		
	'The Fairies' (Allingham)	Song	A JWC	Oct. 1905
	'Golden Guendolen' (Morris)	Song	A JWC	Nov. 1905
1906–7	Symphony in F minor (2 movements)	Orchestra	MS	1906
	'The Enchanted Fiddle' (Anon.)[1]	Song	JWC	1906
	'Magnificat' (St Luke)	Song	A JWC	
	Symphony in F (2 movements) (Opus 8)	Orchestra	MS	3.4.07
	Fatherland (J. L. Runeberg/C. Bax)	Tenor, Chorus & Orch.	A JWC	1907
	'A Milking Sian' (Fiona MacLeod)	Song	JWC	1907
	String Quintet in G	Str. Quintet		
1907–8	*A Song of Life and Love*	Orchestra		
	A Song of War and Victory	Orchestra		

[1] See p. 99, n 2.

Date of Composition	Title	Scoring	Publisher	Date(s) on MSS
1908	'The Flute' (Björnson)	Song	M/C	1908
	Into the Twilight	Orchestra	MS	1908
	Lyrical Interlude	Str. Quintet	M/C	
	Moy Mell (The Happy Plain)	Two pianos	JWC	1908–1917
	'Shieling Song' (Fiona MacLeod)	Song	JWC	1908
1909	*In the Faery Hills*	Orchestra	M/C	1909
	Festival Overture	Orchestra	MS	Oct. 1909; Orchestrated March 1911; revised Nov. 1918
	'A Christmas Carol' (15th c.)	Song	JWC	Christmas 1909
1910	Sonata No. 1	Violin & Piano	M/C	I—2.2.10 II—8.2.10 III—undated Revised March 1915
	Rosc Catha	Orchestra	MS	Nov. 1910
	Sonata No. 1 in F sharp minor	Piano	M/C	Summer 1910 Revised 1917–21
	Enchanted Summer (Shelley)	Two sopranos Chorus & Orch.	R M/C	Dec. 1910
	'A Lullaby' (McCarthy)	Song	E	
1911	Two Russian Tone Pictures *Nocturne—May-Night in the Ukraine National Dance—Gopak*	Piano	JW	

Date of Composition	Title	Scoring	Publisher	Date(s) on MSS
	Tamara (A little Russian Fairytale in action and dance)	Ballet score	MS	1911
	Suite:			
	Waltz			
	Polka			
	Polonaise			
	Buffoon's Dance			
	Galop			
	Apotheosis			
	Christmas Eve	Orchestra	MS	1911
	Christmas Eve on the Mountains		MS	Jan. 1912
1912	Three Pieces	Orchestra	MS	
	Evening Piece			
	Irish Landscape			
	Dance in the Sunlight			
	Four Pieces	Orchestra	MS	1912–13. Title of 3rd not on MS
	Pensive Twilight			
	Dance in the Sun			
	From the Mountains of Home			
	Dance of Wild Irravel			
	Prelude to Adonais	Orchestra		
	Nympholept (Nature Poem)	Orchestra	MS	1912–Feb. 1915
	Mask	Piano		
	Four Pieces	Flute & Piano	M/C	
	Shadow Dance			
	The Princess Dances			

Date of Composition	Title	Scoring	Publisher	Date(s) on MSS
1913	*Naiad*			
	Grotesque			
	Toccata	Piano	M/C	
	Sonata (No. 2 in F)	Piano	MS	Two movements only
	Scherzo	Orchestra	MS	
	Spring Fire	Orchestra	MS	
	The Garden of Fand	Orchestra	M/C	
1914	(Six) Songs from *The Bard of the Dimbovitza* (Vacaresco)	Mezzo soprano & Orchestra	M/C	1, 3, and 5 dated 1914
	'The Well of Tears'			
	'My Girdle I hung on a treetop tall'			
	'Spinning Song'			
	'Misconception'			
	'The Song of the Dagger'			
	The Happy Forest	Orchestra	M/C	Short score 13.5.14 Orchestrated 1921
	Three Roundels (Chaucer)	Voice & Piano	MS No. 2—JWC	1—20.10.14 2—1914 3—31.10.14
	'Welcome Somer'			
	'Your eyen two'			
	'Of her Mercy'			
	In the Night (Passacaglia)	Piano	MS	6.11.14
1915	*The Princess's Rose-Garden*	Piano	Au	10.1.15
	The Maiden with the Daffodil	Piano	JW	23.1.15
	Legend	Violin & Piano	Au	Feb 1915
	Quintet in G minor	Piano and Str. Quartet	M/C	13.4.15

Date of Composition	Title	Scoring	Publisher	Date(s) on MSS
	Apple-Blossom-Time	Piano	Au	May 1915
	Sonata No. 2 in D	Violin & Piano	M/C	
	In a Vodka Shop	Piano	Au	
	Sleepyhead	Piano	Au	
	A Mountain Mood	Piano	JWC	
	Winter Waters (Tragic Landscape)	Piano	JWC	Sept. 1915
1916	*Ballade*	Violin & Piano	JWC	
	Quartet No. 1 in G major	Str. Quartet	M/C	
	Folk Tale	Cello & Piano	JWC	
	Dream in Exile	Piano	JWC	
	Nereid	Piano	JWC	24.3.16 MS entitled 'Ideala'
	Elegiac Trio	Flute, Viola & Harp	JWC	
	In Memoriam (also entitled *An Irish Elegy*)	Cor Anglais, Harp & Str. Quartet	M/C	
	'Parting' (Æ)	Song	M/C	
1917	*Between Dusk and Dawn (or Between Twelve and Three)*	Ballet score		
	Symphonic Scherzo	Orchestra	MS	1917, revised 1933
	Symphonic Variations	Piano and Orch.	MS 2 pianos —M/C	
	Tintagel	Orchestra	M/C	
	November Woods	Orchestra	M/C	
1918	*The Frogskin*	Ballet score		Short score dated 1917

Date of Composition	Title	Scoring	Publisher	Date(s) on MSS
	A Romance	Piano	AHC	
	On a May Evening	Piano	AHC	
1919	*The Slave Girl*	Piano	AF	
	What the Minstrel Told Us	Piano	AF	
	Quintet	Harp & Str. Quartet	M/C	
	Whirligig	Piano	JWC	Summer 1919
	Sonata No. 2 in G	Piano	M/C	26.7.19
1920	*The Truth about the Russian Dancers*	Ballet score	MS	5.2.20
	Suite:			
	Overture			
	Karissima plays golf			
	Bridal Procession			
	Child's Dance			
	Finale			
	Phantasy	Viola & Orch.	M/C	
	Summer Music	Orchestra	M/C	Piano score entitled 'Idyll'
	Lullaby	Piano	M/C	27.4.20
	A Hill Tune	Piano	M/C	
	Burlesque	Piano	M/C	
	Country Tune	Piano	M/C	
	Mediterranean	Piano	M/C	Orchestrated 1921
	The Devil that tempted St Anthony	Two pianos	M/C	
	The Poisoned Fountain	Two pianos	M/C	

Date of Composition	Title	Scoring	Publisher	Date(s) on MSS
	Traditional Songs of France:	Voice & Piano	M/C	July–Aug. 1920
	'Sarabande'			
	'Langueo d'amours'			
	'Me suis mise en danse'			
	'Femmes, Battez vos Marys'			
	'La Targo'			
	A Rabelaisian Catechism: La foi d'la loi	Voice & Piano	MS	16.8.20
1921	Five Irish Songs:	Voice & Piano	M/C	
	'The Pigeons' (Colum)			1.3.21
	'As I came over the grey, grey hills' (Campbell)			28.2.21
	'I heard a piper piping' (Campbell)			undated
	'Across the Door' (Colum)			18.2.21
	'Beg-Innish' (Synge)			19.2.21
	Mater Ora Filium (Anon.)	Unacc. Motet for Double Chorus	M/C	
	Of a Rose I sing a song	Small Chorus, Harp, Cello & Bass	M/C	
	Now is the Time of Christmas	Male Chorus Flute & Piano	M/C	
	Fanfare for a Hosting at Dawn	Woodwind, Brass & Percussion	(1)	
	Symphony No. 1 in E flat	Orchestra	M/C	Piano score 1921 Full score 8.10.22

1 Published in periodical *Fanfare*, ed. Heseltine and Leigh Henry.

Date of Composition	Title	Scoring	Publisher	Date(s) on MSS
1922	Sonata	Viola & Piano	M/C	9.1.22
	Three Irish Songs (Colum): 'Cradle Song', 'Rann of Exile', 'Rann of Wandering'	Voice & Piano	M/C	Feb. 1922
	This Worlde's Joie (14th c.)	SATB unacc.	M/C	14.3.22
	Quartet in one movement	Piano & Str. Quartet	M/C	Summer 1922
	Quintet	Oboe & Str. Quartet	M/C	Christmas 1922
1923	*The Boar's Head*	Carol for unacc. male chorus	M/C	
	To The Name above every Name	Chorus & Orch.	M/C	16.3.23
	Saga Fragment	Piano & Orch.	MS	Scored version of Piano Quartet
	Sonata	Cello & Piano	M/C	7.11.23
	St. Patrick's Breastplate (Irish-Gaelic)	Chorus & Orch.	M/C	Dec. 1923
1924–5	Symphony No. 2 in E minor & C	Orchestra	M/C	Short score 1924 Full score March 1926
	Quartet No. 2	Str. Quartet	M/C	5.2.25
	Fantasy Sonata	Viola & Harp	M/C	
	Cortège	Orchestra	MS	Geneva 1925
	'Carrey Clavel' (Hardy)	Song	M/C	6.8.25
1926	Romantic Overture	Chamber Orch.	M/C	Apr. 1926
	Walsinghame (16th c.)	Tenor, Chorus and Orch.	M/C	May 1926
	Sonata No. 3	Piano	M/C	23.11.26

Date of Composition	Title	Scoring	Publisher	Date(s) on MSS
1927	Sonata No. 3	Violin & Piano	M/C	
	Three Songs from the Norse:	Voice & Piano	MS	
	'Irmelin Rose' (Jacobsen)			16.4.27
	'Land Vaaren Komme' (Jacobsen)			20.4.27
	'Venevil' (Bjornson)			June 1927
	Hardanger	Two pianos	M/C	May 1927
	Northern Ballad (?)	Orchestra	MS	Short score (untitled except for 'III')[1] 26.10.27
	Northern Ballad	Orchestra	MS	Short score November 1927 Full score 1931
1928	I Sing of a Maiden (15th c.)	Five-part small chorus	M/C	
	Paean	Piano	M/C	
	Sonata in F	Violin & Piano	MS	Sept. 1928
	Three Pieces (Arranged from score of The Truth about the Russian Dancers)	Piano	M/C	
	Ceremonial Dance			
	Serpent Dance			
	Water Music			
1929	Symphony No. 3	Orchestra	M/C	Full score Feb. 1929
	Overture Elegy and Rondo	Orchestra	M/C	
	Legend	Viola and Piano	M/C	

[1] The title *Northern Ballad* is given here since the MS was found with the other two works bearing this title. The discrepancy in dates, however, suggests that it may well be a third movement to some other projected work (see p. 149).

Date of Composition	Title	Scoring	Publisher	Date(s) on MSS
	Winter Legends	Piano & Orch.	MS	Short score I—23.10.29 II—29.10.29 III—4.12.29 Full score 3.4.30
1930	Nonet	Fl, Ob, Cl, Hp. & Str. Quintet	M/C	Jan. 1930
	Symphony No. 4	Orchestra	M/C	1930—I
	Overture to a Picaresque Comedy	Orchestra	M/C	19.10.30
1931	*Red Autumn*	Two pianos	M/C	
	The Tale the Pine Trees Knew	Orchestra	M/C	Short score 2.10.31 Full score Dec. 1931
	Symphony No. 5	Orchestra	M/C	Dec. 1931–March 1932
1932	Symphonietta	Orchestra	MS	
	Sonata No. 4	Piano	M/C	
	Concerto	Cello & Orch.	M/C	Full score 19.12.32
1933	*Prelude for a Solemn Occasion*	Orchestra	MS	Full Score Feb. 1933
	Sonatina	Cello & Piano	M/C	29.9.33
	Northern Ballad No. 2	Orchestra	MS	Dec. 1933–Jan. 1934
1934	Concerto	Fl, Hp., Ob. & Str. Quartet	MS	June 1934
	Sonata	Clarinet & Piano	M/C	
	Octet	Hn., Piano & Str. Sextet	MS	
	Symphony No. 6	Orchestra	M/C	Oct. 1934
	Eternity (Herrick)	Voice & Orchestra	MS	16.11.34

Date of Composition	Title	Scoring	Publisher	Date(s) on MSS
1935–6	The Morning Watch (Vaughan)	Chorus & Orch.	M/C	
	Threnody and Scherzo	Bn., Hp. & Str. Sextet		
	Rogues Comedy Overture	Orchestra		
	Quartet No. 3 in F	Str. Quartet	M/C	23.9.36
	Overture to Adventure	Orchestra	M/C	Oct. 1936
1937–8	London Pageant(ry)	Orchestra	MS	
	Concerto	Violin & Orch.	M/C	March 1938
1939	Symphony No. 7	Orchestra	MS	
	Rhapsodic Ballad	Unacc. Cello	M/C	
1943	Legend-Sonata	Cello & Piano	M/C	Feb. 1943
	Work in Progress Overture	Orchestra	MS	
	Fantasia on Polish Christmas Carols	Women's voices &	M/C	
	'God is born'	Strings		
	'In Nightly Stillness'			
	'In the manger He is lying'			
	'Lullay Dear Jesus'			
	'Merrily to Bethlehem'			
	Malta G.C.	Film score	MS	
	Suite:			
	Old Valletta			
	Air Raid			
	Gay March			
	Intermezzo			
	Work and Play			
	March			

Date of Composition	Title	Scoring	Publisher	Date(s) on MSS
1944	*A Legend*	Orchestra	MS	2.5.44
1945	*Nunc Dimittis*	SATB and Organ	M/C	
	Gloria	SATB and Organ	M/C	
	Te Deum	SATB and Organ	M/C	
	Suite on the name Gabriel Fauré	Str. Orch. and	MS	Piano score 1945
		Harp		Scored 28.8.49
	Prelude			
	Barcarolle			
	Polka			
	Intermezzo (Storm)			
	Quodlibet			
1946	*Trio in B flat*	Piano, Violin, Viola	M/C	9.1.46
	Morning Song (Maytime in Sussex)	Piano & Orch.	MS	
	Five Greek Folksongs (Calvocoressi)	SATB	M/C	
	'Miracle of St Basil'			
	'The Bridesmaid's Song'			
	'In Far-off Malta'			
	'The Happy Tramp'			
	'A Pilgrim's Chant'			
1947	*O Dame get up and bake your pies*	Piano	M/C	
	(Variations on a North Country Carol)			
	Fantastic March	Piano	MS	30.1.47
	Romanza	Piano	MS	11.2.47
	Idyll	Piano	MS	19.2.47
	Phantasie	Piano	MS	12.3.47
	Two Fanfares (for the Royal Wedding)	Brass	MS	
	Epithalamium (Spenser)	SATB (unis.) & Organ	M/C	2.9.47

Date of Composition	Title	Scoring	Publisher	Date(s) on MSS
1948	*Oliver Twist* Suite: *Prelude* *Flight* *Chase* *Romp* *Finale*	Film score	MS[1]	
1948–9	Concertante for three solo instruments	Cor Anglais, Cl., Hn. & Orch.	MS	
	Magnificat	SATB and Organ	M/C	
	Concertante for Piano (L.H.)	Piano and Orch.	MS	
	Journey into History	Documentary film score		
	Coronation March	Orchestra	MS[2]	
1953	'What is it like to be young and fair' (C. Bax)[3]	SSCCT unacc.	M/C	

[1] Two lyrical pieces for piano published Chappell 1948.
[2] Piano arrangement published Chappell.
[3] Contribution to 'A Garland for the Queen'.

The following MSS are undated:

Concertino for piano and strings (sketch only)
Allegro III (possibly from above)
Legends No. 1 for piano (MS in possession of John Simons)
Music for *St George and the Dragon*
    MSS in British Museum containing:
    Prelude in B flat
    Allegretto in F
    Gavotte in A minor
    Allegro Moderato
    Ceremonial Dance
    Chorus of Ecclesiastics TTBB
    Dance and SA chorus
    Chorus 'Alas for a defenceless land'
    Interlude for organ
    Lament 'What is past hope' (SATB and Bar. solo)
    The coming of Spring (SATB)
    Once in this land (SATB)
    Moderato grazioso ('a few women's voices')
    In time long past (Voice & piano)
    The Dragon's Song (Bar. and Brass)
Piano Sonata in B flat major 'The Salzburg' (in 18th-century style).

Bax also wrote very many songs in addition to those included in the foregoing list. A list, undoubtedly incomplete, is given below:

1905–1910

From the uplands to the sea	Morris
Green Branches	MacLeod
The White Peace	MacLeod
A Hushing Song	MacLeod
I fear thy kisses	Shelley
The Twa Corbies	Border Ballad
The Kingdom	Ruckert
Isla	MacLeod
Heart O'Beauty	MacLeod
Longing	MacLeod
The Hills of Dream	MacLeod
Landscape	Jacobsen
O Dewy Flower	Jacobsen
The Wood Lake	Leuthold
Aspiration	Dehmel (C. Bax)
A Lyke-Wake Dirge	Border Ballad
Marguerite	Morris
The Garden by the Sea	Morris
Love Ode	Hartleben
Beloved, even in dreams	Ruckert

Home   Dehmel
Enlightenment   Dehmel
To Eire   Cousins

1911–1917
The Journey   Dehmel
Flight   Dehmel
The Dead Child   Meyer
Spring Showers   Ruckert
Faith   Ruckert
Fremkind   Ruckert
The Bridal Prayer   Dehmel
O Mistress Mine   Shakespeare
I Know myself no more   Æ (Russell)
The Splendour Falls   Tennyson
Go, Lovely Rose   Waller

1918–1920
Jack & Jone   Campion
The Maid and the Miller   Trad.
O Dear What can the matter be   Trad.
I Have house and land in Kent   Trad.
Variations on Cadet Rousselle   Orchestrated by Goossens
Trois enfantines   Trad. French
Youth   C. Bax
Green Grow the Rashes   Burns
Far in a western brookland   Housman
When I was one-and-twenty   Housman
Le Chant d'Isabeau   French-Canadian
Midsummer   C. Bax

1920–1953
Watching the Needle Boats at San Sabba   Joyce
Dermot Doun McMorna   Colum
Wild Almond   Trench
The Market Girl   Hardy
On the Bridge   Hardy
I heard a soldier   Trench
Out and Away   Stephens
Dream Child   Newton

The most complete list of Bax's music is that compiled by Graham Parlett (limited edition, Triad Press, 1972).

A discography of Bax's works, by R. L. E. Foreman, appeared in *Recorded Sound*, Nos. 29–30 Jan/April, 1968.

See also R. L. E. Foreman's bibliography in *Current Musicology*, No. 10, 1970, Columbia University.

Index